The Courts and
Standards-Based
Education Reform

BENJAMIN
MICHAEL
SUPERFINE

The Courts and Standards-Based Education Reform

OXFORD
UNIVERSITY PRESS

2008

OXFORD
UNIVERSITY PRESS

Oxford University Press, Inc., publishes works that further Oxford University's objective of excellence
in research, scholarship, and education.

Oxford New York
Auckland   Cape Town   Dar es Salaam   Hong Kong   Karachi   Kuala Lumpur   Madrid   Melbourne
Mexico City   Nairobi   New Delhi   Shanghai   Taipei   Toronto

With offices in
Argentina   Austria   Brazil   Chile   Czech Republic   France   Greece   Guatemala   Hungary   Italy   Japan
Poland   Portugal   Singapore   South Korea   Switzerland   Thailand   Turkey   Ukraine   Vietnam

Copyright © 2008 by Oxford University Press, Inc.

Published by Oxford University Press, Inc.
198 Madison Avenue, New York, New York 10016

Oxford is a registered trademark of Oxford University Press
Oxford University Press is a registered trademark of Oxford University Press, Inc.

Library of Congress Cataloging-in-Publication Data

Superfine, Benjamin.
   The courts and standards-based education reform / Benjamin Michael Superfine.
      p. cm.
   Includes bibliographical references and index.
   ISBN 978-0-19-533748-8 (alk. paper)
   1.   Educational accountability—Law and legislation—United States. 2.   Educational tests and measurements—Law
and legislation—United States. 3.   Education—Finance—Law and legislation—United States. 4.   Education—
Standards—United States.   I. Title.
   KF4150.S87 2008
   344.73'079—dc22

                                                                                                2008009319

1 2 3 4 5 6 7 8 9

Printed in the United States of America on acid-free paper

Note to Readers
This publication is designed to provide accurate and authoritative information in regard to the subject matter covered.
It is based upon sources believed to be accurate and reliable and is intended to be current as of the time it was written.
It is sold with the understanding that the publisher is not engaged in rendering legal, accounting, or other professional
services. If legal advice or other expert assistance is required, the services of a competent professional person should be
sought. Also, to confirm that the information has not been affected or changed by recent developments, traditional
legal research techniques should be used, including checking primary sources where appropriate.

*(Based on the Declaration of Principles jointly adopted by a Committee of the
American Bar Association and a Committee of Publishers and Associations.)*

TO ALISON, MOM, AND DAD

CONTENTS

ACKNOWLEDGMENTS

This book could never have been written without the help of many people.

As a graduate student at the University of Michigan, several of my professors pushed my thinking in ways that directly contributed to this book. I would like to especially thank Roger Goddard, Cecil Miskel, Pamela Moss, and Maris Vinovskis.

I am grateful to the faculty at the College of Education at the University of Illinois at Chicago. I am especially grateful to Dean Vicki Chou and Mark Smylie, who provided me with the opportunity and space to complete this book.

Several people provided excellent feedback on particular chapters or drafts of this book: Alison Castro-Superfine, Roger Goddard, Michael Heise, David Mayrowetz, Len Reiser, Jim Ryan, Mark Smylie, and an anonymous reviewer. Their comments and advice were invaluable, and this book is significantly better for their gracious efforts. Of course, all mistakes and omissions are my own.

My parents, Ann and Stan Superfine, have contributed to this book in more ways than I can count. Their immense love and support have been endless.

Lastly, I would like to thank my wife, Alison Castro-Superfine. Her thoughts have consistently shaped my thinking about my own work and the world more broadly, and she is nothing short of my perfect intellectual companion. Much more importantly, I can never fully express how much her love, support, and patience mean to me, as well as everything else she brings to the table.

CHAPTER ONE

Introduction

Since the Supreme Court decided *Brown v. Board of Education* in 1954, the courts have become an increasingly important force in education policy.[1] Judicial rulings in areas such as desegregation, school finance reform, and the education of students with disabilities and limited English proficiency have markedly changed the education policy landscape. By interpreting both federal and state constitutional and statutory provisions, judges have crafted rulings that have affected virtually all levels of the United States education system. As plaintiffs continue to litigate claims regarding their educational rights, it appears that the courts' role in education policy will only continue to grow.

Since the mid-1980s, the concept of standards-based reform also has become increasingly important in education policy. In contrast to the bulk of education reform movements that litter U.S. history and have often been described as "faddish," the standards-based reform movement has exhibited a good deal of durability. Although the standards-based reform initially began in the states, the federal government began to get involved in the standards-based reform movement in the mid-1990s. Under the No Child Left Behind Act of 2001 (NCLB), every state was required to implement standards-based reform policies with a significant focus on holding schools accountable for their performance.[2] Every state has complied to some extent with this requirement and has some sort of standards-based reform policy in place.[3]

Until recently, the courts have had little involvement with the standards-based reform movement. While the courts had addressed the legality of educational testing practices since at least the 1970s, these testing practices generally were not part of standards-based reform systems.[4] Since the late 1990s, however, the courts have increasingly considered issues regarding standards-based reform. This book examines the recent convergence of the courts' growing role in education policy and the standards-based reform movement. In particular, this book examines the ways in which courts have addressed issues related to standards-based reform, and building on this analysis, considers how the courts should address such issues in the future.

The convergence of the courts and the standards-based reform movement is an extremely important development in the history of U.S. education policy. Even without judicial involvement, standards-based reforms have transformed and likely will continue to transform education policy in the U.S. Aimed at boosting the quality of education provided to students, standards-based reform entails an increased focus on the academic achievement of students and fundamental changes in the structure of the U.S. education system. For much of U.S. history, localities were primarily responsible for deciding what students should know and be able to do. Standards-based reform relocates the decision-making processes about student learning. As this strategy is currently being implemented, states identify the knowledge and skills that students should learn through the specification of *content standards*. These standards are to provide a concrete articulation of the level and type of student learning that other education policies, such as those regarding curriculum, pedagogy, teacher education, professional development, and testing, are meant to support. As standards have often been construed in the recent policy context, they can also provide an anchor for policies that are aimed at holding students and schools accountable for their performance.

The insertion of the courts into the standards-based reform movement raises the stakes of the already politically charged decisions about the design and implementation of standards-based reforms. Despite their prevalence, standards-based reforms repeatedly have resided at the center of often heated disagreements about their efficacy and desirability. On one hand, some have hailed standards-based reforms as the remedy to the problems facing the U.S. education system—through an emphasis on specific levels of academic achievement (and often consequences tied to these levels of achievement), standards-based reforms can ensure that schools provide students with a high-quality education and sufficient opportunities to learn. On the other hand, many have attacked standards-based reforms as overly intrusive and demanding. For example, critics have argued that standards-based reforms entail an array of requirements with which states, districts, and schools have little capacity to comply.[5] Citing issues such as "teaching to the test," critics have also argued that the institution of standards-based reforms has resulted in undesirable consequences in the classroom. It is in this divisive political climate that reformers have begun to look to the courts as a force that can address perceived problems in the ways that standards-based reforms are designed and implemented. By looking to the courts as a vehicle for policy change, reformers are now enabling the courts to decide some of the most contentious and often important issues facing the standards-based reform movement as it continues to grow and change.

The increasing presence of the courts in the standards-based reform movement, however, requires the courts to address types of questions with which they have relatively little experience. Courts have often examined education policies in areas such as the treatment of underrepresented groups and the intersection of schooling and religion. In these types of cases, courts have generally conducted detailed constitutional or statutory analyses and ruled accordingly. When addressing legal questions about standards-based reforms, the courts are forced to delve much more deeply into the details of education policies than they have in the past. Instead of addressing abstract legal principles to determine whether a policy is constitutionally permissible, courts must examine nuanced distinctions between different policy choices in a context of empirical uncertainty. In short, the courts' role in education policy is undergoing a serious shift, and the courts' ability and willingness to assume new modes of reasoning in education cases may determine much of the future of standards-based reform.

By its nature, an examination of the convergence between the standards-based reform movement and the courts entails an interdisciplinary approach. The education system and the legal system have never been wholly distinct from each other (though educators and lawyers may sometimes treat the systems as otherwise). The education system is a complex social system constituted by various entities (such as students, teachers, administrators, schools, districts, and states) and relationships between these entities. The legal system includes several requirements (generally in the form of laws, court decisions, and regulations) that entities, such as courts, apply to the education system. In some cases, the law may regulate almost every aspect of an educational phenomenon, while in other cases, the law may almost completely ignore an educational phenomenon. In order to understand how the courts have addressed standards-based reforms and how they can do so better, it is essential to examine the applicable legal rules and doctrines, the institutions that apply these rules and doctrines, what standards-based reforms are, and the broader educational context in which standards-based reforms are situated.

This book accordingly draws from both legal and educational perspectives to understand the courts' involvement with standards-based reforms. Without an examination of both the legal and education policy issues at play, it is impossible to craft a complete or balanced analysis. The history of and major theoretical and empirical research into standards-based reforms constitute the analytical touchstones for much of this book—an understanding from an educational perspective of what standards-based reforms are, their underlying purposes, the problems these reforms have faced, and the context in which these reforms are situated, is critical for analyzing how the courts have addressed standards-based reforms. An understanding of how the courts have addressed major education policy issues in the past and the forces that have influenced such treatment is also quite useful for understanding the courts' treatment of standards-based reforms. Guided by such legal and educational insights, this book examines and analyzes the major areas in which the courts have interpreted and applied a variety of legal doctrines and requirements to issues regarding standards-based reforms.

On a broad level, this book argues that the courts have thus far addressed standards-based reforms in an ineffective (and sometimes problematic) fashion, but that there may be a more effective role·for the courts to assume. The courts have examined standards-based reforms through a variety of legal frameworks, including those traditionally used in the context of testing cases and school finance reform litigation. Relying on insights from educational and legal research, this book examines and critiques the major areas in which courts have addressed standards-based reform and the ways in which the courts have employed these frameworks. This book specifically highlights how well the courts are positioned—given the law, their institutional characteristics, and standards-based reform policies themselves—to craft effective rulings in cases involving standards-based reforms. Building on this analysis, this book outlines a broad approach that the courts could take to address standards-based reform policies in a more effective fashion.

This book primarily focuses on the courts' treatment of standards-based reform in relation to two major goals of standards-based reforms: aligning various education policies to decrease uncoordinated, and sometimes conflicting, policy mandates for educators and administrators, and ensuring that more high-quality instruction and content are delivered to students. This book further focuses on the courts' treatment of major problems that standards-based reforms (and related accountability policies) have faced in effecting such changes, including lack of financial and physical resources, implementers' lack of knowledge, and lack of political will needed to effect the changes entailed by these policies at various levels. Especially given the courts' historical involvement with issues of educational equity, this book also focuses on the courts' treatment of inequitably distributed "opportunities to learn" the content included in standards, and the potentially negative effects of standards-based accountability policies on various groups of students.

Based on a detailed discussion of the purposes, successes, and problems of standards-based reforms, this book examines the major areas of litigation in which the courts have addressed issues related to the design and implementation of these policies. The courts began to consider issues directly relevant to standards-based reforms in the 1970s. Building on the wave of civil rights law that grew in the decades after *Brown*, courts repeatedly analyzed the justifiability of educational testing practices. While most of the testing practices analyzed by courts during this time were not part of the standards-based reform movement (as the movement did not gain significant momentum until the end of the 1980s and beginning of the 1990s), the legal doctrines created by courts to govern educational testing practices still persist. Indeed, courts recently have applied such doctrines to standards-based testing practices. Based on insights from legal and education policy perspectives, this book considers how courts have applied these doctrines and the utility of these doctrines in the specific context of standards-based reform policies.

This book also examines how courts have addressed the recent surge of claims that plaintiffs have brought to influence the implementation of NCLB, the federal law that required states to administer standards-based testing and accountability systems. Since NCLB was passed, it has experienced several implementation problems. For example, state standards have differed drastically in quality, states have had great difficulty implementing required standards-based testing and accountability mechanisms, and states appeared to lack sufficient fiscal and technical capacities to implement these mechanisms fully. Many critics have also highlighted that the testing and accountability requirements of NCLB have inequitably affected certain groups of schools and students more than others. As plaintiffs have recently targeted these issues with a variety of different legal theories, courts have already considered a number of issues grouped around federally-driven standards, testing, and accountability mechanisms. Again based on insights from legal and education policy perspectives, this book analyzes how courts have addressed issues of federally-driven standards, testing, and accountability.

In addition to examining issues related to standards-based reform in the context of cases aimed directly at influencing these reforms, courts have regularly begun to address standards-based reform in another context—that of school finance reform litigation. As standards and testing have become increasingly prevalent, data from standards-based tests have begun to constitute critical evidence in school finance cases. Moreover, as issues related to school governance have also become increasingly important in school finance cases, the extent to which states have implemented systems of standards and accountability has become a key issue in such cases. Using legal and education policy perspectives, this book examines how courts have used doctrines traditionally associated with school finance reform litigation to address standards-based reforms.

Notably, this book does not examine every instance in which the courts have addressed issues related to standards-based reform. For example, courts ruling in desegregation cases have analyzed student achievement data from large-scale testing programs to determine the extent to which districts were integrated.[6] However, because these cases generally did not involve direct examinations of systems of standards and testing or their effects, these cases offer only limited insight into the ways in which the courts have addressed and may address standards-based reforms. Courts have similarly examined student achievement data in cases involving the constitutionality of school choice programs, such as vouchers.[7] In *Bush v. Holmes*, the Florida Supreme Court specifically examined the constitutionality of Florida's voucher program, which was tied to the state's standards-based reform policy.[8] However, while voucher schemes have often fallen squarely under the political spotlight, their ultimate impact on the education policy landscape has been quite limited—under one recent count, only about 50,000 students nation-wide use publicly-funded vouchers, and due to political and legal barriers, voucher schemes do not appear to be rapidly spreading throughout the country.[9] This book accordingly does not deeply discuss litigation involving issues like desegregation or vouchers that has only an attenuated relationship with standards-based reforms or an ultimately limited influence on standards-based reform systems around the U.S.

It is a particularly opportune time to examine the ways in which the courts have begun to address standards-based reforms. At least over the past 50 years, judicial decisions have produced widespread changes in education policy. As discussed in the following section, however, evaluations of the effectiveness of major court-driven reforms in education have been mixed. Due to problems such as courts' lack of competency to deal with technical matters of education policy, empirical uncertainty in education cases, vague legal doctrine, and political opposition to education reform, courts historically have had difficulties crafting rulings that effect productive education reform. Researchers have specifically criticized court-driven school reforms for their inattentiveness to sound policy knowledge—instead of crafting decisions that ultimately increase the quality of education being provided to various types of students, courts have sometimes followed paths that are arguably justifiable only from a legal perspective. Researchers accordingly have called for more scholarship that addresses the courts' role in education not only from a legal perspective, but from an education policy perspective as well.[10] This book specifically responds to the call for more interdisciplinary scholarship in the field.

Moreover, this book is particularly timely in that it assesses how courts have addressed standards-based reforms at a somewhat early stage of the convergence between the two. Standards-based reforms are among the most important education reform strategies being implemented in the U.S. today. They may have the potential to remedy a number of problems that plague the U.S. education system, such as the persistent achievement gap between white and minority students and the lagging performance of U.S. students in comparison to their international peers.[11] Although courts have certainly heard claims regarding the justifiability of educational testing practices for decades, courts only have begun to consider issues directly involving standards-based reforms over approximately the past decade. The usefulness or desirability of the courts' role in shaping standards-based reforms at this early stage is as of yet unclear. Because the courts have played such an important role in shaping education policy in the past, the time is now ripe to analyze the ways in which courts have shaped and should shape the course of standards-based reforms as such reforms continue to be implemented and change the educational landscape around the country.

The Courts' Involvement with Education

Today, almost every area of public education is governed by a complex web of laws rooted in a variety of different legal sources. As mentioned above, education was traditionally considered a function of state and local governments. As such, most of the law governing education stems from state-level sources. Every state constitution contains an "education" clause that specifies at least some vague legal duty that a state has to provide its citizens with a system of public schooling.[12] For example, many of these education clauses require states to provide their citizens with a "thorough and efficient" system of public schooling.[13] A huge body of state-level statutory and administrative law also governs many aspects of education. State law covers topics ranging from the compulsory attendance of students and the hiring and firing of teachers to school governance and finance.

In the 20th century, federal law also became a significant source of legal mandates regarding education. While the sheer volume of federal education law is not nearly as large as state education law, federal law has been responsible for some of the most visible and fundamental changes in the schooling process. The Equal Protection Clause of the U.S. Constitution constituted the legal provision under which the Supreme Court decided *Brown v. Board of Education* and declared racial segregation in public schools illegal.[14] After *Brown*, the

Equal Protection Clause continued to constitute the legal basis employed by federal courts to find various instances of segregation in public schools unconstitutional. Federal laws, such as the Civil Rights Act of 1964 and the Education for All Handicapped Children Act, built on the principles articulated in *Brown* and established a set of statutory civil rights mandates governing the treatment of students in the public education system.[15] In 1965, the U.S. Congress passed the Elementary and Secondary Education Act (ESEA), which has provided and continues to provide billions of dollars of grants for the compensatory education of economically disadvantaged students.[16]

Up until the 20th century, however, the courts had little involvement with issues related to education. Before the 20th century, there were fewer laws governing education, and plaintiffs brought very few claims regarding educational issues.[17] The plaintiffs who brought educational claims primarily focused on issues that fit into the standard categories of common law—most early education cases dealt with "normal" legal issues such as property, contracts, and torts.[18] Indeed, many citizens during this time viewed education as a sort of sacred institution and were loath to bring claims challenging foundational aspects of the education system.[19] Because the law governing education during the 19th century was somewhat inchoate, however, some plaintiffs brought suits to remedy resulting ambiguities—due to conflicts between state constitutions, statutes, and regulations, it was often unclear which authorities were responsible for educational decisions, such as those regarding the use of land grants for educational purposes.[20] As states released complicated regulations regarding educational decisions and related procedures at the end of the 19th century, litigation provided interested parties with a way to address unfavorable decisions made by educational administrators.

In the 20th century, the rate of litigation greatly increased, and courts became an increasingly important locus for educational decision making. In the Progressive Era of the early 20th century, education reformers pushed for centralization in the governance of schooling.[21] During this time, the legal and bureaucratic structure governing education grew quickly and became much more complicated. Plaintiffs challenged certain aspects of the new programs and governance structures entailed by centralization and bureaucratization. Some plaintiffs attacked the consolidation of schools or attempted to receive benefits from new transportation programs. Under new laws governing the hiring and firing of teachers, other plaintiffs increasingly challenged employment decisions. But even with the increased judicial involvement in education during the first half of the 20th century, plaintiffs generally did not bring claims regarding social issues, such as race, ethnicity, class, or religion, that challenged fundamental aspects of public education.[22] To be sure, some claims regarding social issues were brought during the beginning of the 20th century. For example, in the foundational case *Meyer v. Nebraska*, a teacher of German challenged the constitutionality of a state statute forbidding the teaching of a modern foreign language to any child who had not finished the eighth grade.[23] And in another foundational case *Pierce v. Society of Sisters*, an order of Catholic nuns challenged the constitutionality of a state statute requiring children to attend public instead of private schools.[24] However, most educational claims were not directed at these sorts of issues.

In the second half of the 20th century, the character of the courts' involvement with education changed dramatically. Beginning primarily in 1954 with *Brown*, courts began to get involved in "public law litigation," or litigation aimed at reforming institutional structures through judicial rulings that arguably put the courts in the place of policymakers.[25] In this type of litigation, the legal process proceeds in a somewhat nontraditional fashion—instead of focusing on the application of relatively narrow legal rules and/or principles to the actions of the particular parties involved in a case, the legal process in public law litigation is generally more flexible, deals with broader legal principles and sometimes unrepresented parties, and addresses perceived harms that result from more diffuse institutional behavior.[26] As a result, courts ruling in public law litigation exercise much flexibility when considering potential remedies and often craft broad, forward-looking remedies that appear legislative in character to address such harms. Of course, few (if any) lawsuits in education represent "pure" cases of public law litigation, and education cases generally fall somewhere on a spectrum that ranges from purely public law to purely private, or more traditional, law. Indeed, the cases examined in this book fall at various points on this spectrum.

After the Supreme Court decided *Brown*, reformers seeking to influence the fundamental structure of the U.S. education system launched a wave of public law litigation over the following decades aimed at segregation and its effects. In the decade and a half after *Brown*, the Supreme Court repeatedly ruled that the Equal Protection Clause of the U.S. Constitution precludes segregation.[27] And although the initial court-ordered desegregation proceeded only at "all deliberate speed," the Supreme Court eventually ordered full integration "forthwith."[28] Given the early success of desegregation litigation in court, the number of cases aimed at segregation exploded in the 1960s.[29] Today, the Equal Protection Clause of the U.S. Constitution still serves as the basis for litigation in high-profile education cases such as *Grutter v. Bollinger*, where the Supreme Court addressed the issue of affirmative action and held that race can serve as a factor for making admissions decisions in the higher education setting.[30]

Springing from the socially-minded desegregation cases, reformers also began to bring suits aimed at reforming state systems of financing public schools. Due to states' traditional method of financing public schools on the basis of local property taxes, the amount of funds available for public schooling can differ drastically from district to district within a state. Consequently, per-pupil expenditures often differ drastically as well. Attempting to remedy these funding disparities, reformers attacked school funding structures through the courts beginning in the late 1960s and early 1970s. Early attempts at influencing state systems of school finance under the federal Equal Protection Clause were somewhat successful in federal court.[31] However, when the Supreme Court considered reformers' federal equal protection argument in 1973, the Court held that funding disparities from district to district are not unconstitutional.[32] Since this ruling, reformers have turned to state courts and brought claims under provisions in state constitutions. Reformers addressing school finance systems in state courts have met varying degrees of success. Although claims attempting to equalize educational funding have faced several problems, newer legal theories centering on the concept of educational "adequacy" appear to be more successful.[33] Accordingly, some form of school finance litigation has been brought in at least 45 states.[34]

In addition to deciding cases on the basis of constitutional provisions in the second half of the 20th century, courts have decided an increasing number of education cases under federal statutes. With the passage of the Civil Rights Act of 1964, the U.S. Congress established statutory protections for victims of discrimination.[35] In this law, Congress explicitly offered legal relief for U.S. citizens who are subject to discrimination on the grounds of race, color, or national origin under any program or activity receiving federal funds. Moreover, under the Civil Rights Act, Congress authorized the federal government to withhold funds from entities that practice discrimination and authorized the U.S. Department of Justice to file civil rights cases. Immediately following the passage of this law, federal courts entered a rare period of clear and effective leadership in dismantling desegregation as they coordinated their efforts with those of the other governmental branches.[36] In addition to affecting desegregation, the Civil Rights Act has provided the basis for judicial determinations that specify how the government must provide equal educational opportunities to students with limited English proficiency.[37] Moreover, reformers have used the Civil Rights Act to challenge the justifiability of large-scale educational testing practices.[38]

Over the past 50 years, courts have similarly heard a number of cases regarding the rights of students with disabilities. With the passage of Section 504 of the Rehabilitation Act of 1973, Congress established the right of disabled students to be protected from discrimination in public education.[39] In 1975, Congress passed the Education for All Handicapped Children Act.[40] Later renamed the Individuals with Disabilities Education Act (IDEA), this law provides that students with disabilities must receive a free appropriate public education and the related services and support that they need to achieve. Under these statutes, courts have heard an array of claims aimed at boosting the quality of public education for students with disabilities. In particular, courts have focused on the integration of disabled students into classrooms with their nondisabled peers and the types of supports that disabled students need to succeed in regular classrooms.[41]

Although the types of cases mentioned above are considered to fall within some of the more landmark areas of court-driven education reform of the past 50 years, courts have begun to hear many other types of cases as well. Plaintiffs have brought education claims in areas such as the place of religion in public schools, gender equality, rights of privacy, student discipline, and free speech, to name but a few.[42] Indeed, judicial decisions in these areas have dramatically affected the education policy landscape as well. In short, the courts have transformed from an institution that rarely addressed education into an institution that now addresses a broad range of sometimes foundational and system-wide educational issues. In doing so, courts have become important drivers of education reform and policy.

EVALUATIONS OF COURT-DRIVEN REFORM IN EDUCATION

Despite the increasing presence of major court-driven reform efforts over the past 50 years, evaluations of these efforts have been somewhat mixed. When other governmental branches fail to address perceived policy problems, the courts offer reformers a potential means to overcome political inertia and affect governmental decision making.[43] In addition to requiring other governmental branches to take policy actions they may find undesirable for any number of reasons, court decisions can provide "political cover" for policy-makers to act in cases where the political climate does not readily favor policy change.[44] Given their comparative insulation from the political process and the nature of the adversarial process, the courts also constitute an institution that generally engages in a fairly evenhanded brand of decision making.[45] That is, compared to the decision-making processes of legislative and executive entities, the adjudicative process equalizes the representation of positions and how information is conveyed to the decision maker. The courts accordingly constitute a venue where underrepresented groups can argue for the value of different policy choices before a governmental institution that is generally more impartial than a legislature or agency.[46] Indeed, reformers have used the courts to bring legitimacy to efforts to address various social problems, such as segregation, that have impacted underrepresented groups.[47]

The courts, however, also possess several limitations in their abilities to effectively shape education policy. Because the costs of litigation are quite high, many issues involving policy never enter the courts in the first place.[48] When education policy issues are heard by the courts, countervailing political forces may prevent judicial orders prescribing unpopular changes from being fully or effectively implemented.[49] Indeed, as noted above, the courts have had some of their greatest success in effecting education policy change when they have acted in concert with other governmental branches to achieve a shared goal, such as desegregation, that involves a significant amount of political resistance. The courts have also faced several difficulties dealing with technical or scientific issues of education policy.[50] Although the courts have some tools available to them that can help them sort through such issues, they have faced many difficulties understanding scientific (and particularly statistically oriented) arguments undergirding factual claims, and they may be misled into a "false sense of security" about the validity of claimed facts.[51] Indeed, the empirical uncertainty characterizing several important educational issues can exacerbate the effects of such institutional capacity problems.[52]

Elements of educational litigation more directly related to legal rules and doctrines have limited the courts' effectiveness as well. Because many public law cases are brought under legal theories based on broad constitutional provisions, the legal rules and doctrines at play in public law litigation in education may be quite ambiguous.[53] These rules and doctrines accordingly may offer courts little concrete guidance for finding constitutional violations in public law litigation or crafting remedies in response to such violations. Legal scholars have also argued that the courts are not legally justified to craft rulings that require them to make difficult and sweeping policy choices in the face of vague legal doctrine—making such policy choices is more properly thought of as the province of a legislature, and by usurping the power to make such choices, the courts violate the separation of powers principle.[54] In perhaps the harshest and most famous critique of the courts' role in public law litigation focusing on education, Gerald Rosenberg concluded that courts can "*almost never* be effective producers of significant social reform."[55]

The effects of various types of educational litigation reflect these mixed evaluations. As a partial result of court orders to desegregate schools, massive integration in public schools occurred between 1968 and 1972.[56] By the 1980s, the SAT scores of African-American students rose, and the achievement gap between African-American and white students substantially narrowed.[57] However, high levels of desegregation persist in schools.[58] The achievement gap between African-American students and white students in mathematics, reading, and science has proven persistent as well.[59] And minority students have continued to be more likely to drop out of high school than white students.[60] The courts' failure to craft effective desegregation rulings can be partially explained by a political climate that has been extremely hostile to desegregation.[61] But other factors have heavily contributed to the courts' ineffectiveness as well. Due at least in part to somewhat vague and confusing legal doctrine, and courts' perceived incapacity to craft effective rulings without clear guidance, several federal courts have rushed the dismantling of desegregation plans and assumed with little evidence that these plans failed.[62] Moreover, several external factors, such as residential housing patterns, have impacted efforts to desegregate schools and have proven difficult for courts to overcome.[63]

Evaluations of the results of school finance litigation are similarly mixed. School finance litigation has generally reduced the inequality of per pupil expenditures across districts and has resulted in increased funding for many low-funded schools.[64] But in many instances, equalization of education spending within a state did not improve a state's overall education spending, and state expenditures in such states often remained level or decreased.[65] Additionally, even in many cases where school finance litigation increased educational spending, student test scores showed little or no gains.[66] As was true in desegregation litigation, a political climate hostile to change played a large role in limiting the courts' effectiveness in school finance reform. But the difficulty of defining a constitutionally equal or adequate education, empirical uncertainty about key factual issues (such as the impact of money on student achievement), and the courts' seeming lack of competency to make technical educational decisions have also limited the courts' effectiveness.[67]

Court-driven reform in the area of providing students with disabilities with the appropriate education yields similar evaluations. Of all the major areas of court-driven education reforms discussed in this chapter, reform in the education of students with disabilities has perhaps been the most successful. Due to the Education for All Handicapped Children Act, the number of students with disabilities educated in regular classrooms for more than 80 percent of the school day grew from 1.3 million to over 2.4 million between the

1987–88 and 1992–93 school years.[68] However, court-driven reform in this area has generated its share of detractors. Critics have pointed out that students with disabilities are twice as likely to drop out of school as nondisabled students.[69] Moreover, critics have repeatedly highlighted and attacked the large costs of providing a free appropriate education to disabled students.[70]

In short, the courts are a complex institution that has had mixed success in education cases, especially in high-profile litigation in the second half of the 20th century dealing with fundamental, structural issues of the U.S. education system. Judicial decisions and their impact in this area have been influenced by a complex interaction of various elements, including the institutional properties of courts (such as technical competency and legal procedures), participants in a suit, political context, educational subject matter, and of course, relevant legal frameworks and arguments raised by litigants. As this book moves forward, it will highlight such elements and their interactions in particular cases to flesh out how the courts have engaged with standards-based reforms and the ways in which the courts can more effectively address these reforms. In this way, this book is designed to engage in an extremely holistic analysis of the courts' involvement with standards-based reforms. If this book were to analyze only legal doctrine, it would miss several important factors influencing the courts' treatment of this policy. If this book were to analyze legal doctrine in light of education policy research, the analysis would be more complete, but it would still miss the potentially important influence that the institutional processes of courts and the larger political context in which they are situated also have on the courts' treatment of standards-based reform. By examining how these various elements have appeared and interacted with each other in cases addressing standards-based reform, this book can hopefully provide deeper insight into how the courts have engaged in this increasingly prevalent and technical area of education policy

Certainly, it would be overly optimistic to assume that the courts by themselves have the potential to remedy all the concerns raised by all the commentators and critics of standards-based reforms. But it does not appear overly optimistic to assume that the courts can have a significant and positive influence on the standards-based reform movement. If judicial decisions are crafted with a detailed understanding of the policy issues at stake in the cases that involve standards-based reforms, and if courts assume roles and adopt legal frameworks that allow them to avoid many of the major problems they have previously faced, the courts may be able to constitute a desirable institution for influencing standards-based reform policies as they move forward and change the shape of the U.S. education system.

Overview of the Book

This book relies on a variety of sources to understand how the courts have addressed standards-based reforms. In order to flesh out from an educational perspective what standards-based reforms are, the various forms they can take, and the goals they are meant to accomplish, this book looks to the work of education historians, researchers, and theorists. In order to articulate the major successes and pitfalls experienced by standards-based reforms, this book relies on several implementation reports and empirical studies that have been conducted since standards-based reform became a prevalent education strategy in the U.S. And in order to situate standards-based reforms in the broader context of policy, public opinion, and important contemporary events, this book looks to sources such as the *Congressional Record* and newspapers.[71]

As this book concentrates on the ways in which the courts have addressed standards-based reforms, this book also relies upon several different types of legal sources. These sources include cases, statutes, regulations, constitutions, briefs, complaints, and orders. Because the basic function of the courts is to interpret and apply the law, legal rules and doctrines in large part determine how well courts are positioned to rule on issues before them.[72] Legal sources such as constitutions, statutes, and regulations articulate an often complicated and intertwined body of legal rules and principles. Cases demonstrate how courts have interpreted and applied these legal rules and principles in given instances, and other documents (such as briefs and orders) can help flesh out the judicial processes employed in these cases. An examination of such legal sources therefore allows us to analyze how courts have treated standards-based reforms and how courts are more generally positioned to address issues related to standards-based reforms as such issues become more prevalent in the legal setting.

Throughout this book, these sources will be discussed in various ways. At times, this book will read much like a law review article as it discusses doctrinal trends and examines the state of the law in various areas. At other times, this book will read more like a work of history or social science, as it includes detailed case studies to capture the institutional processes and contexts of various lawsuits that addressed standards-based reforms. Moreover, this book includes some parts that are focused solely on education policy research and the history of standards-based reforms before any judicial involvement in this field. To bring together these various disciplinary perspectives on the courts and standards-based reform, a concluding section at the end of each chapter analyzes the interaction between courts' institutional characteristics, the relevant legal frameworks, and the underlying educational research—the complex interaction between these different elements appears to have strongly influenced how the courts have approached standards-based reform and arguably how the courts have approached education policy more generally.

The structure of this book is divided into six primary parts in addition to the Introduction. In Chapter Two, this book situates standards-based reforms in their historical and theoretical contexts, and includes much of the education policy information needed to provide an analytical backdrop for analyzing the courts' treatment of standards-based reforms. This chapter begins with a brief history of standards-based reforms and accountability policies, and discusses the major historical and educational problems standards-based reforms were designed to address. Then, this chapter focuses on the theories underlying standards-based reform. This section particularly highlights the ways in which standards based reform entails a fundamental restructuring of the U.S. education system around rigorous, shared goals for students and the possibility of instituting tests and accountability systems tied to such goals.

After examining the theories underlying standards-based reforms, this chapter turns to key developments in the standards-based reform movement in the 1990s. This chapter discusses the growth and blending of standards-based reforms and accountability mechanisms at the state level and traces the federal government's increasing involvement in the standards-based reform movement. This part particularly highlights the design and implementation of the Goals 2000: Educate America Act and the Improving America's Schools Act—two federal statutes that were passed in 1994 under the Clinton administration and aimed at instituting standards-based reforms around the country—and how standards-based reforms were actually designed and implemented across the U.S. Indeed, researchers conducted many of the major studies on standards-based reform in the 1990s, and such studies can offer much insight into the most significant pitfalls and opportunities entailed by standards-based reform. Finally, this chapter discusses the design and implementation of standards-based reforms during and after 2002 by focusing on the design and implementation of NCLB.

In Chapters Three through Five, this book analyzes the major ways in which the courts have addressed standards-based reform against the historical and theoretical backdrop described in Chapter Two. Chapter Three specifically focuses on the ways in which courts have treated issues related to high-stakes testing—a practice that hinges an individual student's ability to graduate, be promoted from one grade to another, or be placed in a particular track, on the results of a test.[73] Even before the standards-based reform movement began, states were already engaged in the activity of high-stakes testing, and courts had begun to work out principles of appropriate test use. Because the law governing high-stakes testing directly deals with issues of both testing and accountability, an examination of this law is critical for understanding the ways in which standards-based reforms are governed by pre-existing legal doctrines. Moreover, high-stakes testing cases offer invaluable insight into the ways in which courts have engaged with social science evidence directly related to standards-based reform and central concepts of the theories underlying standards-based reform, such as opportunity to learn. This chapter particularly examines the high-stakes testing doctrine in the four major areas in which it has been used by courts: intentional discrimination, preserving or furthering the effects of prior segregation, the disparate impact of testing practices, and ensuring that students receive their proper due process protections. Because a broad overview of the relevant law may miss important nuances about the characteristics and nature of the judicial process in high-stakes testing cases, this chapter also includes case studies of two important high-stakes testing cases—*Debra P. v. Turlington* and *GI Forum v. Texas Education Agency*.[74]

Then, this chapter analyzes the extent to which the high-stakes testing litigation enables courts to effectively address issues related to modern standards-based reform policies. This chapter concludes that, while courts can effectively govern limited aspects of standards-based reforms in the context of high-stakes testing litigation, this type of litigation does not allow courts to effectively address several of the problems that standards-based reforms have faced thus far. The viability of high-stakes testing litigation as a way to influence the implementation of testing practices has rapidly decreased in recent years. Moreover, the application of the legal frameworks governing high-stakes testing can tax the capacities of the courts to make decisions in an area that is characterized by scientific uncertainty and where the line between educational and legal standards has become blurred. The legal frameworks governing high-stakes testing also were developed in the wake of the civil rights era and not specifically designed to regulate standards-based reforms. As such, high-stakes testing litigation can result in the judicial adoption of an ineffective lens for assessing the design and implementation of modern standards-based reforms and related accountability systems.

In Chapter Four, this book turns to the type of litigation that reformers have more recently used in efforts to regulate the development and implementation of standards-based reforms. This chapter examines the litigation generated directly in response to NCLB and focuses on the ways in which courts have addressed NCLB-related claims. This litigation is especially important for considering the relationship between the courts and standards-based reform because the requirements of NCLB directly apply to and govern the standards-based reforms and accountability systems currently being implemented in every state. Entities such as private individuals, nonprofit organizations, teachers' unions, and school districts have all brought suit to influence NCLB's design and implementation. This chapter focuses on the major cases that have been brought for several different purposes by the various entities in this field.

In order to complete such an analysis, this chapter includes case studies of NCLB-related litigation in the three major areas in which such litigation has occurred: cases focusing on the implementation of NCLB accountability sanctions, cases focusing on the justifiability of student and school performance determinations, and cases focusing on the underlying capacities possessed by various entities to respond to NCLB requirements. Based on such case studies, this chapter concludes that the legal frameworks employed in these cases were generally not structured in ways that enabled courts to easily order changes in standards-based reform and accountability policies. Moreover, this chapter concludes that NCLB-related litigation has poorly framed many of the problems facing standards-based reform and accountability policies, and that several key issues surrounding NCLB's design and implementation have largely remained hidden from judicial analysis in this context.

In Chapter Five, this book examines the convergence of standards-based reform and school finance reform litigation. While school finance reform litigation has not traditionally involved issues related to standards-based reform, it has begun to do so since the late 1990s. In addition to examining school finance schemes, courts ruling in school finance cases have considered an array of related issues implicated by plaintiffs' legal theories. Courts hearing school finance cases have examined several different sorts of educational inputs (such as physical facilities and teacher quality) that bear upon students' educations, and these courts have even begun to consider issues directly related to standards, testing, and accountability systems. In order to provide the background necessary to understand these cases, this chapter first provides a brief overview of the history of school finance litigation and the legal issues that have typically shaped school finance litigation.

Then, this chapter examines the three major ways in which issues related to standards-based reform have emerged in school finance litigation: First, legislatures have responded to court orders that their education systems are not constitutionally adequate by building systems of standards and accountability—according to these legislatures, the institution of standards-based reforms and related accountability systems, in addition to altering their education funding systems, constitutes their chosen method for providing students with constitutionally adequate educations. Second, courts have used content standards and data from standards-based assessments to determine whether states have actually provided students with constitutionally adequate educations. Third, courts have begun to order states to implement standards-based reform and accountability systems as a means of providing students with constitutionally adequate educations. Courts addressing standards-based reforms in this fashion have generally considered the institution of these policies as a potential answer to the concern that simply ordering states to provide students with an adequate education cannot alone boost student performance. This chapter includes case studies of five recent school finance cases to detail the particular ways in which these issues have emerged. This chapter concludes that courts have most effectively addressed standards-based reform in the context of school finance litigation for a variety of reasons, including the shape of the relevant legal concepts, the history of school finance litigation, and the courts' active attempts to capitalize on their strengths and minimize their weaknesses in this field.

In Chapter Six, this book synthesizes the analyses conducted in the previous chapters and offers concluding thoughts. First, this chapter includes an overview and analytical summary of the major crosscutting issues and themes of the book. Second, this chapter situates the analyses in the larger context of recent developments in public law litigation across various domestic policy fields. Lastly, this chapter provides recommendations for how litigants and the courts should proceed to effectively address standards-based reform and accountability policies through litigation. These recommendations are largely based on recent developments in school finance litigation that appear to have well positioned the courts for addressing major issues related to standards-based reforms and related accountability policies.

The Intended Audience

As this book takes an interdisciplinary approach to the examination of how the courts have addressed standards-based reforms, this book is aimed at several different audiences. First, this book is aimed at lawyers and legal researchers. This book deals extensively with what the law is and can be. The courts are the main object of inquiry, and the courts are, of course, one of the major institutions shaping the legal community. By examining the ways that courts have addressed standards-based reforms, lawyers and legal researchers can gain a better understanding of how the courts work in a rather new area of law. In doing so, lawyers and legal researchers can gain knowledge that allows them to analyze, argue about, and shape the law more effectively.

This book is also aimed at policymakers. Education law and policy is a field that is rapidly evolving. As this book reflects, new laws and policies play a central role in shaping the direction of this field. In designing laws, policymakers not only have to consider the actual rules that they build into laws, but also how such rules will be interpreted and enforced. Indeed, implementation is a crucial stage in the policy process. In designing policies, policymakers thus must consider how the power to interpret and enforce policies should be divided between different branches of government. While the underlying goals of some policies may be better achieved through the enforcement of administrative agencies, the underlying goals of other policies may be better achieved through judicial action. Standards-based reform is a field in which the courts have had little effect thus far but appear as if they will have an increasingly important effect as this strategy continues to be implemented in the states. By examining how courts have addressed and may address standards-based reforms, policymakers can gain greater insight into the effects of past policies and how to design more effective policies in the future.

Finally, this book is aimed at education researchers. As standards-based reforms have been designed and implemented in the past, these reforms have constituted a major object of education research. Education researchers have repeatedly analyzed, critiqued, supported, attacked, and made recommendations regarding standards-based reforms. As this book demonstrates, the courts are beginning to constitute an increasingly important institution that determines how standards-based reforms are designed and implemented. However, the considerations with which courts must contend with regard to standards-based reforms may not be transparent to education researchers. Standards-based reforms are embedded in a complex web of legal rules and principles that often have no immediately obvious relation to the reforms themselves. This book can help education researchers gain a greater understanding of the legal rules, doctrines, and institutional pressures that ultimately shape standards-based reforms.

Because this book is intended for such a wide audience, I have made efforts to ensure that all of its parts are understandable to different groups. In places, I have thoroughly explained legal concepts that may seem basic to lawyers, and I have extensively discussed educational insights that may seem basic to those in the education community. In this way, I hope to have crafted a piece of scholarship that not only investigates a new trend but is also accessible and useful. Hopefully, this sort of approach can make the courts a more effective venue for addressing fundamental issues of education policy.

CHAPTER TWO

Standards-Based Reform and Accountability Policies

Currently, standards-based reforms are ubiquitous across the United States. Under state and federal law, every state is required to have put in place standards-based reform policies. The standards-based reform movement primarily began in the mid-1980s and entails fundamental changes in the structure of the U.S. education system—standards-based reform policies require an increased focus on the academic achievement of students, a relocation of the decision-making processes about what students should learn, and the alignment of different types of education policies (such as those regarding curriculum, testing, and the professional development of teachers) toward shared goals. Since standards-based reform policies began to be implemented in the U.S., they have also become significantly blended with federal- and state-level policies to hold schools, and sometimes students, accountable for their performance on tests. As such, the standards-based reform movement may have the potential to increase the quality of education provided to all students in the U.S. and to reduce inequities among the educational opportunities provided to these students. But at the same time, standards-based reform policies have faced several problems and continue to raise concerns among critics. Some of the most significant concerns focus on the failure of these reforms to effectively change teaching and learning at the classroom level and the inequitable and arguably undesirable effects of the accountability mechanisms that have become a central part of these reforms.

In order to provide the needed context for an analysis of the ways in which the courts have addressed standards-based reforms and provide an "analytical touchstone" to evaluate this treatment, this chapter engages in a detailed discussion of the standards-based reform movement. This chapter discusses the history of standards-based reforms, the theories underlying standards-based reforms, and research on the implementation of these reforms. Because standards-based reforms have become so blended with accountability policies, this chapter also discusses the growth of accountability policies in the U.S. and how these policies have tied into the standards-based reform movement.

This chapter particularly focuses on two major goals of standards-based reform and accountability policies: aligning various education policies to decrease uncoordinated, and sometimes conflicting, policy mandates for educators and administrators, and ensuring that more ambitious instruction and high-quality content are delivered to students. In examining the implementation of standards-based reform and accountability policies, this chapter also focuses on major barriers that have decreased the effectiveness of these policies, including a lack of financial and physical resources, lack of knowledge, and lack of political will needed to effect the changes entailed by these policies at various levels and especially at the classroom level. Moreover, this chapter focuses on the implications of these policies for educational equity, which is one of the major areas in which the courts have traditionally driven education policy—the concept of "opportunity to learn" for certain groups of students and the potentially negative effects of these policies on these students constitute especially important focal points for the courts. This chapter also highlights certain technical problems that have riddled the design and implementation of these policies, such as problems implementing accountability systems that yield valid interpretations about student and school performance. In short, this chapter is meant to provide a detailed picture of the fundamental changes standards-based reforms are aimed at effecting in the U.S. education system, an understanding of the changes that have actually occurred, and the major opportunities and pitfalls of the standards-based reform movement as it moves forward. In doing so, this chapter sets the stage for a nuanced examination of how the courts have engaged with this movement, grounded in knowledge from the field of education policy.

A Brief History of Standards-Based Reform and Accountability Policies

Although standards-based reform emerged in the 1980s, it represented the convergence of several historical, political, and intellectual forces present throughout U.S. history and the 20th century in particular. This section discusses these forces and some major historical events in order to provide the needed context for a detailed discussion of standards-based reforms throughout the rest of this book. While this discussion is far from comprehensive about the various forces and events that influenced the development of standards-based reforms, this section focuses on what many observers have considered the most important forces and events prefiguring the standards-based reform movement.

As discussed above, the standards-based reform movement entails significant changes in the traditional structure of the U.S. education system. For much of U.S. history, educational decision making was very decentralized, as teachers and local school boards possessed much of the power to determine how and what students learned.[1] Teachers often worked in isolated classrooms and made most of the decisions regarding the education of their students by themselves. Administrators, who generally possessed administrative skills instead of pedagogical skills, oversaw teachers. Assessments were used in classrooms primarily to divide students into tracks or for diagnostic purposes—assessments could help teachers and administrators see whether students were learning the knowledge and skills embodied in loosely defined state curricula.[2] Schools were primarily accountable to districts, which were in turn accountable to local school boards. Parents could also hold schools accountable for their performance by "voting with their feet" and moving to areas served by higher-performing schools.

This is not to say that there were no broader standards that applied to schools. In the earliest days of formal schooling in the U.S., the curriculum embodied in a limited number of textbooks constituted a de facto curriculum for many schools and provided a sort of national standard.[3] Though somewhat varied, college entrance requirements before the 20th century also provided a sort of standard for schools. In 1892, the National Education Association (NEA) convened the Committee of Ten, a panel that issued a report calling for new curricular standards for all students, including those who would not go to college.[4] Although the recommendations of the Committee were not adopted, other de facto standards were promulgated in the form of various tests taken by students. Building on the intelligence testing movement that had emerged during World War I to predict the performance of soldiers at various tasks, the College Entrance Examination Board began to administer the Scholastic Aptitude Test (SAT) in 1926 to predict the readiness of high school students for college.[5] By the 1950s, the use of this test had become widespread, and although the College Entrance Examination Board claimed that the SAT was not designed to guide school standards, it likely constituted an important influence on what students were taught. Textbooks, developed by private companies and used in a wide range of classrooms, continued to standardize what was taught in schools as well.[6] But there were no formal standards guiding what students were taught through this time.

In the second half of the 20th century, the quality of public education came under increasing scrutiny, and both public and governmental attention focused on the quality of schools. *Sputnik's* launch in 1957 generated significant concern that the U.S. was not keeping pace with its international competitors and that the U.S. education system needed to produce more technologically capable students.[7] Given the additional focus on schools during the civil rights era as an institution that could remedy serious societal problems, drops in student performance on the SAT in the late 1960s and early 1970s also drew significant attention to the quality of schooling.[8] Student performance on the National Assessment of Educational Progress (NAEP), a federally-funded standardized test administered to a group of randomly selected students around the country, largely confirmed the trends in student performance indicated by the SAT.[9]

In this climate of increased political attention to education, states increasingly became involved with educational decision making and accountability with the enactment of minimum competency tests (MCTs) throughout the 1970s. Responding to critiques that the awarding of academic diplomas reflected unjustified social promotion and low academic standards, MCTs measured basic skills in subjects such as reading, writing, and mathematics. The use of accountability measures such as MCTs also reflected a growing concern that reformers could not improve the quality of schooling by simply increasing the level of resources, or inputs, provided to schools—the landmark "Coleman Report," published by a group of prestigious researchers in 1966, was interpreted by many as casting doubt on the direct relationship between educational resources (including funding, facilities, and curriculum) and student performance.[10] By 1979, 36 states had adopted some form of MCT, and 18 states required students to pass these tests in order to receive diplomas.

Despite the focus of these tests on boosting students' educational performance, the effects of these tests raised serious concerns—in almost every state that implemented a graduation test, at least 30 percent of the affected students initially failed the test, and African-American students failed the tests at a significantly higher rate than white students.[11] Indeed, the widespread use of MCTs in the 1970s reflects at least two major tensions in the historical purposes of testing in the U.S. that continue to apply today: First, while the demand for tests largely stems from the demand for fair treatment of all students, the use of tests often raises its own questions of fairness.[12] Second, while tests have consistently been used to ascertain the effects of schooling on students, testing has also been used extensively as an accountability mechanism to manage school systems that are perceived as inefficient and to influence curriculum and pedagogy.[13]

The publication of *A Nation at Risk*, a report drafted by a federally appointed panel in 1983, further intensified the public scrutiny of education. Proclaiming that the American education system was failing to educate students in a world characterized by fast economic and social changes, *A Nation at Risk* famously stated, "[T]he educational foundations of our society are presently being eroded by a rising tide of mediocrity that threatens our very future as a Nation and a people."[14] The report accordingly called for several reforms, including more rigorous expectations for students, better teacher preparation, and spending more time on learning. After the publication of *A Nation at Risk*, researchers released a slew of reports that similarly decried the state of the U.S. education system.[15]

This attention to the quality of schooling, focused by the publication of *A Nation at Risk*, served as an impetus for further reform and public support of reform. States began to get involved in educational decision making to a greater extent. In addition to administering MCTs, several states became involved in the "excellence movement" and engaged in a wide range of education reforms, including increasing graduation requirements, lengthening the school year, increasing requirements for teacher certification, and restructuring statewide systems of school finance.[16] This reform movement, however, prompted criticism of its own. Complaining that the reforms of the excellence movement were too "top down," critics called for more "bottom up" or local reforms, such as more time for teachers to plan together, and school-site management.[17] During the mid- to late-1980s, these movements converged as Lamar Alexander, the chair of the National Governor's Association, prominently called for a "horse trade." Under this trade, districts, schools, and teachers would be given increased flexibility in exchange for submitting to accountability measures. If schools agreed to become accountable for student performance, states would allow schools to pursue their own education reform. Unfortunately, none of the reform movements that emerged in the 1980s appeared to significantly change the education provided to students; the education reforms were generally unrelated to each other and sometimes contradictory, and despite the presence of these reforms, there was little change in student achievement.[18]

Reacting at least in part to the seeming inability of U.S. education reform efforts to effectively leverage change, researchers looked to the education systems of other countries.[19] Researchers highlighted that, in contrast to the U.S. education system, some foreign education systems were very centralized—these education systems were often characterized by a national curriculum that specified what students were to learn and therefore provided a stable foundation for a variety of policies that ranged from testing to teacher development. Many countries with these types of more centralized education systems notably outperformed the U.S. on international assessments. Thus, it appeared that the *coherence* of education policies to work together toward specified learning goals might be a key ingredient for enacting effective education reform.

It was precisely around this notion of coherence and the goal of more rigorous content for all students that reformers began to develop a new type of education reform. In the mid-1980s, California began to adopt sets of curriculum frameworks and assessments tied to these frameworks. A few other states, such as Kentucky and South Carolina, adopted reforms in a similar vein. These frameworks constituted specifications of what students should know and be able to do in different subjects, and they were to serve as the basis for the institution of education policies ranging from testing to the adoption of textbooks. In 1989, the National Council of Teachers of Mathematics (NCTM) published the *Curriculum and Evaluation Standards for School Mathematics* (*NCTM Standards*), the first extensive set of standards developed by a professional organization.[20] The *NCTM Standards* called for significant changes in the ways that mathematics was taught and learned— in contrast to learning basic skills, these standards called for students to engage each other in discussion about different concepts and to provide explanations for their thinking, and for teachers to facilitate discussions and to ask questions in ways that further their students' thinking. These standards were also to constitute a model that could be used by states or other entities attempting to institute a more coherent type of education reform around a high-quality vision of teaching and learning.

The Charlottesville Education Summit, a meeting between the administration of President George H. W. Bush and the nation's governors in September 1989 at the University of Virginia, also constituted a significant event that shaped the standards-based reform movement in its earliest stages. At this meeting, the Bush administration and the nation's governors forged a bipartisan agreement about the need for national performance goals for students. As a result of the discussions at the summit, the National Governors Association announced six goals for education in 1990.[21] In doing so, the governors paid specific attention to the traditional allocation of educational decision making authority—the governors explicitly indicated that a new "Federal-State Partnership" would need to be developed in order to enable the U.S. to achieve these goals. Thus, by the end of the 1980s and beginning of the 1990s, several different historical forces and entities, ranging from federal and state-level governmental officials to education researchers, were converging on the idea of restructuring the U.S. education system around rigorous, shared goals for students and the possibility of instituting tests and accountability systems tied to such goals.

Theories of Standards-Based Reform

By the beginning of the 1990s, fairly detailed theories about standards-based reform had begun to emerge. At this time, many used the term *systemic reform* to refer to standards-based reform. Although the term systemic reform has since fallen out of favor, the logic of systemic reform persists and underlies current standards-based reform policies mandated at both state and federal levels. Generally, systemic reform referred to the idea that standards or curriculum frameworks should provide an anchor for the development and implementation of coherent education policies—as some researchers had begun to highlight, the U.S. has traditionally maintained a multi-layered and fragmented system of education governance.[22] In this system, policy mandates, guidelines, incentives, sanctions, and programs at federal, state, and local levels interact with each other to create uncoordinated, and sometimes conflicting, demands for educators and administrators. By implementing systemic reform policies based around rigorous standards specifying what students should know and be able to do, policymakers could reduce this incoherence, and thereby boost the quality of education provided to students at the classroom level and reduce inequities in educational opportunities available to students. The idea of systemic reform, however, has been defined differently by different researchers, policymakers, and organizations. Thus, although systemic reform theories generally focus on the same core elements (such as high quality standards and increasing policy coherence), the components of systemic reform vary from theory to theory.[23]

The concept of systemic reform as defined by Marshall Smith and Jennifer O'Day in the early 1990s is perhaps the most influential construction of this theory. Although many of the key ideas underlying the concept of systemic reform were present before Smith and O'Day articulated their vision of systemic reform, their work crystallized several of these ideas in a persuasive and analytical form. Many of Smith and O'Day's ideas drew from the types of education reforms that had begun to be implemented in some states, such as California, during the 1980s and that researchers had begun to highlight in foreign countries. Their ideas also drew from the "effective schools movement," a strand of education research generally asserting that enacting isolated and individual reforms is not the most effective way to change schools.[24] Instead, reforms must work together to produce changes in school culture, which would significantly contribute to the effective functioning of schools.

Smith and O'Day particularly emphasized that, in order to influence what students were learning, change ultimately needed to occur at the most basic level of education—in classrooms and in schools.[25] In order to effect this sort of change through policy, O'Day and Smith identified three primary components of systemic reform:

1) Curriculum frameworks that establish what students know and be able to do would provide direction and vision for significantly upgrading the quality of the content and instruction within all schools in the state . . .

2) Alignment of state education policies would provide a coherent structure to support schools in designing effective strategies for teaching the content of the frameworks to all their students. Novice and experienced teachers would be educated to understand and teach the new challenging content, and teacher licensure would be tied to demonstrated competence in doing so. Curriculum materials adopted by the states and local districts, as well as state assessments of student performance, would reflect the content of the curriculum frameworks. The integration of these and other key elements of the systems would act to reinforce and sustain the reforms at the school building level.

3) Through restructured government systems, schools would have the resources, flexibility, and responsibility to design and implement effective strategies for preparing their students to learn the content of the curriculum frameworks to a high level of performance. This flexibility and control at the school site is a crucial element of the system, enhancing professionalization of instructional personnel and providing the basis for real change in the classroom.[26]

Two particular features of these components should be highlighted. First, these components focus on the notion of coherence or alignment. The components include the specification of challenging content that all students must learn, and the alignment of education policies, possibly ranging from the selection of textbooks to teacher development, around this content. Indeed, largely mirroring the focus of the *NCTM Standards*, Smith and O'Day emphasized that such content should entail higher-level cognitive goals that emphasize complex thinking skills and that aim at helping students actively draw connections between knowledge.[27] Attaining such goals requires substantial changes in the ways in which many subjects are taught and learned, as many teachers have traditionally focused on isolated facts and skills.

Second, these components position states as essential units in promoting systemic reform—O'Day and Smith's idea of systemic reform concentrates on upgrading educational quality within states and the alignment of statewide policies to achieve this goal. Still, O'Day and Smith expressly suggested that schools should be given a certain degree of flexibility to develop their own educational strategies. So, while O'Day and Smith focused on states as the primary drivers for educational changes, they also emphasized that the creation of a balanced approach, incorporating local decision making, is crucial for leveraging systemic change.

O'Day and Smith additionally noted that one of the "chief concerns" of systemic reform is the "equality of educational opportunity."[28] As one of the major justifications for their focus on equality of educational opportunity, O'Day and Smith emphasized trends in test scores, social and economic conditions, and instruction of poor and minority students. The authors concluded that, while poor and minority students had made educational gains in the 1970s and 1980s, the gap between these students and wealthier and nonminority was no longer continuing to close. Thus, O'Day and Smith asserted that systemic reform should improve the educational conditions of poor and minority students. O'Day and Smith accordingly emphasized that systemic reform includes the goals of providing challenging content for *all* students and providing strategies capable of reaching *all* schools.

To this end, O'Day and Smith argued that "opportunity to learn" standards (OTL standards) should be created. As they asserted, "Policy coherence may be a necessary prerequisite to systemic reform, but we cannot imagine that it is sufficient."[29] OTL standards would describe the resources that must be in place to enable teachers and schools to implement coherent education policies around challenging content. O'Day and Smith particularly indicated that these standards should be parsimonious and well focused, provide operational specifications for assessing whether a school is giving its students the opportunity to learn the content and skills set out in the curriculum frameworks, and offer the promise of allowing a clear linkage between inputs and outputs. Here, O'Day and Smith noted that a systemic reform strategy should align the "fundamental elements of the education infrastructure," including teacher training, certification, continuing professional development, curriculum materials, school curriculum, and assessment, to provide a different way of thinking "about the essential resources and practices of a high-quality school."[30]

Finally, O'Day and Smith argued for some form of accountability based on standards. The authors considered a variety of problems in using standards for improvement and accountability purposes, including conceptualizing and measuring the standards, deciding who should perform assessments, and the wide range of effects that standards could potentially have on schooling. Still, O'Day and Smith asserted that standards could be used to provide the public with information about the performance of schools, provide information to policymakers about schools that need help, and institute rewards and sanctions for school performance. Although these authors did not concretely specify any particular accountability strategy as integral to the concept of systemic reform, they clearly emphasized that assessment of student and school performance is important for systemic reform.

As noted above, various individuals and organizations proposed other versions of systemic reform. While some of these versions are very similar to O'Day and Smith's, other versions include components that do not seem to fit easily into O'Day and Smith's vision. For example, Chester Finn, a former Assistant Secretary of Education under President Ronald Regan, argued for a version of systemic reform that generally comports with Smith and O'Day's.[31] However, Finn also argued that curriculum frameworks should be established at the national level instead of the state level, that students should not be allowed to graduate from high school until they demonstrate their competency on national examinations tied to the curriculum frameworks, and that OTL standards should not be developed. University of Wisconsin professor William Clune conceptualized systemic reform in a similar way as Smith and O'Day, but broke down the concept of systemic reform into five primary components instead of three and seemed to suggest that more decentralized efforts could lead to effective reform.[32]

Some researchers have paid particular attention to the notion of OTL standards. Researchers had focused on the concept of opportunity to learn for at least 30 years before the seminal work of Smith and O'Day.[33] Like Smith and O'Day, these researchers were generally concerned about the variation in learning opportunities available to various groups of students and the resulting differences in student achievement. These researchers focused on differences in physical resources (such as textbooks and other instructional materials), curricular content, teacher qualifications, and pedagogical strategies employed by teachers.[34] Through the end of the 1980s and beginning of the 1990s, the concept of opportunity to learn became increasingly important as not just an academic issue but a policy issue as well—it represented for many a useful and emotive construction to address substantive differences in educational opportunity. The OTL standards suggested by Smith and O'Day, and discussed by other researchers, represented the way in which the concept of opportunity to learn could be embedded in education policies.

Like systemic reform, however, the concept of opportunity to learn has been defined by researchers in several different ways.[35] For example, some defined opportunity to learn primarily in terms of concrete resources, such as money and curricula. Others defined the concept as including school personnel, school processes, and other organizational features, such as school leadership, in addition to more concrete resources. Moreover, depending on political philosophy, OTL standards could be defined as requiring that all students receive the same learning opportunities or alternatively that students with fewer educational opportunities receive increased learning opportunities to enable them to meet set standards that apply to all students.[36] So, although there was much attention to the concept of opportunity to learn and push among the educational community for the construction of OTL standards, there was nothing approximating a universally accepted definition. As discussed later in this chapter, the fate of OTL standards in the political arena in the 1990s constituted a major event in the history of standards-based reforms, and as discussed in Chapter Three, courts gave much attention to the concept of opportunity to learn in high-stakes testing cases. Indeed, this concept will repeatedly surface throughout this book as it discusses various ways in which policymakers and courts have struggled to address educational problems.

In short, while there is no single or universally accepted theory of systemic reform or standards-based reform, proponents have generally called for challenging content, policy coherence, and some form of accountability to fundamentally restructure the U.S. education system. While there is similarly no universally accepted construction of opportunity to learn, researchers and policymakers have often focused on this concept as well and have looked to it as an important aspect of standards-based reforms to ensure that the necessary substantive resources are provided to all students in order to help them learn the skills and knowledge entailed by standards.

The Growth of Standards-Based Reform and Accountability Policies

Throughout the 1990s, standards-based reform and related accountability policies became increasingly popular around the U.S. at both the state and federal levels. As mentioned above, some states had begun implementing policies in the 1980s that set the stage for the standards-based reform movement in the 1990s. For example, California adopted challenging curriculum frameworks in the mid-1980s and continually revised them in the following years.[37] In the 1980s, Texas also adopted a set of "Essential Elements" in 12 core areas of knowledge, and Connecticut adopted the Common Core of

Learning, a set of voluntary general skills and outcomes for public schooling.[38] By the mid-1990s, various elements of standards-based reform policies were prevalent around the country—by 1996, 44 states had completed a math content standards document, and 38 states had instituted or were in the process of developing teacher licensure criteria linked to state standards.[39] Various states, such as Kentucky and Massachusetts, had also begun to institute accountability sanctions for low school or student performance on tests aligned with state standards.

Still, the implementation of several other elements of standards-based reforms proved to be much slower. By 1996, only 21 states had completed a math performance standards document.[40] Because performance standards detail specifically what students need to do in order to demonstrate that they have learned the content embodied in content standards, they constitute a critical element for the implementation of standards-based reform policies. Similarly, only 16 states had established a statewide mathematics assessment aligned with state standards by 1996, and only Kentucky had in place an assessment program fully consisting of innovative components like performance-based assessments and portfolios of students' work.

The standards-based reform movement, however, did not entirely occur at the state level. The federal government also played a significant role in shaping the standards-based reform movement and blending these reforms with accountability. In particular, federal laws passed in 1994 focused on further spurring the development and implementation of standards-based reforms and related accountability mechanisms at the state level. The passage of these laws added the weight of the federal government to the standards-based reform movement already growing around the U.S. and positioned the federal government as one of the most important players in this movement through the present day. Both the shape and implementation of federal law during the 1990s offer important insight into the ways in which standards-based reform and related accountability mechanisms have developed and the major types of problems these policies continue to face.

FEDERAL INVOLVEMENT IN STANDARDS-BASED REFORM IN THE 1990S

As noted in the Introduction, the federal role in education had traditionally been small but grew quickly after World War II. While the federal government had provided funds to states for educational purposes with laws such as the National Defense Education Act and Elementary and Secondary Education Act (ESEA), the federal government generally did not delve into microlevel education policy decision making. The Charlottesville Education Summit, however, signaled a profound shift in the federal role, as the federal government began to get deeply involved in setting goals for students and considering ways to restructure the U.S. education system. Indeed, although President George H. W. Bush did not initially alter his federal initiatives in response to the formulation of the national goals, he did attempt to involve the federal government more formally in the standards movement with the 1991 proposal of a bill titled the America 2000: Excellence in Education Act.[41] This bill was aimed at enabling students to meet the national education goals through the creation of "world-class" standards in five core subjects, the development of assessments to measure student performance, increased flexibility and accountability at state and local levels, and increased school choice options for parents. Because America 2000 faced a great deal of political opposition in Congress, largely based on concerns about the institution of school choice and voluntary national standards and tests, the bill was never enacted.[42]

But by the time President William Clinton took office, the idea of creating a piece of federal legislation aimed at leveraging standards-based reform around the country had gained a good deal of momentum. As discussed above, researchers were beginning to offer detailed arguments about the desirability of systemic reform, and states were increasingly implementing elements of standards-based reform policies. Moreover, Marshall Smith, who had worked with Jennifer O'Day to articulate one of the most influential conceptions of systemic reform, became the Under Secretary of Education in the Clinton administration. By signing into law the Goals 2000: Educate America Act in March 1994, President Clinton was able to incorporate systemic reform principles into federal law.[43]

The most fundamental components of Goals 2000 provided grants to states to develop their own content and performance standards and assessment systems aligned with these standards.[44] States were also to align curricula and instructional materials with these standards and to develop OTL standards. Goals 2000 further provided for the creation of national content and performance standards and national OTL standards that would serve as a model for states and could be voluntarily adopted by them.[45] In order to provide some sort of quality control for these different types of standards, Goals 2000 provided for the creation of the National Education Standards and Improvement Council (NESIC).[46] NESIC was to be composed of 19 members appointed by the President, and was required to certify and review state content and performance standards, national content and performance standards, state OTL standards, and national OTL standards. In doing so, NESIC would constitute a weak but clearly federal form of accountability over state educational decision making. In order to additionally hold states accountable for their use of Goals 2000 funds, the law required states to submit plans to the U.S. Department of Education (ED) specifying how such funds would be used.[47] While the passage of these federal-level accountability mechanisms proved difficult in Congress, largely because many conservatives strongly believed that Goals 2000 represented the unjustifiable expansion of federal power, Congress ultimately passed the law by bipartisan votes in both the House and Senate.

Building on the passage of Goals 2000, the 1994 reauthorization of the ESEA was framed by the principles of standards-based reform and accountability embodied in Goals 2000. Although the ESEA (and Title I in particular) was the most high-profile education law when President Clinton took office, most legislators did not attempt to reauthorize the ESEA until after Goals 2000 had been passed.[48] When Congress did reauthorize the ESEA with the passage of the Improving America's Schools Act (IASA) in October 1994, the ESEA was changed to complement Goals 2000.[49] Under the IASA, Title I conditioned the receipt of its funds upon the development of standards and assessment systems in each state. These standards and assessment systems were precisely the ones addressed by Goals 2000.

The IASA also required states to hold schools accountable for the performance of all students—under the IASA, states were required to test students at least once in grades three through five, once in grades six through nine, and once in grades ten through twelve. Moreover, the IASA required states to determine whether schools and districts were making adequate yearly progress (AYP) in bringing student performance on state assessments up to state standards, to identify schools that failed to make AYP for two consecutive years for school improvement, and to implement corrective action if needed.[50] The IASA also required states to align their Title I programs with these accountability policies to ensure that "disadvantaged" students were held to the same high standard as other students and to leverage the implementation of coherent education policies. The 1997 revisions to the Individuals with Disabilities Education Act later required states to include students with disabilities in state and district assessment programs (with appropriate accommodations), and to disaggregate and report the performance of these students.[51] As Goals 2000 was aimed at providing the federal direction and capacity for standards-based education reform, Title I of the IASA was aimed at providing incentives to do so.

Despite the bipartisan passage of Goals 2000 and the IASA, political controversy about federally-driven standards-based reforms and accountability surfaced soon after the passage of Goals 2000. Conservative groups like the

Christian Coalition and Women for America raised local opposition across the country against Goals 2000 in response to the spread of federal control.[52] Several members of Congress also spoke out against federal involvement in education and introduced several bills that would either repeal Goals 2000 entirely or eliminate some of its key provisions, especially after Republicans gained control of both houses of Congress in the beginning of 1995.[53] Several members of state governments voiced concerns about the intrusiveness of Goals 2000 into fundamental matters of state education policy as well.[54] In the face of these continuing attacks on the federal involvement in education, the Clinton administration proved reluctant to enforce Goals 2000 provisions—although few states had submitted plans within two years of the enactment of Goals 2000, states continued to receive Goals 2000 funds.[55]

In 1996, a little more than two years after Goals 2000 was passed, President Clinton signed into law P.L. 104–34—an appropriations bill that set the permanent 1996 budget and eliminated the most controversial language from Goals 2000, including the requirement that states submit school improvement plans to ED. While states were still technically required to make plans, states could receive Goals 2000 funds simply by making assurances to ED that the plans were indeed being made. The appropriations bill also eliminated NESIC and removed all references to OTL standards from Goals 2000. In short, P.L. 104–34 removed the accountability mechanisms from Goals 2000 and relieved the Clinton administration from the difficulty of enforcing controversial Goals 2000 mandates in an extremely hostile political climate.

Without federal willingness to enforce Goals 2000, however, states used their Goals 2000 money for a variety of uncoordinated educational activities, such as educational technology.[56] Indeed, states ultimately devoted only about five percent of their Goals 2000 funds to building and implementing standards and assessments.[57] And although states were required to construct systems of standards, assessments, and accountability in receipt for Title I funds under the IASA, they lagged far behind their statutory timelines for the development of these systems. As a result of political pressure and these ostensible failures, Goals 2000 was de-emphasized during the remainder of President Clinton's term—the administration largely abandoned Goals 2000 and focused instead on the upcoming reauthorization of the ESEA and unrelated categorical programs like the Reading Excellence Act and the Class-Size Reduction program. A similar attitude dominated Congress, as it allowed the authorization for Goals 2000 to lapse in 1999. Despite the seemingly bipartisan consensus about the desirability of standards-based reform, a hostile political climate reduced the effectiveness of federal, legislative efforts to leverage the development of standards-based reforms and to specify the opportunities students need to learn the material in state standards.

IMPLEMENTATION OF STANDARDS-BASED REFORMS IN THE STATES IN THE 1990s

As federal and state governments increasingly devoted attention to building standards-based reforms and related accountability systems in the 1990s, the structure of states' education systems began to change. This change, however, was not uniform across the U.S., and as is often the case with education policies, the policies governing standards-based reform at the state level were rarely, if ever, implemented in complete accordance with their underlying logic. Moreover, the policies that were implemented sometimes had unintended effects, especially at the classroom level. This section discusses the major trends in the implementation of standards-based reform and accountability policies in the 1990s that still appear to persist through the mid- to late-2000s. This section particularly focuses on the implementation of major elements of these policies: standards, curricula, assessments, accountability systems, and professional development. Then, this section discusses the ways in which instructional practices have changed and the known effects of these reforms on student performance.

Standards

As the documents that specify the substantive set of skills and knowledge that students are to learn, standards arguably constitute the most critical element of a standards-based reform system. By 1999, 48 states plus Puerto Rico and the District of Columbia had developed content standards, and 21 states plus Puerto Rico had developed performance standards.[58] By 2001, all states except Iowa had content standards in place in reading and math, and Iowa had submitted evidence to ED that it had content standards. Still, states faced significant challenges putting in place all the necessary standards. By 2001, only 28 states had approved performance standards.[59] Because performance standards are so related to the development of final assessments, it is clear that many states did not meet the timelines set forth in Title I of the IASA and did not have fully functioning standards-based reform systems.[60]

In addition to the challenges faced by states of drafting standards, the quality of the standards that states actually made was somewhat varied and sometimes low. Because each state drafted its own standards, at least three different groups—The Council for Basic Education, the American Federation of Teachers, and the Fordham Foundation—examined the varying quality of standards across states. While these groups generally disagreed about the quality of standards in each state, the groups all agreed that the quality of standards was not consistent from state to state.[61] For example, the Council for Basic Education found that, out of 42 states evaluated in English, 7 states had very rigorous standards, 21 states had rigorous standards, and 14 states had standards that were not rigorous.[62] Out of 43 states evaluated in mathematics, 16 states had very rigorous standards, 24 states had rigorous standards, and three states had standards that were not rigorous. The Fordham Foundation strikingly concluded that 30 states combined mediocre, poor, or no standards with weak accountability policies, while 12 states combined mediocre or inferior standards with high-stakes accountability systems.[63] The Fordham Foundation also found that several states' standards were very vague. Although the fundamental idea underlying standards-based reform entails the creation of high-quality and challenging standards for all students, achieving this goal consistently in all states has proven quite elusive.

Curricula and Assessments

While states had been using textbooks and assessments for several decades and for several different purposes before the standards-based reform movement began, restructuring state education systems by aligning curricula and assessments with standards has proven quite challenging as well. Researchers have estimated that 75 percent to 90 percent of classroom instructional time is structured by curricula contained in textbook programs.[64] Because textbooks have historically been produced by private companies that are heavily influenced by the pressures of market forces, textbooks have generally been structured to satisfy a few large buyers, such as textbook adoption committees in Texas and California.[65] Such market pressures drove the construction of textbooks and curricula through the 1990s and persist through the present.[66] As a result, the alignment between curricula and standards in states has been and remains to be uncertain. Moreover, textbooks and other physical elements of curricula (such as manipulatives) have sometimes been missing in classrooms, especially in the case of high-poverty schools with limited resources.[67]

Restructuring state education systems in accordance with a heavy focus on assessments aligned with standards has also proven quite challenging. By the 1999–2000 school year, statewide assessment systems for standards-based reform purposes were prevalent. Forty-eight states were using state assessments as the principal indicator for performance in mathematics and English or reading.[68] Despite the prevalence of statewide assessments, the development and administration of these assessments has proven difficult. Personnel at both state and district levels appear to have lacked sufficient technical knowledge and political will for developing and administering standards-based assessments (which were precisely the sorts of capacities Goals 2000 was aimed at increasing).[69] As a result, many state and district personnel reported little or no progress toward reaching these goals during the late 1990s.[70]

Studies focusing on the state-level implementation of assessments further bore out some of these concerns. Several studies raised specific concerns about the *validity* of state assessment systems. Generally speaking, the concept of validity is employed by psychometricians to refer to the extent to which the interpretations and uses of test scores are justifiable. While psychometricians have defined validity in several different ways in well over half a century of considering this concept, major professional organizations of the psychological and educational communities (including the American Educational Research Association) have come together to create the *Standards for Educational and Psychometric Testing* (*AERA Standards*), a document indicating that several different types of evidence should be considered to ensure the validity of a testing practice.[71] For example, evidence should indicate that the content included on tests well represents the content intended to be assessed, that performance on tests corresponds to behavior in the real world, and that the internal structure of tests represents the domain of knowledge or skills being assessed.[72]

Given that validity focuses on the match between a testing practice and the skills and knowledge that the testing practice is intended to measure, establishing that testing practices are valid is crucial for implementing standards-based reforms—in order for state education policies to be coherent, testing practices must yield valid interpretations about the extent to which students know the content and skills embodied in standards. However, state assessments have failed to be consistently well aligned with state standards, and sometimes the alignment between state tests and state standards has been so weak that tests used in one state have had a greater alignment with standards used in another state.[73] Because of the difficulty and expense of developing and administering tests that yield valid inferences about higher-order thinking skills, statewide assessment systems have also tended to focus on basic skills instead of the more difficult skills included in some sets of standards.[74] As a result of such challenges, states have often purchased "off the shelf" tests from testing companies.[75] Because commercially developed tests must appeal to wide markets, most commercial tests generally focus on basic skills as well.

States have faced especially difficult challenges implementing testing practices that are valid with regard to students with limited English proficiency (LEP) or disabilities. In the case of LEP students, performance on a test may improperly reflect language comprehension in addition to (or instead of) students' mastery of the content.[76] The presence of certain "accommodations," such as additional time to complete tests, does not necessarily solve such validity issues. Many states have also relied heavily on norm-referenced tests instead of criterion-referenced tests to measure student performance in relation to state standards.[77] Criterion-referenced tests generally enable states to make more valid interpretations of student performance in relation to standards.[78] In the specific case of LEP students, the use of norm-referenced tests can exacerbate extant validity issues.[79] It has similarly proven difficult to assess the knowledge and skills of students with various disabilities, even when various accommodations are permitted.[80] Indeed, validating testing practices is an extremely difficult and technical process that poses particular challenges for states with regard to students with disabilities and limited English proficiency, especially in a context of limited knowledge and limited political will to implement valid testing practices at state and district levels.

Accountability

Although accountability policies focused on schools arguably do not constitute a necessary element of a standards-based reform system, they accompanied the development and implementation of standards-based reforms around the U.S. While many components of standards-based reforms are aimed at focusing policy mandates in a coherent way for the education of all students and at providing various entities with the capacities to effect instructional change, accountability systems have somewhat different goals. Accountability systems are generally aimed at motivating various entities to change their behavior through the collection of information about their performance and the application of rewards or sanctions based on such performance. Moreover, accountability systems can arguably provide motivation for affected entities to develop capacities for change if they do not already possess such capacities.

Like state standards and testing practices, accountability systems differed dramatically across the states.[81] By the 1999–2000 school year, 33 states set performance goals for schools or districts (generally on the basis of scores on criterion- and norm-referenced tests) and held these units directly accountable for meeting these goals. Nineteen of these states included noncognitive indicators, such as graduation rates, in their accountability systems. The performance goals for schools under these accountability systems varied widely across states—the percentage of students in a school expected to meet basic or proficient standards varied significantly, and schools in some states had to meet multiple performance thresholds (such as maintaining sufficient performance on tests and a sufficient graduation rate). States also defined AYP under the IASA differently—while some states required all schools to meet an absolute target, other states held schools accountable for relative growth in relation to their starting points and/or for narrowing the achievement gap. Only six states accounted for subgroup performance, such as the performance of minority students or LEP students, in schools.

As a result of failure to meet performance goals, schools were subject to a number of possible accountability sanctions, including mandatory development of improvement plans, mandatory technical assistance, on-site audits or monitoring by state officials, probationary status or placement on a state warning list, loss of state accreditation status, transfer or replacement of instructional or administrative status, mandatory provision of options for students to transfer schools, state takeover or reconstitution, and school closure. So, while states had begun to develop standards-based accountability systems in the 1990s, the implementation of these systems was quite varied across the states in both character and strength.

Although the IASA required states to implement unitary assessment systems for Title I schools and non-Title I schools to ensure that all students were held to the same standards and treated fairly, states also faced significant challenges fulfilling this requirement. By the 2000–2001 school year, only 22 states had unitary systems in place that held all schools or districts to the same standards, regardless of their Title I status.[82] Twenty-eight states had dual systems of accountability in which Title I schools had different standards or only Title I schools were held accountable. Twelve states with dual systems had established one system of accountability for all schools and separate systems for Title I schools. Moreover, many states provided different types of assistance to Title I schools than to non-Title I schools. The prevalence of such dual systems appears to have stemmed from a number of interrelated factors, including differing purposes of the two systems, differences in the administrative units that identified schools as failing, and general problems in implementation and administrative coordination.[83]

Several of these administrative problems resided in state departments of education. Many administrators indicated that they did not have adequate staff and felt that they were unable to meet the technical assistance needs of local districts (again demonstrating the lack of capacity that Goals 2000 was to provide).[84] In this context of limited capacity, many administrators also indicated that they did not know what to measure for accountability purposes, and they were reluctant to link program success to student achievement. Similar problems faced district level personnel as well—while the vast majority of district personnel believed that they understood what it took to establish standards-based accountability systems, very few district personnel believed that establishing such systems constituted a major change, and about one-third of district personnel included in a survey reported little to no progress in linking school or district accountability to student performance.[85] As was also the case with establishing assessments linked to standards, establishing school and district level accountability systems is an extremely difficult and technical process, especially in a context of limited technical knowledge and potentially limited political will. These challenges, in combination with the flexibility permitted under federal law, appear to have largely driven the variable shape and strength of accountability systems around the country. As discussed further below, accountability systems have not consistently resulted in their intended effects and have sometimes resulted in quite negative effects on the behavior of educators, who are the primary entities targeted by accountability systems.

Professional Development

Given that a central part of the logic of standards-based reform is changing teachers' practice to reflect state standards, reformers have focused on professional development as another key element of standards-based reform. Teachers have often struggled to alter their behavior to educate students in accordance with the instructional principles and content embodied in standards.[86] For these individuals, it is not enough to simply teach harder; instead, teaching in accordance with state standards, and a curriculum and test aligned with these standards, demands a different educational approach. High-quality professional development tied to the skills and knowledge embodied in standards can arguably help teachers gain the skills they need to change their practice.

Although high-quality professional development is difficult to definitively define, education researchers and practitioners have reached a national consensus that this kind of professional development includes at least six components: High-quality professional development must show teachers how to connect their work to standards for student performance, must immerse participants in model inquiry forms of teaching, must be intensive and sustained, must engage teachers in concrete teaching tasks and be based on teachers' experiences with students, must focus on subject matter knowledge and deepen teachers' skills, and must be connected to other aspects of school change.[87] In some cases, professional development that comported with this vision appears to have significantly altered teachers' instructional practices.[88] For example, in one study of the implementation of California's mathematics curriculum frameworks, researchers focused on elementary school teachers' opportunities to learn the content embodied in these frameworks and concluded that high-quality professional development was a key element spurring changes in teachers' practices.[89] However, it is important to note that only about 10 percent of the teachers examined in this study received what were considered strong learning opportunities through professional development. Various factors influenced the professional development actually received by the teachers, including the delegation of public authority for providing professional development to private firms without strong guidance, the range of professional development providers and professional development opportunities accordingly available to teachers, and teachers' expansive freedom to choose their professional development.

Focusing on the support provided by states to teachers, other reports have similarly found that many states have not provided teachers with the guidance they needed to effectively employ instructional strategies aligned with curricular standards—while teachers generally receive a substantial amount of professional development throughout their careers, such professional development has not proven consistently sufficient to leverage changes in teachers' practice.[90] Indeed, there is historically little research on the quality of professional development that teachers have actually and typically received in the context of standards-based reform efforts.[91] So, while high-quality professional development may have the potential to leverage changes in teachers' practice in accordance with state standards, the quality of professional development that teachers have actually received appears to be uncertain and likely uneven.

Instruction

Given that the central goal of standards-based reform is ultimately to change what occurs in the classroom and to thereby boost the learning opportunities of all students, examining the impact of standards-based reform and accountability policies on instruction is critical—the classroom is where the proverbial rubber hits the road for standards-based reform. Several researchers have examined the extent to which teachers' instructional practices comported with their states' standards and tests. As some researchers have found, instructional practices in a state were generally no more aligned to that state's test than it was aligned to the tests of other states, suggesting that standards-based reform has not brought instruction into alignment with states' tests.[92] Similarly, in a study about the effects of testing systems on social studies teachers in New York, one researcher found that testing systems did not have a direct influence on how teachers made decisions about content or pedagogy.[93]

This is not to say, however, that standards-based reform has been entirely unsuccessful at changing teachers' practice. As discussed above, many elementary school teachers in California who received high-quality learning opportunities adopted new instructional practices that comported with the principles of instruction embodied in the state's mathematics curriculum frameworks.[94] However, many of these teachers also adopted new instructional practices for mathematics in a piecemeal fashion and resisted changes in fundamental aspects of their teaching practices. Other researchers have observed similar patterns elsewhere. For example, one researcher examined the instructional practices of language arts teachers in a district working to align its instructional policies to support high-quality learning goals consistent with a state's standards-based reform policies.[95] On the surface level, these teachers' instructional practices largely reflected the district's messages about high-quality instruction. But a closer look at these instructional practices at the level of implementing specific tasks and engaging in classroom discourse revealed that some essential dimensions of classroom practice were resistant to change.

A particularly important factor influencing these teachers' response to reform efforts appears to have been the teachers' prior knowledge, experiences, and orientations toward the principles of teaching and learning embodied in reform efforts. Other researchers have confirmed the important role that such personal traits play in the implementation of standards-based reforms at the classroom level.[96] Indeed, such beliefs can play a particularly potent role in guiding teachers' instructional practices in high-poverty schools.[97] In the case of one state implementing standards-based reform in the late 1990s, researchers found that teachers generally taught basic skills to students instead of engaging in more rigorous instruction where teachers believed that poor students were not capable of learning challenging skills and content.[98]

In addition to the personal beliefs and experiences of teachers, several other intangible factors appear to have influenced the implementation of standards-based reforms at the classroom level. Some researchers have pointed to the "internal accountability" of schools as an important capacity for implementing standards-based reform effectively.[99] The term internal accountability refers to collective views held by schools about what students need in order to learn and to well-developed organizational processes to actualize these beliefs. Thus, schools with a high degree of internal accountability possess shared expectations about student performance and instructional practice, and have a high degree of school-wide coherence. Principals have proven to be key figures in fostering internal accountability within schools—principals can manage the curriculum, teacher assignment, various physical and financial resources, and focus teachers' attention on the skills and knowledge embodied in the standards. Unfortunately, many principals appear to have lacked the skills to provide this sort of leadership, and the technical assistance provided to principals in failing schools around content, standards, and testing has generally proven ineffective.[100] As a result, the support in turn provided to teachers and the environments created in schools regarding instruction have varied drastically.[101]

The school district has proven to be another important administrative unit that has influenced the extent to which teachers have changed instructional practices in accordance with standards.[102] Districts can articulate clear and coherent goals for schools, and can be a source of both pressure and support for schools. However, the will of district officials to provide a clear vision of instructional change and an understanding of the reforms by district officials have constituted key factors influencing the extent to which districts have promoted instructional change.[103] Moreover, larger districts generally appear to have possessed greater resources to support schools in implementing standards-based reforms, and districts with high levels of political flexibility have also provided effective support.[104] Thus, in addition to the characteristics of particular teachers, certain characteristics of schools and districts, such as political will and knowledge about reform, have also significantly influenced the extent to which standards-based reform has leveraged instructional change at the classroom level.

The presence of accountability systems tied to states' standards-based reform policies has had important effects on educators as well. Educators have had mixed responses to accountability systems.[105] Some educators have indicated that accountability systems are beneficial because these systems focus attention on instruction and student performance. On the other hand, many educators have criticized accountability systems on several grounds, including operational and technical aspects of these systems, overly high expectations for students, and the resulting impetus to narrow the range of content taught to reflect only what is tested. Despite these mixed reactions, accountability systems have generally influenced instructional practices in schools—schools have adopted a range of instructional reforms, including adoption of new curricula arguably aligned more closely to standards, new basic skills and advanced courses, and remedial programs like test preparation. Such changes, however, have rarely altered teachers' instructional practices in fundamental ways. Furthermore, researchers have generally found that tests have focused schools and teachers on the content embodied in tests at the expense of untested content, and that tests have focused a significant number of teachers on decontextualized test preparation activities.

In addition to the sheer presence of accountability systems, the strength of such systems has played an important role in structuring schools' and teachers' responses. Stronger state accountability systems have produced a greater response in high schools for focusing instruction on the skills and knowledge embodied in state standards.[106] Still, high schools have exhibited a great deal of variability in their response to accountability systems, regardless of whether they were situated in a state with a strong or weak accountability system. Indeed, this variability reinforces the importance of will and capacity for instructional change at both the school and district level as important factors influencing the responses of educators to external policy change.[107]

Accountability systems tied to state standards have important implications for equity of instruction within schools. Some accountability systems, such as Texas' in the 1990s, required the disaggregation of school-level student performance data using certain categories, including the performance of specific minority groups and LEP students. In at least some cases, the accountability system's disaggregation requirement generated a shared focus among educators on learning for all students.[108] At the same time, however, accountability systems have created inequities in the type of instruction received by students. In schools with greater numbers of low-income students, teachers engaged in a large amount of very focused, decontextualized test preparation as pressure to perform on the test mounted.[109] Thus, exhibiting major historical tensions in the theory of testing, modern accountability systems have focused educators on issues of equity while simultaneously raising questions of fairness.

Student Performance

Given that the ultimate goal of standards-based reform and accountability policies is to increase the academic performance of all students and to promote educational equity for all students, student performance trends constitute a critical piece of information for understanding the effects of these policies. Because differences in assessments across states make it difficult to track student achievement on a nationwide basis, the NAEP constitutes a useful instrument for observing large-scale changes in student achievement. The NAEP is consistent across the states, and while the NAEP does not align with state tests, it provides independent measures of student achievement in mathematics and reading. Nationwide NAEP scores rose very slightly in both reading and mathematics for all schools from 1992 to 1999.[110] For example, reading scores for nine-year olds rose by one point during this time period, and mathematics scores for nine-year olds rose by three points. NAEP scores in the highest-poverty schools rose at a slightly greater rate during this time period. For example, reading scores for nine-year olds in the highest poverty schools rose by six points, and mathematics scores for nine-year olds rose by four points. However, longer-term trends from the late 1980s to 1999 indicate a widening of the achievement gap in NAEP scores between high- and low-poverty schools—the achievement gap between high- and low-poverty schools during the 1990s was approximately equal to a difference of three grade levels. Thus, it is very difficult to conclude from nationwide NAEP scores that standards-based reform and accountability systems were having their intended effects on student performance during the 1990s. Given the significant impact of NCLB on the policy landscape beginning in early 2002, this chapter will continue its discussion of nationwide trends in NAEP scores where attention is devoted to NCLB and its effects, and the recent directions in which standards-based reforms have begun to turn.

Despite the inconclusiveness of data from the administration of the NAEP in the 1990s, data from assessments in some states and localities during this time seem to support the efficacy of standards-based reform to increase student performance. As discussed above, California was one of the first states to seriously implement standards-based reform policies. During the mid-1990s, California aligned transitional high school mathematics courses with high quality standards. As part of this effort, California provided professional development to high school teachers regarding the content and pedagogy necessary to teach in accordance with the standards. Students enrolled in courses with teachers who received this professional development had a greater chance than general track students to complete college preparatory coursework by the end of high school.[111] These students also exhibited greater achievement gains than students in general mathematics. Another study focusing on standards-based education reform in California yielded similar findings in regard to elementary students.[112] As discussed above, many elementary school teachers who received high-quality professional development changed their instructional practices accordingly, and their students exhibited achievement gains on mathematics tests. The students of teachers who received professional development unaligned with the curriculum, however, did not exhibit the same achievement gains. Similar trends have emerged in some other states as well.[113] For example, in Michigan and Connecticut, student achievement in mathematics increased on the NAEP after both states began to initiate standards-based mathematics reforms.

Researchers have additionally focused on the influence of accountability systems on student performance. Upon examination of test results in Texas and North Carolina, both of which instituted strong accountability systems with consequences for schools and districts in the early 1990s, some researchers found that these states made much larger gains on the NAEP between 1992 and 1996 than other states.[114] Other researchers similarly found that states with strong accountability systems aimed at schools and districts made larger gains on the NAEP between 1996 and 2000.[115] However, focusing on the technical aspects of test construction and dropout rates in the specific case of Texas, some researchers concluded that the "Texas Miracle" was nothing more than a myth.[116] These researchers also found that the achievement gap between African-American and white students in Texas was large and increasing slightly, and that the implementation of Texas's accountability system may have increased the dropout rate of the state's lowest performing students. Researchers have similarly disagreed about the effects of the implementation of high-stakes accountability policies on student achievement in Chicago.[117] And even where one researcher concluded that achievement gains in Chicago were real, he also found that student performance gains generally occurred on test items that reflected mastery of basic skills.[118] In a broad study of high-stakes testing programs in 18 states, some researchers concluded that accountability systems have had no effect or even a negative effect on student performance.[119] So, likely reflecting the uneven implementation of standards-based reform and accountability policies at various administrative levels, and the potentially negative effects of overly strong accountability measures, the evidence of the impact of these policies on student achievement is quite mixed.

No Child Left Behind

Despite the array of challenges facing standards-based reform and accountability policies, both governmental and public attention continued to focus on these policies through the beginning of the 21st century. In January 2002, President George W. Bush signed No Child Left Behind (NCLB), a sweeping law that reauthorized the ESEA for the first time since the IASA and that solidified the federal government's role in the standards-based reform movement.[120] Building on the previous requirements of the IASA and the strong standards-based accountability systems implemented in Texas while Bush was governor of the state, NCLB required states that receive Title I funds to develop standards and assessments, and to hold schools and districts accountable for their performance on the assessments. If schools and districts failed to meet their performance goals, a variety of administrative sanctions were prescribed. While the statutory provisions governing standards and assessments were not entirely new at the federal level, the accountability mandates included in NCLB were unprecedented; the federal government had never before specified in such detail the steps that states, districts, and schools must take to increase student performance if schools failed to perform adequately.

According to its statutory text, the primary purpose of NCLB was to "ensure that all children have a fair, equal, and significant opportunity to obtain a high-quality education and reach, at a minimum, proficiency on challenging State academic achievement standards and academic assessments."[121] In order to achieve this purpose, NCLB specified in great detail the specific means that must be used. NCLB required states to submit plans specifying how they would comply with the requirements of NCLB.[122] Moreover, NCLB required states to adopt their own challenging academic standards in reading, mathematics, and science that described at least three levels of achievement—basic, proficient, and advanced.[123] NCLB also required each state to adopt a system of assessments to monitor the progress of student achievement in relation to state standards.[124] Through the 2004–2005 school year, states were required to administer reading and mathematics tests at least once annually to students in three different grades.[125] Beginning in the 2005–2006 school year, states were required to administer these tests at least once annually to students in grades three through eight, and once annually to students in grades ten, eleven, or twelve.[126] States were also required to begin administering science tests in the 2007–2008 school year.[127]

In addition to increasing the amount of testing required under the IASA, NCLB significantly strengthened and focused the requirements governing statewide accountability systems. Like the IASA, NCLB required states to ensure that all of their schools and districts make "adequate yearly progress" (AYP).[128] In order to comply with this mandate, states were required to define for themselves what constitutes an acceptable annual increase of student proficiency on state assessments. This annual increase must have included separate objectives for economically disadvantaged students, students from major racial and ethnic groups, students with disabilities, and LEP students.[129] NCLB also required states to ensure that each of these student subgroups reaches proficiency within 12 years of NCLB's enactment, or by 2014. NCLB importantly stated that state assessments must be used for purposes for which the assessments are valid, reliable, and consistent with nationally recognized professional standards, and that AYP determinations must be statistically valid and reliable as well.[130]

While NCLB required students in all schools to take state assessments, only schools that received Title I funds were accountable for making AYP. If a school failed to make AYP, the school became subject to a variety of accountability measures: NCLB required a school that failed to make AYP for two consecutive years to be identified for school improvement. When a local educational agency (LEA) (which is generally equivalent to a school district) contained a school labeled for school improvement, the LEA was required to provide all students enrolled in that school with the option to transfer to another public school within the LEA.[131] If a school failed to make AYP after its first year of identification for school improvement, NCLB required the school's LEA to make "supplemental educational services" available to all of its students.[132] Supplemental services providers generally provided extra tutoring to students, and under NCLB, these providers were required to have a demonstrated record of effectiveness, to be selected by parents, and to be approved by the proper state.[133]

If a school failed to make AYP after its second year of identification for school improvement status, NCLB required that school to be identified for corrective action.[134] Once a school was identified for corrective action, that school's LEA was required to implement at least one out of the six following actions:

(i) Replace the school staff who are relevant to the failure to make adequate yearly progress. (ii) Institute and fully implement a new curriculum, including providing appropriate professional development for all relevant staff, that is based on scientifically based research and offers substantial promise of improving educational achievement for low-achieving students and enabling the school to make adequate yearly progress. (iii) Significantly decrease management authority at the school level. (iv) Appoint an outside expert to advise the school on its progress toward making adequate yearly progress . . . (v) Extend the school year or school day for the school. (vi) Restructure the internal organizational structure of the school.[135]

If a school failed to make AYP after its first year of identification for corrective action, the school's LEA was required to implement one out of another set of even more demanding actions:

(i) Reopening the school as a public charter school. (ii) Replacing all or most of the school staff (which may include the principal) who are relevant to the failure to make adequate yearly progress. (iii) Entering into a contract with an entity, such as a private management company, with a demonstrated record of effectiveness, to operate the public school.

(iv) Turning the operation of the school over to the State . . . (v) Any other major restructuring of the school's governance arrangement that makes fundamental reforms.[136]

NCLB also contained some provisions directed at ensuring that states, districts, and schools possessed the capacity to implement these NCLB accountability requirements. The law required the U.S. Secretary of Education to provide states, at their request, with technical assistance to develop and implement standards and assessments, and for making AYP determinations.[137] The law also allowed ED to provide grants to states for the implementation of school improvement measures and for states in turn to award subgrants to districts and schools for this purpose. In specific regard to the subgrants, NCLB provides that the subgrants must be of "sufficient size and scope" to support required school improvement and corrective action activities.[138] However, NCLB also capped the amount available through these subgrants at $500,000 per school and indicated that states may prioritize the distribution of such funds on the basis of need and commitment to ensuring that the funds will be used properly.[139] Accordingly, some language in NCLB appears to have allowed school improvement grants to be insufficient for the purpose of providing schools and districts with the financial capacity to implement NCLB consequences effectively. Similarly, NCLB set a funding floor for the creation of assessments, but as discussed later, the funding provided above this floor has proved insufficient for this purpose.[140]

NCLB further provided that states must "establish a statewide system of intensive and sustained support of improvement" for LEAs to increase the opportunity for students to meet state standards.[141] In order to accomplish this task, states were required to provide "support and assistance" to LEAs with schools that had failed to make AYP and create "school support teams" to review all facets of a schools operation and to collaborate with parents and staff.[142]

NCLB also contained provisions requiring states to ensure that all public school teachers in core subjects were "highly qualified" by the end of the 2005–2006 school year. The definition of a highly-qualified teacher (HQT) varied for different types of teachers—current teachers had different requirements than new teachers, and elementary teachers had different requirements than middle or high school teachers. However, NCLB generally required teachers to be fully certified and to have demonstrated their knowledge and skills by taking sufficient academic coursework in their field, by passing a state test, or by successfully completing a rigorous state evaluation.[143]

In order to accomplish these goals, Congress provided for large increases in education funding. Upon NCLB's passage, ED's discretionary budget was increased to $48.9 billion.[144] This figure represented an increase of 15.9 percent—the largest in the history of ED. NCLB funds were also authorized at higher levels than ever before in the history of the ESEA. For its first year of implementation, NCLB was authorized at $26.4 billion. In its second year, it was authorized at $29.2 billion, and in its third year, it was authorized at $32 billion. Notably, these authorization levels were the outcome of much congressional debate featuring vastly different positions regarding the funding that states need to effectively implement the new requirements of NCLB and help students reach proficiency—while leaders of both parties generally agreed that federal funds needed to be used more efficiently, Democrats called for much more funding than Republicans, and the final funding levels represented serious political compromises.[145] Indeed, NCLB contains the "Unfunded Mandates Provision," which prohibits federal officers or employees from mandating states and localities to spend funds for costs not paid for by NCLB.[146] This provision has become particularly important in the debates that surround the implementation of NCLB and cases launched to influence it.

THE IMPLEMENTATION OF NCLB

Since NCLB was passed, the implementation of several of its key provisions has proven quite difficult. The lack of adequate funding for NCLB testing and accountability mandates appears to have constituted one of the most serious NCLB implementation problems. As states began to implement NCLB, they were experiencing one of the worst fiscal crises since World War II. In 2003, states faced a combined budget gap of $17.5 billion, and 31 states faced deficits.[147] Nevertheless, congressional appropriations fell markedly short of NCLB authorization levels, and the costs for states to implement NCLB have proven to be very high.[148] For example, the General Accounting Office estimated that it would cost $1.9 billion between FY 2002 and FY 2008 for states to implement the simplest types of testing programs, and more sophisticated testing systems could cost up to $5.3 billion.[149] As a result, the cost of test development and administration exceeded NCLB funding in several states, and it would have been extremely expensive for states to have expanded the question types they used to increase the validity of their testing practices.[150] States similarly appear to have lacked the fiscal capacities necessary to fully implement the consequences for failure to make AYP. The implementation of the school choice and supplemental services provisions has already proven costly in states, and as NCLB continued to be implemented, the cost of implementing other NCLB accountability mandates has mounted as well.[151]

Some reports also argued that states lacked the funds necessary to bring their students up to the proficient level as required by NCLB.[152] As a result of such concerns, a variety of individuals and organizations have repeatedly attacked NCLB funding levels and have labeled NCLB an "unfunded mandate."[153]

In addition to these funding issues, states have faced several other problems implementing consequences for school failure to make AYP. States have not come close to offering public school choice to all students who were required to receive the option.[154] An array of factors not directly related to funding conspired to lower the capacities of schools and districts to implement the choice provisions, including an insufficient number of receiving schools, insufficient amount of space, countervailing state policies, and overly tight timeframes. Indeed, due to their inabilities to offer public school choice, many districts instead offered supplemental services.[155] Nevertheless, states have faced significant problems implementing the supplemental services provisions of NCLB. Student access to supplemental services providers has not been consistent across the states, and the amount and quality of services provided to students appears to have varied dramatically.[156]

The HQT provisions of NCLB have also proven difficult for states to implement effectively. Just before NCLB began to be implemented, only a little over half of U.S. secondary teachers could be considered highly qualified.[157] Efforts to raise the number of HQTs have faced many problems. Severe teacher shortages have plagued staffing efforts in high-need subjects, and many states have broadly distributed Title II funds, which have generally been earmarked for preparing, training, and recruiting high-quality teachers and principals, instead of focusing these funds more narrowly on schools that have not met the HQT requirements.[158] In addition, states have faced difficulties implementing information systems to track teacher qualifications data, and states consequently appear to have lacked the information necessary to direct resources where they were most needed, such as in high-poverty schools, for boosting teacher quality. Given these difficulties, many states have developed low standards for defining what constitutes an HQT.[159]

Perhaps most importantly, many problems regarding states' standards and testing practices have surfaced. Since NCLB was passed, the quality of content standards developed by states has continued to vary dramatically across states, and the quality of some states' standards has been rated as quite low.[160] Similar issues have also surfaced in states' systems for determining whether schools make AYP. As states had the power to somewhat set their own definitions of AYP under NCLB, states used a variety of methods to determine whether schools made AYP. States set first year AYP goals at very different points.[161] Moreover, states used different methods to determine whether schools made AYP from year to year—as one implementation report indicates, three states that were surveyed created a system in which schools would make AYP by making generally equal annual increases in student progress, but 14 states staggered improvement over two- or three-year intervals rather than one-year increments, and 18 states used a combination method. An additional factor that has proven particularly detrimental to the statistical justifiability of AYP decisions stems from decisions about the minimum number of students necessary to constitute an assessable subgroup for AYP purposes. Researchers have suggested that many states have set the number of students sufficient to constitute an assessable subgroup as too low and consequently risked over-identification of the number of schools that fail to make AYP.[162] As a result of varying standards, tests administered by states, and methods of determining AYP, researchers have questioned the validity of AYP determinations under NCLB.[163]

States have also implemented the major school support and assistance provisions of NCLB in varied ways. Strategies implemented by states include the provision of or grants for school improvement, assigning a state-approved school support team to review school operations and make recommendations, providing assistance to schools through institutions of higher education, educational service agencies, or private providers, and assigning a distinguished principal and/or teacher to work with a school.[164] In response to such strategies, district superintendents indicated that they needed more help in several areas, including notifying parents that a district needs improvement, implementing a new curriculum based on state and local content standards, and authorizing students to transfer from district schools to schools in a higher-performing district. Moreover, it appears that almost half of the schools in corrective action or restructuring did not receive any of the required support from their district.[165]

In the midst of the various implementation problems that NCLB has faced, NCLB appears to have spurred some changes at the school and classroom level. On one hand, it appears that NCLB has focused educators on state standards, the performance of various subgroups of students in relation to these standards, and on using data effectively to inform classroom practices.[166] On the other hand, NCLB appears to have intensified the pressure and expectations placed on teachers to the extent that they have often felt overwhelmed. In this climate, teachers have faced increased pressure to "teach to the test" and thereby engage in activities such as teaching students how to fill in answer sheets and focusing narrowly on test-taking skills.[167] These effects appear to have been exacerbated in high-poverty areas where schools faced a significant risk of failure to make AYP. Moreover, some teachers appear to have facilitated cheating to raise test scores of their students, and significant questions remain about the extent to which NCLB has leveraged classroom practice into closer alignment with state standards.

Since NCLB was enacted, several groups have attempted to link NCLB with student achievement trends. The conclusions reached by these groups have been mixed. The Bush administration focused on NAEP results, released in July 2005, that more progress was made by nine-year-olds in reading in the last five years than in the previous 28 years combined, that nine-year-olds had their best scores in reading and mathematics in this history of the NAEP, and that achievement gaps in reading and mathematics between white and African-American and between white and Hispanic nine-year-olds were at an all-time low. Based on these results, the Bush administration concluded that NCLB "is working."[168] Other organizations, such as Education Week, Education Trust, and the Northwest Evaluation Association, found that student performance on state tests was rising nationally and that achievement gaps were narrowing or staying the same.[169]

However, the Northwest Evaluation Association also found that student growth rates have decreased and that student growth in every ethnic group has slightly decreased since NCLB was implemented.[170] Moreover, NAEP scores did not show consistent rises in student performance in reading and mathematics between 2002 and 2005 or a narrowing of the achievement gap in all tested grades.[171] And as noted by the Center on Education Policy, some portion of student performance gains may have been due to increased student learning, but another portion may have been due to a narrow focus on content covered on state tests and changes in state testing practices allowed by ED's shifting position on this issue.[172] As a result, it is extremely difficult to make simple conclusions about the causal impact of NCLB on student achievement.

Still, it is clear that NCLB has had a significant impact on the labels attached to schools. In 2005, 16 percent of all schools and 20 percent of all districts failed to make AYP. For the 2005–2006 school year, 14 percent of Title I schools were in school improvement, but only about three percent of these schools were subject to corrective action. NCLB has notably affected urban districts significantly more than suburban or rural districts.[173] In 2005, 50 percent of urban school districts failed to make AYP, while 20 percent of all districts failed to make AYP. In the same year, 72 percent of urban districts had at least one school that failed to make AYP, while 31 percent of all districts had at least one school that failed to make AYP. The inequitable effects of the AYP provisions likely stemmed from several interrelated factors, including the larger size of urban districts, the presence of a greater number of subgroups in urban districts, and the presence of more low-income students in urban districts.[174] So, NCLB appears to have exerted significantly more pressure on urban districts with poor and minority students that other types of districts.

Due at least in part to the difficulties that states and schools have had implementing NCLB provisions and making AYP, NCLB has been the object of several political attacks. Governors have sent letters to ED criticizing the application of the new federal requirements to their states and asking for more flexibility.[175] Bills or resolutions to opt out of or limit federal funding under NCLB were introduced in several states, and several bills calling for changes in NCLB have also been proposed in the U.S. Congress.[176] In response to such political pressure, ED has loosened some key NCLB requirements and regulations, especially those governing the requirements for including LEP students and students with disabilities in AYP calculations.[177] But ED has still displayed more willingness to enforce this federal law than it had displayed toward other federal laws (such as Goals 2000) in the past, particularly in regard to its core provisions regarding the implementation of standards and assessments.[178] ED has withheld federal funds from states for failure to comply with such provisions, and state officials have voiced a belief that NCLB is being strongly enforced.[179] It is precisely in this context of strong enforcement, increased accountability, limited capacity and political will, and inequitable effects on schools, that NCLB has spurred several high-profile lawsuits.

High School Exit Exams

As discussed earlier in this chapter, states had been implementing high-stakes testing practices since the 1970s. Many states still implement various types of high-stakes practices, and about half of them implement high school exit exams—twenty-five states currently implement or plan to implement high school exit exams by 2012.[180] By this time, an estimated 70 percent of high school students and 81 percent of minority students will be enrolled in schools in states that plan to have these exams in place. Although these exams had traditionally tested basic skills and were not integrated into states' broader standards-based reforms, many states have begun to align high school exit exams with state standards. In 2006, 15 out of 22 states implementing high school exit exams used standards-based exams, and by 2012, 17 out of the 25 states implementing these exams are to use standards-based exams. All states using standards-based exit exams tested students in English language arts or reading and mathematics, and some states tested students in science and social studies. Moreover, in 2006, 20 states used high school exit exams to meet NCLB testing requirements for high school students.[181] Thus, high school exit exams are rapidly becoming integrated into standards-based reform policies.

Like NCLB testing practices, there has been substantial variation in high school exit exam testing practices. The pass rate on high school exit exams has varied significantly from state to state. Because of factors such as differences in students, content and difficulty of tests, alignment of tests with state standards, and student familiarity with the test, pass rates of students taking an exit exam for the first time in 2005 ranged from 70 percent in some states to 90 percent in others.[182] Like NCLB testing practices, high school exit exams also have had significant inequitable effects. Gaps in pass rates between African-American and white students for first time test takers averaged 20 to 30 percentage points in most states. The gaps between Latino and white students were slightly smaller. Students with disabilities faced particular problems passing exit exams, as most strongly exemplified by the 16 percent pass rate for students with disabilities who took the exit exam for the first time in Maryland during 2005. As the standards-based reform movement becomes increasingly blended with the high school exit exam movement, standards-based reforms will become even more focused on accountability, which will in turn put increased pressure on students, teachers, schools, and districts to increase student performance on tests aligned with standards.

Discussion and Conclusion

Since the mid-1980s, standards-based reform policies have become pervasive in the U.S. These policies are aimed at leveraging fundamental changes in the structure of the U.S. education system in response to problems highlighted by both researchers and policymakers. While there are several potential problems that these policies can address, two particularly stand out. First, these policies are aimed at remedying the lack of policy coherence in the U.S. education system, which has created uncoordinated, and sometimes conflicting, policy mandates for educators and administrators at various levels. Second, these policies are aimed at remedying the lack of high-quality instruction and content delivered to students. By addressing both of these problems, standards-based reforms are ultimately aimed at raising student performance and at decreasing inequities in student performance. In this sense, the standards-based reform movement is a natural continuation of prior large-scale education policy movements like desegregation and school finance reform.

In order to leverage such changes in the U.S. education system, theories of standards-based reform have generally included several common elements—high quality standards, aligned curricula, aligned tests, and aligned teacher educational programs and professional development. Although many disagree on the appropriate role of accountability mechanisms in standards-based reforms, such mechanisms have become increasingly prevalent and blended with these reforms to put increased pressure on students, teachers, schools, and districts to change their behavior. At the same time, the federal government has become increasingly involved in guiding the standards-based reform movement and has provided a strong push for increasing the focus on accountability in states' standards-based reform policies.

While the core features of the theory underlying standards-based reform appear very promising and tightly linked with what appears to be serious systemic problems in the U.S. education system, several significant issues have emerged since states began to implement standards-based reform policies. Individuals at an array of administrative levels appear to have lacked the knowledge needed to effectively implement these policies, such as the technical skill needed to implement more valid testing practices at scale. Similarly, administrators may not have possessed sufficient knowledge to support instructional practices aligned to standards. Indeed, as the education researcher Steven Raudenbush argued about the general state of educational knowledge, "Knowledge about how to use resources in instruction is key, yet woefully lacking."[183] Compounding this lack of knowledge, financial and physical resources appear to have been limited for supporting the administrative changes needed in all states and districts and for supporting the instructional changes needed in all schools.

Various political forces have also had a significant impact on the implementation of standards-based reform and accountability policies. Educators and administrators have sometimes lacked the political will to change their instructional and administrative practices to support student learning in a way that reflects challenging standards, especially in schools in high-poverty areas. With the unwillingness of the Clinton administration to enforce Goals 2000 in a hostile political climate, funds that should have been spent on boosting states' capacities for change were not. Given the more recent political focus on outcomes and accountability, states and districts have channeled most of their attention to complying with the accountability mandates of NCLB instead of providing schools with additional support, and they have accordingly implemented systems of school support under NCLB that have varied widely in features and in quality. The political context in which standards-based reform policies have been situated has also proven particularly influential. For example, the political history of California strongly contributed to the wide array of professional development opportunities available to teachers in California, and the political structure of the U.S. ultimately shaped the development of standards and accountability systems as a partially state-by-state enterprise. In the context of this federalist political structure and political pressure to produce students that score well on tests, states have crafted standards of dramatically different quality and accountability systems that define AYP quite differently.

Such political forces have proven especially influential with regard to the implementation of one of the most important elements of standards-based reform theories—OTL standards. As discussed above, political pressure, centered on the proper relationship between the state and federal governments, led to the demise of the opportunity to learn provisions in Goals 2000, and OTL standards were never created. While the conceptual shape of opportunity to learn was never fully clear and long contested by various groups, this idea was central in early theories of standards-based reform; the concept built on the notion that there are structural inequities in the U.S. education system and that particular attention should be given to the various opportunities that are shaped by these inequities to help all students learn the knowledge embodied in standards. While NCLB devoted some attention to students' opportunities to learn with provisions such as those governing HQTs and support for low performing schools, the notion of opportunity to learn has largely faded from the political discourse, and there are few formal political and legal structures in place that address opportunities to learn in direct relation to standards. As a result, current policies governing standards-based reform largely focus on outputs instead of the inputs needed to help all students learn the content and skills in standards.

In the context of this complicated interaction between knowledge, various types of resources, and political context, the standards-based reform movement has not yet fully achieved its primary goals. While states have made significant progress instituting certain elements of standards-based reform and accountability mechanisms required under state and federal law, fundamental features of teachers' instructional practices have proven difficult to alter. As two education historians, David Tyack and Larry Cuban, have noted, the fundamental "grammar of schooling" is quite resistant to change.[184] For many of the reasons discussed above, various education reforms have changed the surface of educational practices for short periods of time, but few have fundamentally changed the core of what and how students are taught. The standards-based reform movement thus far seems to reflect such common characteristics of education reform movements. Still, the standards-based reform movement has proven markedly durable since it emerged (unlike many other education reform movements in U.S. history), and it may simply require more time for standards-based reforms to penetrate more deeply into the structure of the education system.

Moreover, the implementation of standards-based reform policies may have exacerbated inequities in the structure of the U.S. education system in some key respects. While these policies have focused educators', administrators', and policymakers' attention on educational inequities, it is far from clear whether the various necessary capacities are in place to help all students learn the skills and knowledge embodied in standards. Indeed, without such capacities, the pressure of strong accountability mechanisms appears to have led to instructional problems, such as decontextualized test preparation, in high-poverty schools and for students who have more difficulty reaching proficiency on these tests. In light of such problems, it has proven very difficult to determine the effects of standards-based reform and accountability policies on student achievement, and these policies have generated a significant amount of attention and criticism among educators, administrators, policy-makers, parents, and the general public.

As this book is being completed in early 2008, the U.S. Congress has begun to consider the reauthorization of NCLB, and the final shape and requirements are thus far unclear. At this point, it appears that NCLB will change in some key respects. For example, Congress may alter the AYP provisions to account for growth of school performance and may alter the consequences for poor performance. However, it also appears that the fundamental shape of the law will remain the same—the law will still likely include a significant focus on standards-based reform and holding schools accountable for performance, and will devolve a substantial amount of authority to states to make decisions in these areas. Many of the major issues discussed in this chapter that directly revolve around NCLB's design and implementation will likely persist, and the historical issues associated with standards-based reform and accountability policies will certainly remain.

The lawsuits discussed in the following chapters reflect these issues. In line with the notion that traditionally underrepresented groups can use the courts as a venue to have their claims heard, concerns about the inequitable conditions of education and the related effects of standards-based reform and accountability policies drove most of these lawsuits. In such lawsuits, certain educational issues repeatedly emerged—guided by litigants' arguments and the appropriate legal frameworks, courts often focused on students' opportunities to learn, the validity of testing practices, the resources available for instruction, and the theoretical underpinnings of standards-based reform and accountability policies as tools that could boost the educational performance of all students. At the same time, courts often ignored certain important issues highlighted in this chapter, such as the sometimes low quality of state standards, the lack of knowledge needed to effectively implement standards-based reform and to effectively use resources in instruction, and the difficulty of fundamentally changing teachers' practice. Still, such litigation addressed these standards-based reform and accountability policies from a variety of different angles, and plaintiffs, defendants, and judges utilized very different legal structures to frame perceived problems in these policies—all in the context of the courts as a venue for governmental decision making that entails certain institutional characteristics. Using this chapter and the previous discussion about the characteristics of courts in education cases as an analytical backdrop, the next chapter focuses on lawsuits that have appeared in a high-profile and often divisive legal context—that of high-stakes testing.

CHAPTER THREE

High-Stakes Testing Litigation

Although the standards-based reform movement did not emerge until the mid-1980s, a body of law began to develop in the 1970s that has governed and continues to govern important elements of standards-based reform and accountability policies. As discussed in Chapter Two, several states enacted minimum competency tests (MCTs) and high-stakes testing practices in the 1970s in order to boost the quality of education provided to students and to motivate students. Such high-stakes testing practices generally hinged decisions about the tracking, promotion, or graduation of students on the results of a test and often had inequitable effects on minority students, students with disabilities, and students with limited English proficiency (LEP). As a result, these testing practices generated a wave of litigation focused on protecting students against what was perceived as discriminatory governmental decision making.

An examination of the high-stakes testing cases is critical to the central aim of this book—how the courts have addressed and can address standards-based reform and accountability policies—for several reasons. Large-scale testing constitutes a central element of these policies, and high-stakes testing litigation has historically been the flagship type of litigation that plaintiffs have used to address these sorts of testing practices. As such, the cases governing high-stakes testing practices constitute comparatively the most developed source of legal mandates regarding large-scale testing practices. Although the body of law governing high-stakes testing practices has been applied by courts to accountability policies that were not necessarily linked to standards-based reform, courts have applied this law to modern standards-based accountability policies as well. Perhaps most importantly, these cases offer a window into the ways in which courts have conceptualized high-stakes testing practices and opportunities to learn, and have linked these educational concepts with legal concepts. These cases thus offer invaluable insight into the courts' abilities to engage with educational issues central to standards-based reform and how the law can frame the ways in which courts have engaged with such issues.

Given that the cases addressing high-stakes testing practices have focused on discrimination, these cases are largely grounded in the logic of the civil rights movement and accordingly stem from legal sources that were generally built to govern instances of discrimination—Title VI of the Civil Rights Act of 1964 (Title VI), Title IX of the Education Amendments of 1972 (Title IX), Section 504 of the Rehabilitation Act of 1973 (Section 504), the Equal Educational Opportunities Act of 1976, and Title II of the Americans with Disabilities Act of 1990 (Title II) constitute the major statutory sources that govern the use of tests for high-stakes purposes.[1] The Fifth and Fourteenth Amendments of the U.S. Constitution also constitute important legal sources that govern high-stakes testing practices. These federal constitutional provisions and statutes, regulations implementing the statutes, and judicial interpretations of these legal sources form a legal framework that governs discrimination in four major high-stakes testing contexts—intentional discrimination, preservation of the effects of prior segregation, disparate impact, and due process. Given the federal character of the legal requirements governing high-stakes testing, high-stakes testing litigation has generally occurred in federal courts.

This chapter examines the law governing high-stakes testing in each of these areas and includes a detailed discussion of two major cases in which courts have applied this law—*Debra P. v. Turlington* (*Debra P.*) and *GI Forum v. Texas Education Agency* (*GI Forum*).[2] The discussion of these two cases highlights important details of the judicial processes in the high-stakes testing field that would otherwise remain hidden if one examined only the broad legal mandates in the relevant cases. *GI Forum* is especially important because it involves the application of the legal framework governing high-stakes testing to a state's standards-based testing system that held both students and schools accountable for educational performance. Based on this examination, the institutional characteristics of courts, and the discussion of standards-based reform in the previous chapter, this chapter analyzes the ways in which courts are positioned to address standards-based reforms and related accountability systems in the context of high-stakes testing litigation. This chapter concludes that, while high-stakes testing cases are extremely important for protecting the educational rights of minority students and other traditionally underserved groups of students, these cases (and the legal frameworks guiding them) are becoming increasingly less viable and apply to modern standards-based reform policies only to a limited extent. Moreover, these cases are characterized by scientific uncertainty and have taxed the capacities of the courts in certain key respects. As such, high-stakes testing litigation does not well position the courts to become an effective venue for shaping standards-based reform and accountability policies as they move forward.

Intentional Discrimination

The issue of intentional discrimination has surfaced several times in the testing context. Under the Equal Protection Clause of the Fourteenth Amendment of the U.S. Constitution, governmental entities are generally precluded from intentionally discriminating against individuals on the basis of race, national origin, or sex. An array of federal statutes also precludes governmental entities from intentionally discriminating against individuals on the basis of race, national origin, sex, or disability. Such discrimination is only legally acceptable in cases where it is "narrowly tailored" to further a "compelling governmental interest."[3] Courts have found instances of intentional discrimination acceptable under this standard only very rarely and primarily in the affirmative action context.[4] Because states, school districts, public schools, and public school employees are governmental entities, these entities are all precluded from intentionally discriminating against individuals.

Where governmental entities have made high-stakes decisions that have impacted groups of students unequally, affected students have brought claims that these governmental decision makers have engaged in intentional discrimination. For example, in *People Who Care v. Rockford Board of Education*, minority students scored lower than white students on a standardized test administered by a school district and were accordingly more likely to be assigned to a lower level class than the white students.[5] Because the federal trial court in this case found no acceptable explanation for the district's actions, the court found that intentional discrimination was present and ordered the district to stop engaging in such testing practices. However, because courts are generally loath to ascribe the intention to discriminate to school officials, findings of intentional discrimination in the testing context are rare. Moreover, under *Washington v. Davis*, a case decided by the Supreme Court in 1976, courts cannot find that governmental entities have engaged in intentional discrimination solely on the basis of a policy's disproportionate impact on some group, such as a racial minority.[6] Even if such disproportionate impact was foreseeable or actually anticipated by the governmental entity that instituted the policy, this disproportionate impact by itself cannot prove intentional discrimination.

Judicial deference to the reasons offered by educational officials to explain why high-stakes testing practices with a disproportionate impact were instituted and continued after the impact was known have also made it difficult for plaintiffs to successfully argue claims of intentional discrimination in the high-stakes testing context. For example, in *Debra P. v. Turlington*, a case discussed in more detail later in this chapter, a court examined the constitutionality of a high-stakes graduation test that had a disproportionate impact on

African-American students.[7] The *Debra P.* court found that this testing practice was not instituted to discriminate against African-American students, but was instead instituted to identify and provide remedial instruction to those students who needed it. In fact, in *People Who Care v. Rockford Board of Education*, the appellate court that heard the case reversed the trial court decision that found intentional discrimination because of the justifications proffered by school officials.[8] Thus, although intentional discrimination is prohibited by federal statutory and constitutional mandates, it is very difficult to invalidate any testing practice on these grounds.

Preserving or Furthering the Effects of Prior Segregation

Under well-established Supreme Court precedent, the Fourteenth Amendment of the U.S. Constitution prohibits governmental practices that preserve or further the effects of prior *de jure* school segregation—the type of segregation mandated by law that was deemed unconstitutional in *Brown v. Board of Education*.[9] The Equal Educational Opportunities Act of 1976 similarly prohibits governmental practices that preserve or further the effects of prior *de jure* school segregation.[10] In cases where school districts have not erased the effects of prior *de jure* segregation, these districts are under a "heavy burden" to prove that policies which preserve or further the effects of segregation have an important justification.[11] The primary type of justification that would survive such judicial scrutiny involves the targeting of better educational opportunities to students who need them in order to remedy the effects of prior segregation. Plaintiffs have often pointed to such legal requirements in attempts to invalidate high-stakes testing practices.[12]

Defendants in the high-stakes testing context, however, have been fairly successful at convincing courts that testing practices with disproportionate impacts do not preserve or further the effects of prior *de jure* segregation. Defendants have successfully argued that too much time has passed since a system of *de jure* segregation was fully dismantled in their area and that a high-stakes testing practice with a disproportionate impact therefore does not preserve or further the effects of prior *de jure* segregation.[13] And as noted above, defendants have successfully argued that a high-stakes testing practices with a disproportionate impact have provided disadvantaged students with benefits, such as remedial classes.[14] As it has become increasingly difficult to successfully identify instances in which *de jure* segregation persists (because courts have deemed many previously segregated school systems to be desegregated), claims regarding prior *de jure* segregation in the context of high-stakes testing have become uncommon.[15] Thus, although it is still possible to invalidate testing practices on the basis of preserving or furthering the effects of prior *de jure* segregation, this type of legal action has become increasingly rare.

Disparate Impact

Although the U.S. Constitution has been interpreted by the Supreme Court as unable to support claims aimed at high-stakes testing practices solely on the grounds of disproportionate impact, federal statutes have supported such claims. To be precise, regulations promulgated by the U.S. Department of Education (ED) to implement Title VI, Title IX, Section 504, and Title II have been interpreted to support such claims.[16] While courts have been reluctant to find that most testing practices constitute instances of intentional discrimination, almost all high-stakes testing practices do have a disproportionate impact on the basis of ethnicity, LEP status, or disability status. Thus, the regulations implementing Title VI, Title IX, Section 504, and Title II have constituted some of the primary legal grounds on which plaintiffs have sued to influence the administration of high-stakes testing practices.

In order to determine whether a policy or practice that results in a disproportionate impact is illegal, courts have developed the "disparate impact" test. This test has guided judicial examinations into the justifiability of practices with a disproportionate impact by specifying the factors relevant to a determination of illegality, the weight of these factors, and the order in which judges should examine these factors. Courts employing the disparate impact test have generally asked three questions to determine whether a high-stakes testing practice with a disproportionate impact is impermissible: First, does the practice result in a sufficiently substantial disparity in educational benefits provided to students on the basis of race, national origin, sex, or disability? Second, is the practice educationally necessary or justified? Third, is there an equally effective alternative practice that results in less disparity?

In order to answer the first question—whether the practice results in a sufficiently substantial disparity—the Supreme Court indicated that "statistical disparities must be sufficiently substantial that they raise . . . an inference of causation."[17] In the case of testing, the statistical disparity is generally reflected in the test scores of different suspect groups, such as minority students or LEP students. Although the Supreme Court has not precisely defined what constitutes a sufficiently substantial statistical disparity, many lower courts have addressed this question and have articulated similar but slightly different standards.[18] For example, one of the most common tests, employed by both federal courts and the Equal Employment Opportunity Commission in the employment context, identifies an adverse racial impact where the members of a particular racial group are selected at a rate that is less than four-fifths of the rate at which the group with the highest rate is selected.[19] Under the disparate impact test, the plaintiff has the burden of establishing that a testing practice has resulted in a sufficiently substantial statistical disparity.[20]

If a plaintiff successfully establishes that a sufficiently substantial statistical disparity exists, a court proceeds to the second prong of the disparate impact test: determining whether the practice is educationally necessary or justified. In this step, the burden shifts to the defendant to prove that the practice is in fact necessary or justified.[21] While there are always many factors to consider in determining whether a practice is necessary or justified, courts have consistently examined certain factors in making this determination. Courts have particularly examined whether a practice serves legitimate educational goals of the institution in question.[22] As was true with courts examining whether educational institutions have intentionally discriminated against different disadvantaged groups, courts applying the disparate impact test have generally deferred to educational institutions to define their own legitimate goals. Thus, courts have tended to focus on the fit between the practice and an institution's goals—courts have examined whether there is a "manifest relationship" between the practice and the institution's goals.[23]

In the specific case of high-stakes testing practices, courts have repeatedly examined the validity of a testing practice to determine whether there is a sufficient fit between the testing practice and the educational institution's goals. As discussed in Chapter Two, validity is a technical term used by the psychometric community and generally refers to the justifiability of interpretations and uses of test scores. For example, in *Larry P. v. Riles*, California used standardized intelligence tests to place students into special classes for the educable mentally retarded. The use of this test resulted in a disproportionate impact on African-American students, and the plaintiffs brought a Title VI disparate impact claim. In examining the educational necessity of the testing practice, the *Larry P.* court examined the following three factors:

> (1) placement is based on a variety of information and evaluation tools that are non-discriminatory, and not solely on IQ tests; (2) the tests are validated for black schoolchildren, and therefore accurately reflect mental retardation in black children; and (3) blacks have a higher percentage of mental retardation than whites.[24]

Thus, the *Larry P.* court focused on whether interpretations that specific students were mentally retarded were supported by sufficient psychometric evidence about the use and interpretations of the test scores in question.

In order to determine whether these types of interpretations are sufficiently valid, courts have examined several different aspects of test construction. The *Standards for Educational and Psychometric Testing (AERA Standards)* (also discussed in Chapter Two) outline an array of different types of empirical and theoretical evidence that can be used to validate a testing practice. For example, in order to validate a testing practice, the *AERA Standards* indicate that psychometricians can examine the extent to which the content covered on a test is aligned with the knowledge and skills that are to be assessed or the extent to which test results correlate with empirical observations of behaviors in a real-world, non-test environment. Indeed, courts have often looked to the *AERA Standards* to guide their examinations of the validity of high-stakes testing practices.[25] Moreover, in line with the *AERA Standards*, courts have repeatedly examined where "cut scores" for the placement of individuals into different groups are located, and courts have examined whether high-stakes decisions are based on the results of one particular test or several different factors.[26]

Furthermore, courts have focused on the purposes for which tests are used when examining the validity of testing practices. For example, in addition to focusing on the evidence of whether the test in question measured what it was supposed to measure, the *Larry P.* court also focused on the specific consequences resulting from the administration of the test. The court wrote:

> [T]he question for predictive validity in schools is not whether standardized intelligence tests predict future performance generally ... but whether the tests predict specifically that black elementary schoolchildren (as opposed to white elementary schoolchildren) who score at or below 70 on the IQ tests are mentally retarded and incapable of learning the regular school curriculum.[27]

By breaking down validity in this fashion, the court indicated that a testing practice must be validated in the specific context in which it is used. Thus, the same testing practice may be valid for one purpose (say, determining whether students are capable of learning the regular school curriculum and placed into particular classes) but not for another. According to the *Larry P.* court, the specific consequences of test failure (or success) must be aligned with valid interpretations about what a test is supposed to measure.

To be sure, validity has been defined in a number of ways by different courts over time. Although many courts have looked to the *AERA Standards* as a guide to what constitutes validity, courts have not done so consistently.[28]

Moreover, as the *AERA Standards* have been periodically revised, they have articulated sound testing principles differently with each revision. Thus, courts relying on the *AERA Standards* to guide validity inquiries have defined validity differently over time and have required different evidence to demonstrate that a testing practice is sufficiently valid to survive a disparate impact inquiry.[29] Nevertheless, basic principles of validity established by the measurement community have repeatedly guided validity inquiries, and these principles aim at ensuring that tests measure the body of knowledge and skills that they are supposed to measure. So, in the course of examining the educational necessity of a testing practice, legal standards and standards developed by professional educational and psychological organizations have begun to converge. As a result, courts employing the disparate impact test have generally examined the alignment between the knowledge and skills included on a test, the knowledge and skills students are supposed to possess, and the ultimate purposes of the test. Exactly what courts examine to determine whether a testing practice is sufficiently valid and thus educationally necessary, however, has differed from case to case.

In the third and final prong of a disparate impact analysis, a court examines whether an equally effective alternative practice exists and results in less disparity.[30] A court reaches this question if a defendant successfully proves that a practice with a disproportionate impact is necessary or justified. In the third step, the plaintiff has the burden of establishing that such an alternative practice exists. In examining the feasibility of an alternative practice, courts have examined various factors, such as cost and administrative burden.[31] Plaintiffs have rarely established that such an equally effective alternative practice exists and results in less disparity.[32]

Applying the disparate impact test in the context of alleged discrimination against LEP students and students with disabilities involves additional legal issues. As Title VI protects individuals from discrimination on the basis of national origin, it also applies to practices that have a disproportionate impact on LEP students. Validity inquiries under the educational necessity prong of the disparate impact tests involving LEP students must deal with an array of factors that complicate the process of validation. For example, cultural biases and language barriers make it difficult for a testing practice to yield valid interpretations about what LEP students know and can do.[33] So, courts applying the disparate impact test to the high-stakes testing of LEP students must address several additional educational issues in determining whether a testing practice results in an impermissible disparate impact.[34]

The testing of students with disabilities also involves additional legal issues. As the regulations implementing Section 504 and Title II of the

Americans with Disabilities Act prohibit discrimination against students with disabilities, the disparate impact test can also be applied to instances where testing practices have a disproportionate impact on students with disabilities. In order to ensure that a testing practice yields valid interpretations about what a disabled student knows and can do (as opposed to a student's disability), accommodations in a testing practice are often appropriate.[35] Common accommodations include tests in large print, tests in Braille print, simplifying the language of directions, and increasing testing time. Indeed, regulations implementing the federal laws prohibiting discrimination against individuals with disabilities articulate requirements regarding validity and accommodations.[36] Mirroring the *AERA Standards*, these regulations specifically indicate that the results of a single test are not sufficient to determine whether a student has a disability or the program in which a student with a disability should be placed.[37]

Despite the number of statutory provisions and cases governing the application of Title VI to high-stakes testing practices, a recent Supreme Court decision has greatly limited the applicability of the disparate impact test. In *Alexander v. Sandoval*, a case decided in 2001, the Supreme Court ruled that the Title VI regulations can no longer support a cause of action based on a claim of an impermissible disparate impact.[38] That is, plaintiffs can no longer bring suit on the grounds of an impermissible disparate impact under Title VI regulations, and a court will no longer examine this type of argument. Title VI, its regulations, and the cases interpreting these regulations still technically constitute good law. But this law must be enforced by ED and not by the courts. In order to make ED aware of instances in which educational entities have violated the requirements governing disparate impact, individuals are permitted to file complaints with ED. However, without the ability to enforce the requirements of Title VI and its regulations in the courts, the ability of the disparate impact test to adequately govern modern high-stakes testing practices is very limited.

Due Process

Finally, several courts have interpreted the due process clauses of the Fifth and Fourteenth Amendments as applicable to high-stakes testing practices. As these courts have indicated, states create an expectation in students that they will receive a diploma. That is, states bestow students with a "property interest" in receiving a diploma. The due process clauses of the U.S. Constitution protect the property interests of individuals and have accordingly been interpreted as requiring certain safeguards to protect individuals from having their diplomas unfairly taken away by the state. Unlike Title VI, the due process clauses apply to all students—every student, regardless of their status as a member of a minority or otherwise underserved group, is accorded the same due process protections. In the case of testing practices, however, groups of students who are disproportionately affected by graduation decisions typically bring suit using due process arguments.

In such cases, courts have ruled that two primary safeguards apply. First, the due process clauses require educational entities to provide adequate notice to students of the test and its consequences. For example, in *Debra P.*, which is discussed in greater detail below, a court indicated that a four-year notice of a test on which decisions about graduation hinged was sufficient to satisfy the requirements of due process. In determining what constitutes adequate notice, courts have examined a variety of contextual factors, including the possibility of retesting and the instructional help that students have received to help them pass the test.[39] Courts have generally referred to the requirement for providing adequate notice as an important aspect of providing "procedural due process" to students.

Second, the due process clauses require students to have an "opportunity to learn" the knowledge and skills assessed by a graduation test. *Debra P.* constitutes the primary case detailing the due process protections involving opportunities to learn that must be provided to students. An appellate court in *Debra P.* court ruled that a state may condition the receipt of a public school diploma on the passing of a test so long as it is a fair test of what has been taught. This court construed such an opportunity to learn in terms of "curricular validity." According to the court, in order for a testing practice involving a property right, such as the receipt of a diploma, to be constitutional, that testing practice must have curricular validity. Exactly what constitutes curricular validity, however, is somewhat unclear. While some courts have construed curricular validity as requiring only that the skills and knowledge tested are included in the written curriculum from which students learn, others have argued that curricular validity requires such skills and knowledge to actually be taught to students in the classroom.[40] Courts have generally referred to the requirement for providing a sufficient opportunity to learn to students as an important aspect of providing "substantive due process" to students. In addition to the requirements governing the disparate impact test under Title VI, the requirements governing curricular validity have constituted the primary legal frameworks that the courts have used to find high-stakes testing practices illegal.

Case Studies in High-Stakes Testing

Because a broad overview of the relevant law may miss important nuances about the characteristics and the nature of the judicial process in high-stakes testing cases, this chapter now focuses on two cases—*Debra P. v. Turlington* and *GI Forum v. Texas Education Agency*. Both of these cases are recognized by lawyers and legal scholars as being very important in the area of high-stakes testing, and by examining these cases in detail, we can gain a better sense of how courts have actually engaged with the primary policy issues in this area.[41]

DEBRA P. V. TURLINGTON

Debra P. originally began in October 1978 when several public school students brought a class action suit against Florida over the administration of State Student Assessment Test, Part II (SSAT II), a functional literacy examination administered to students across the state. Florida had adopted the SSAT II in 1976 pursuant to the state's Educational Accountability Act of 1976.[42] This law established three requirements that Florida students were required to meet in order to graduate from public schools: (1) attain a minimum number of credits, (2) master certain basic skills, and (3) achieve functional literacy as determined by the state Board of Education. In order to accomplish these goals, the law provided for the establishment of remediation classes and a comprehensive testing program to evaluate students' basic skill development at periodic intervals. In 1978, the Florida legislature amended the law to require students to pass a functional literacy examination before they could receive a diploma.[43] The SSAT II was administered pursuant to this requirement. If students completed the minimum number of required high school credits but failed the functional literacy examination, they were to receive only a certificate of completion.

Like many other competency tests administered during the 1970s, the SSAT II resulted in a substantial number of student failures. Thirty-six percent (or 41,724 of 115,901 students taking both the mathematics and verbal sections of the SSAT II) failed one or both sections of the test during its October 1977 administration. Moreover, 78 percent of African-American students failed at least one section of the test, as compared to 25 percent of the white students taking the test. The second administration of the SSAT II yielded similar results, as 74 percent of the African-American students taking the test for a second time failed at least one section of the test, while 25 percent of white students retaking the test failed at least one section. Similar disparities characterized the third administration of the SSAT II, and by May

1979, the failure rate among African-American students was approximately 10 times that of white students. Students from across Florida sued the state in federal court precisely in response to such effects based on four primary grounds: equal protection, due process, Title VI of the Civil Rights Act, and the Equal Educational Opportunities Act.

Debra P. *at the Trial Court Level*

In July 1979, Judge George C. Carr of the Middle District of Florida issued the first ruling in *Debra P.* and found that Florida violated the requirements of equal protection, due process, Title VI, and the Equal Educational Opportunities Act. Judge Carr had presided over the entire trial and was required to analyze an array of complex and sometimes conflicting evidence and testimony. His opinion in *Debra P.* systematically evaluated such evidence and testimony, and the parties' arguments under the bodies of relevant law.

Most of the major claims in the case turned on the concept of validity, which was hotly debated by the several expert witnesses in the case. Throughout the trial, the experts discussed eight different types of validity and focused specifically on two types—content validity and construct validity.[44] According to the defendants' experts, a testing practice has content validity if the content of the test items matches the domain of skills and knowledge intended to be measured. In contrast, the plaintiffs' experts argued that content validity also includes the concept of curricular, or instructional, validity—a type of validity that encompasses whether the test specifications and objectives (and thus implicitly the test items) cover material in the school curriculum and that students have been taught. According to Dr. Walt Haney, one of the plaintiffs' expert witnesses, the testimony regarding content validity in the case was quite complex because it is unclear how deeply into the classroom even an expansive view of content validity should go—such a concept of content validity could extend to curriculum materials, actual instruction, and perhaps even the effectiveness of instruction.[45]

In addition to debating the meaning of content validity, the experts argued about what types of validity should be used to establish the psychometric justifiability of a testing practice. The plaintiffs' experts argued that a testing practice must maintain several types of validity, including an expansive version of content validity (that includes curricular validity) and construct validity, which represented in *Debra P.* the extent to which the SSAT II measured whether students possessed "functional literacy." The defendants' experts argued that the SSAT II only needed to maintain content validity (as narrowly defined above) but that the testing practice had sufficient construct validity anyway.

With passing reference to the then current version of the *AERA Standards* and after examining the historical development of the SSAT II, including studies on any potential test item bias, Judge Carr took a middle position.[46] He was persuaded by the defendants' arguments about how content validity should be defined and found that the SSAT II had adequate content validity. In addition, he found that construct validity was also required and that the SSAT II had adequate construct validity. And as discussed further below, Judge Carr also found important the extent to which the SSAT II reflected the content of curricula and instruction, though not directly through the lens of content validity. Indeed, such constructions of validity and the extent to which curricula and instruction matched the SSAT II ultimately drove most of Judge Carr's opinion in the case and emerged in his discussion of equal protection, Title VI, the Equal Educational Opportunities Act, and due process.

The first claims of the plaintiffs addressed by Judge Carr asserted that the administration of the SSAT II constituted intentional discrimination against African-American students and perpetuated past segregation in violation of the Equal Protection Clause, Title VI, and the Equal Educational Opportunities Act. In order to rule on these claims, Judge Carr started by reviewing the history of public education in Florida, beginning in 1885. Like many states, Florida formally operated a dual school system for most of this time, and the educational facilities and offerings available to African-American students were substantially worse than those available to their white peers. Despite the presence of desegregation decrees in Florida, Judge Carr found that schools across the state continued to be segregated and unequal in various respects (such as facilities, course offerings, and instructional materials) through 1971—a period in which the plaintiffs attended public schools in Florida. Supplementing these findings, Judge Carr found that the denial of diplomas resulted in several extremely negative effects on impacted students, such as a decreased ability to attain a high-paying job. Given such disproportionately distributed opportunities and effects of the SSAT II, Judge Carr found that the administration of the SSAT II violated the Equal Protection Clause and Equal Educational Opportunities Act by perpetuating the effects of past segregation.

Still, Judge Carr did not find that that administration of the SSAT II represented intentional discrimination. Although Judge Carr noted that Ralph Turlington, the state's Commissioner of Education, anticipated a high failure rate for African-American students, the judge framed the SSAT II as tool ultimately used by the state to increase the quality of education for all students across the state. In order to bolster this finding, Judge Carr discussed the validity of the SSAT II and highlighted that it had adequate content validity (as narrowly defined by the defendants) and construct validity. Satisfied that the SSAT II had been properly validated in these two respects, and finding that the state did not intentionally discriminate only because there was a foreseeable disproportionate impact, Judge Carr found that the administration of the SSAT II did not constitute an instance of intentional discrimination.

Judge Carr also found for the plaintiffs using a due process analysis. In order to complete the due process analysis, Judge Carr first determined whether the plaintiffs had a property right at stake. Reasoning that all the plaintiffs (including both African-American students and other types of students) had a property interest in receiving a diploma if they fulfilled the requirements for graduation exclusive of the SSAT II requirement, and bolstering this reasoning with a discussion of relevant Supreme Court precedent, Judge Carr found that all the plaintiffs indeed had a property right in receiving a diploma.[47] Based on this finding, Judge Carr analyzed whether the plaintiffs were accorded the proper due process protections.

In order to complete this analysis, Judge Carr examined an array of evidence, including evidence about the decentralized structure of the education system in Florida (which included 67 autonomous school boards), the great variation in texts and instructional materials used in Florida counties, the failure of most texts to contain all content needed for functional literacy, and the implementation schedule for the SSAT II. Judge Carr particularly focused on the implementation schedule, highlighting that teachers were aware of the objectives of the SSAT II only four months in advance of the first administration of the SSAT II and had only two months of instruction with such knowledge (because teachers were made aware of the objectives of the SSAT II during their summer break). Moreover, Judge Carr focused on the fact that remediation programs held for students who failed the first administration of the SSAT II did not immediately receive instructional materials designed by the state to assist such programs. Perhaps most importantly, Judge Carr found that, although it was impossible to determine if all the skills covered in the SSAT II were actually taught to all students, it was clear that many students had received most of their instruction during years in which the objectives of the SSAT II and diploma sanction were not present. As a result, students were suddenly required to pass a test "constructed under the pressure of time and covering content that was presumed to be elementary but that their schools may or may not have taught them recently, well, or perhaps at all."[48]

Based on these findings, Judge Carr found that the defendants had violated the students' procedural due process rights by failing to give them adequate notice of the graduation requirement and that the defendants had violated the students' substantive due process rights because the SSAT II likely did not match the content that was taught to students over their years of formal schooling. In light of these various findings, Judge Carr ruled that Florida should be enjoined from requiring passage of the SSAT II as a requirement for graduation for four years.

Debra P. *at the Appeals Court Level*

Soon after Judge Carr's decision in *Debra P.*, the defendants appealed, and a three-judge panel in the Fifth Circuit heard the case.[49] This panel released its opinion in May 1981. The panel began its opinion by stressing the familiar sentiment of judges in education cases that courts are not in a position to determine education policy in a state. Still, the panel largely found that Judge Carr had decided correctly. With little additional analysis, the panel accepted Judge Carr's findings that the administration of the SSAT II violated the Equal Protection Clause, Title VI, and the Equal Educational Opportunities Act because it preserved the effects of past segregation in Florida. With little analysis, the panel also found that Judge Carr had correctly ruled that the implementation schedule of the SSAT II did not allow for sufficient notice and accordingly did not provide students with their proper procedural due process protections.

The panel devoted much of its opinion to evaluating Judge Carr's substantive due process analysis. After finding that Florida had failed to provide adequate notice, the panel also emphasized that the due process violation potentially went deeper than the issue of notice:

> When it encroaches upon concepts of justice lying at the basis of our civil and political institutions, the state is obligated to avoid action which is arbitrary and capricious, does not achieve or even frustrates a legitimate state interest, or is fundamentally unfair . . . We believe that the state administered a test that was, at least on the record before us, fundamentally unfair in that it may have covered matters not taught in the schools of the state.[50]

So, the panel also found that Judge Carr was correct that the state may have improperly tested students on material that they did not have the opportunity to learn in school.

But in contrast to Judge Carr, the panel framed this analysis of what was actually taught in terms of validity. With only passing reference to the *AERA Standards* in a footnote, the panel stated that curricular validity encompasses what is actually taught (not just the content that appears in curricula) and that curricular validity is an important component of content validity. Given the lack of direct evidence offered at trial about what students were actually taught, the panel found that the record of the trial was insufficient to prove that the SSAT II measured what was actually taught in Florida schools—indeed, the defendants stipulated before the trial that they made no efforts to determine whether or not the minimum student performance standards were in fact being taught in public schools and did not conduct any formal studies to confirm that such skills and knowledge were being taught. The panel accordingly concluded that Florida had not satisfied the requirements of due process.

Unlike Judge Carr, however, the panel did not simply delay the implementation of the graduation requirements. Explicitly recognizing the interests of Florida in the administration of its minimum competency program, the panel instead remanded the case to the trial court to determine whether the SSAT II was a fair test of what was actually taught. After the panel handed down its decision, a hostile response quickly emerged from within the circuit court. Without a request from either of the parties, a judge on the circuit court requested the court to reconsider the case *en banc*, or to have the decision reconsidered by all the members of the court. A large majority of the court refused to reconsider the case because neither party suggested that the case should be reheard and because the judges in this majority believed that the parties' decisions in such complex litigation are entitled to great deference.[51] Two judges on the Fifth Circuit, however, dissented in the court's denial of the hearing *en banc* that the panel's decision meddled too deeply in education policy. But given the refusal of most members of the court to reconsider the case, *Debra P.* soon returned to the trial level.

Debra P. *on Remand*

After the case was remanded to Judge Carr, he began the difficult task of determining whether the skills and knowledge tested on the SSAT II were actually taught in schools.[52] Following the circuit court's decision, Judge Carr held a series of status conferences aimed at determining the most effective way to comply with the circuit court's mandates and then held a trial on the issue of curricular validity.[53] This trial largely became a battle between conflicting experts, and as Judge Carr noted, the answer to the apparently easy question of what was actually taught turned out to be quite complex. In order to prove that the skills and knowledge tested by the SSAT II were taught in schools, the defendants commissioned IOX Assessment Associates, a private consulting firm, to develop a study. IOX's study consisted of four separate components: (1) a survey sent to every teacher in Florida, (2) a survey sent to every school district and four university laboratory schools in Florida,

(3) a series of site visits to verify the accuracy of the district reports, and (4) a student survey administered by site visitors to 11th grade social studies and English classes.

At trial, three expert witnesses testified for the defendants, on the basis of the data collected by the IOX study, that Florida was teaching what was tested on the SSAT II. Two expert witnesses also testified for the plaintiffs that the survey did not sufficiently support the curricular validity of the SSAT II, primarily because the survey was not a reliable indicator of what actually went on in all classrooms and because the survey revealed large variations in teachers' practices. Describing the importance and difficulty of interpreting the expert testimony in the remand proceedings, Judge Carr wrote:

> As the foregoing outline of the evidence suggests, the resolution of the instructional validity issue depends both on whose experts are believed and on what sort of proof is required. With regard to the former, it is important to understand that the instructional validity issue, and the related concept of minimum competency testing, are relatively new and highly controversial subjects which seem to have polarized the educational community. Thus, in large part, this Court has been called upon to settle not only a legal argument but also a professional dispute. At times, the distinction between these two spheres has blurred . . . unlike some of the other claims made by the plaintiffs at the first trial, the instructional validity issue strikes at the heart of the teaching and learning process.[54]

Given his perceived difficulty of delving this deeply into educational issues, Judge Carr turned back to the law itself. He cited state statutory requirements indicating that the state must periodically examine and evaluate district programs to comply with the law and that districts no longer had the authority to decide that they would not teach certain minimum skills. Moreover, Judge Carr cited requirements that schools needed to submit annual reports of how well school instructional programs were helping students acquire minimum skills and the fact that districts had recently gained access to state-approved instructional materials to implement statutorily mandated curricular objectives. Framing such requirements as bolstering the results of the survey and the testimony of the defendants' experts, Judge Carr was persuaded that students were provided with sufficient opportunities to learn the content included on the SSAT II. As Judge Carr indicated, once certain content is included in the official curriculum and a majority of teachers recognize the content as something they should teach, "the only logical inference is that the teachers are doing the job they are paid to do and teaching these skills."[55]

As a result, Judge Carr ruled that the injunction over the use of the SSAT II as a graduation requirement should not be extended and that Florida could deny diplomas to future students who would take the SSAT II. Upon appeal, the circuit court emphasized that its earlier opinion did not require the state to *directly* prove that the SSAT II covered content taught in the classroom and accordingly affirmed Judge Carr's findings.[56] In short, while *Debra P.* was extremely influential in defining content validity and curricular validity in the context of high-stakes testing for future courts, the case was extremely difficult for judges because it forced them to decide among conflicting evidence and expert testimony about issues that resided at the heart of the educational process. Presented with such conflicting evidence and testimony about educational issues, the courts created law that required the content of high-stakes tests for individuals to match instruction, but ultimately leaned on legal requirements to solve the dilemma of resolving conflicting evidence and expert testimony about educational behavior in the real world.

GI FORUM v. TEXAS EDUCATION AGENCY

While *Debra P.* has been widely recognized as one of the most important cases in the history of high-stakes testing because of its requirements regarding curricular validity, *GI Forum* is also very important—in addition to demonstrating how a court has ruled in a recent high-stakes testing case, the case involved a high-stakes testing policy that was part of a larger effort to implement a modern, statewide standards-based reform and accountability system.[57] The case originally began in October 1997 when the Mexican American Legal Defense and Education Fund (MALDEF) sued Texas on behalf of nine minority students over the administration of the Texas Assessment of Academic Skills (TAAS), an exam that students had to pass in order to graduate from high school.

Texas had adopted the TAAS in 1990 as part of a longstanding effort to overhaul its public education system.[58] Statewide education reform in Texas primarily began in 1979 when the Texas legislature required the state to begin administering the Texas Assessment of Basic Skills (TABS), a minimum competency test without sanctions for students. In 1984, the state legislature passed the Equal Educational Opportunity Act, a law that required the State Board of Education to adopt a statewide curriculum (the Essential Elements) and that was designed to impose an accountability system on schools and students. Under this law, the state Board of Education adopted the Texas Educational Assessment of Minimum Skills (TEAMS), a basic skills exam, that students were required to pass in order to receive a diploma.

In 1990, Texas replaced the TEAMS with the TAAS, which was generally designed to measure mastery of the state curriculum but assessed higher-order thinking skills than the TEAMS.[59] In order to graduate from high school, students needed to pass the reading, mathematics, and writing sections of the TAAS. Texas also used the TAAS to rate the performance of schools and districts, and to provide incentives to schools to perform well. In order to complete these ratings, the state disaggregated the performance of schools and districts by ethnicity and socio-economic status. Incentives for high performance on the TAAS included extra funding, and incentives for low performance on the TAAS included possible closure of schools. Indeed, Texas' accountability system later constituted an important model for No Child Left Behind.

Like the earlier administration of the SSAT II in Florida, the administration of the TAAS resulted in a substantial number of student failures. The first administration of the exit exam TAAS in October 1991 resulted in a 67 percent failure rate for African-American students and a 59 percent failure rate for Hispanic students. Thirty-one percent of white students taking the TAAS also failed. Similar failure rates persisted as the TAAS continued to be administered in the following years. For example, in 1995, 68 percent of African-American students and 63 percent of Hispanic students failed the exit-exam TAAS, and 30 percent of white students failed.[60] In response to these failure rates, MALDEF brought suit on behalf of minority students under many of the same basic theories used in *Debra P.*: equal protection, due process, and violation of Title VI of the Civil Rights Act and the Equal Educational Opportunities Act. In January 2000, Judge Edward C. Prado of the Western District of Texas issued the first and only ruling in *GI Forum* and found that Texas did not violate any legal requirements by using the TAAS for high-stakes purposes. Like Judge Carr, who had presided over the trial in *Debra P.*, Judge Prado was required to sort through a large volume of often technical and conflicting testimony and evidence presented during a trial that lasted for five weeks.

Judge Prado began his decision in *GI Forum* by highlighting some general observations about the case that offer much insight into the intersection of the courts and education policy in the context of high-stakes testing litigation. First, Judge Prado echoed familiar concerns about the role of the courts in education policy—that courts are required to give deference to state's education policies and that courts do not have the expertise or "mandate of the electorate" to justify unwarranted intrusion in curricular decisions.[61] Judge Prado also highlighted a particular issue that he believed was not implicated by the case. He indicated that, despite the strong and diverse opinions surrounding the use of the TAAS, he had not been asked to rule and legally could not rule on the wisdom of standardized examinations— he had no authority to tell Texas what a student should know upon graduation and could only decide whether the exit exam was a fair test of what was taught. Thus, Judge Prado emphasized the limited scope of his analysis in the case. Finally, Judge Prado emphasized the diversity of the expert testimony in the case and the difficulty of determining the quality of the experts— while Texas' experts largely testified about the construction of the TAAS and did so persuasively, the plaintiff's experts offered persuasive testimony about the wisdom of the TAAS as applied to minorities who had not received equal educational opportunities.

Having highlighted these broad issues, Judge Prado proceeded to analyze the evidence and testimony in light of the applicable legal requirements. Some of the plaintiffs' arguments were dismissed before the trial even began. The plaintiffs argued that the defendants had intentionally discriminated against minority students primarily because state officials foresaw that the TAAS graduation requirements would affect these students disproportionately.[62] Like the defendants in *Debra P.*, the *GI Forum* defendants argued in response that Texas was using the TAAS to improve the performance of these students.[63] The plaintiffs also argued that the use of the TAAS perpetuated the effects of past segregation in Texas, while the defendants argued in response that sufficient time had passed since state-mandated segregation and that such effects had sufficiently disappeared.[64] Judge Prado granted summary judgment on both of these issues because he found that there would not be sufficient evidence to support these particular arguments that the plaintiffs had made at trial.

The plaintiffs' Title VI disparate impact claim, however, made it to trial and constituted a central feature of the case. Focusing on the significant statistical disparities between the passage rates for white students and minority students under various statistical analyses, Judge Prado found that the plaintiffs had made the case that the administration of the TAAS had resulted in a sufficiently substantial disparity between minority students and white students.[65] Judge Prado accordingly moved to the second prong of the disparate impact test and emphasized that the defendants simply needed to produce evidence that there was a manifest relationship between the TAAS and a legitimate educational goal to show that the administration of the TAAS was educationally necessary. In order to determine whether the defendants had produced such evidence, Judge Prado examined several different factors, including the overall effectiveness of the test to provide "an objective assessment of whether students have mastered a discrete set of skills and knowledge," the legitimacy of the cut score, whether the TAAS could serve as motivation for students, and whether the TAAS produced higher dropout and retention rates for minority students.[66] After examining such factors, the judge found that the TAAS was educationally necessary.

While several elements of the educational necessity analysis included issues directly related to test validity (such as whether the test effectively measured students' knowledge), it is important to note that Judge Prado did not explicitly indicate the precise place of validity in this analysis. Before evaluating the plaintiffs' Title VI claims in his opinion, Judge Prado explicitly examined how the TAAS was constructed, what validity means in the psychometric context, and the setting of cut scores. Moreover, Judge Prado briefly referenced the then current version of the *AERA Standards* and the testimony of various experts who cited the *AERA Standards* at length in their testimony.[67] In some ways, Judge Prado even appeared to implicitly stretch the concept of validity beyond the sort that was employed by other courts that had similarly examined the legality of testing practices.[68] Still, Judge Prado did not expressly indicate that Texas' testing practice had to be valid in certain respects in order to be educationally necessary, and he was ultimately persuaded that that TAAS was well constructed to serve as a tool for determining students' fitness to graduate. Because Judge Prado then found that the plaintiffs failed to present sufficient evidence that there were other equally effective alternatives to the TAAS, he concluded that the administration of the TAAS did not result in an impermissible disparate impact under Title VI.

The plaintiffs' due process claims also made it to trial. Like the plaintiffs in *Debra P.*, the plaintiffs in *GI Forum* argued that Texas had not provided sufficient notice of the graduation requirement and that the administration of the TAAS lacked sufficient curricular validity. While Judge Prado found that students had property interests in receiving diplomas, he was not persuaded by the plaintiffs' procedural and substantive due process arguments. Because both parties eventually agreed that students had generally received sufficient warning of the TAAS and its consequences, Judge Prado rejected the procedural due process argument. After examining the substantive due process argument, Judge Prado also found that the plaintiffs had received sufficient opportunities to learn the content tested by the TAAS and that the testing practice therefore had sufficient curricular validity.

In order to prove that students in Texas had generally received such opportunities to learn, the state's experts presented an array of evidence during trial—they primarily relied on an examination of the state-mandated curriculum, an examination of curricular materials, surveys of teachers, surveys of district officials, and reviews of the TAAS by educator committees and bias review panels to establish that students had sufficient opportunities to learn the material tested by the TAAS. This evidence was notably different than that presented by the defendants in *Debra P.* during the remand proceedings—in *Debra P.*, the defendants conducted on-site evaluations of districts and schools to determine the extent to which teachers were actually creating sufficient opportunities to learn the content in the curriculum.[69] Still, when combined with the fact that Texas was offering remediation classes to students who needed them, Judge Prado found that such evidence was sufficient to establish the curricular validity of the TAAS. Because he did not find for the plaintiffs in regard to any of their claims, the judge dismissed the case.

Judge Prado's decision in *GI Forum* generated strong reactions. Members of the psychometric community hotly debated Judge Prado's treatment of the issues related to validity in the case.[70] Several researchers also debated the meaning of ostensible gains in student performance during the administration of the TAAS and fought over whether these gains should be labeled a "miracle" or a "myth."[71] Nonetheless, potentially fearing that a conservative Fifth Circuit Court of Appeals would overturn the precedent established in *Debra P.*, the plaintiffs did not appeal the case.[72] Indeed, following *GI Forum*, plaintiffs' success in high-stakes testing litigation continued to be quite limited.[73] As such, the decision in *GI Forum* may constitute a model for how courts continue to decide modern high-stakes testing cases.

Discussion and Conclusion

Although the body of law governing high-stakes testing is not large, it is comparatively the largest and most cohesive set of legal requirements that applies to standards-based reform and related accountability policies. It has developed over decades of judicial interpretation of federal statutory and constitutional provisions, and it is built to govern the use of tests to hold students accountable for their performance. Like much education litigation of the past, high-stakes testing cases have been generated largely in response to various inequities resulting from the implementation of state-level education policies. In this respect, high-stakes testing cases highlight some of the major "pressure points" in state education policies and the unequal educational opportunities provided to these students.

As an examination of these cases indicates, however, it appears to be increasingly difficult for plaintiffs to successfully challenge testing practices under the legal frameworks governing high-stakes testing. Because courts give much deference to states' education policies and the rationales underlying them, it is very difficult for plaintiffs to make successful claims that testing practices constitute instances of intentional discrimination, even if state officials foresaw a disparate impact prior to the implementation of these testing practices. Successful claims that testing practices perpetuate or further the effects of prior segregation also become harder to make every year as state policies become increasingly removed from the last instances of *de jure* segregation in states—while the plaintiffs in *Debra P.* successfully argued in the early 1980s that Florida's testing practices perpetuated the vestiges of prior segregation, the plaintiffs in *GI Forum* unsuccessfully attempted to make the same arguments in the early 21st century about Texas' testing practices. In addition, under the recent Supreme Court case *Alexander v. Sandoval* (which was decided after *GI Forum* was decided), plaintiffs can no longer bring disparate impact claims in federal court under the Title VI regulations. Plaintiffs must instead file complaints alleging an impermissible disparate impact with ED, thus greatly reducing the enforceability of Title VI protections for students. And as one scholar has argued, federal judges appear to have largely spent their reformist impulses in education after decades of difficult, protracted, and often ineffective litigation over desegregation.[74]

While high-stakes testing litigation seems like a natural response to some of the major problems raised by the implementation of modern standards-based accountability systems, a close inspection of major high-stakes testing cases also reveals that such litigation does not well position courts to act effectively in this area. On the surface, the litigation involving high-stakes testing appears to have much to recommend. Through mandates governing curricular validity, such litigation has focused courts on minority students' opportunities to learn, an important element of standards-based reform that has failed to receive continuing attention in the political arena. A focus on minority students' opportunities to learn would seem to accord with one of the primary advantages of the courts as a venue to protect the rights of underrepresented individuals and groups where the political process fails to adequately do so. Indeed, as discussed in Chapter Two, the pressure of strong accountability systems appears to have exacerbated inequalities in educational opportunities without consistent attention to students' opportunities to learn.

The particular manner in which such litigation helps the courts frame the requirements governing curricular validity also appears to have much to recommend. By focusing courts on the alignment between curricular frameworks, tests, curricular materials, and instruction, high-stakes testing litigation has also focused courts on one of the most significant problems facing standards-based reform—where various entities lag in their efforts to align various policy elements under standards-based reform policies, a judicial focus on this alignment could provide a useful additional push in this direction. Because there are pervasive concerns about the validity of ongoing testing practices, attention to validity on a more general level also appears to be a desirable effect of high-stakes testing litigation.

Deeper inspection, however, reveals the limitations of this form of litigation to help courts act effectively in the context of modern standards-based reform and accountability policies. As *Debra P.* and *GI Forum* highlight, different judges have construed the concept of curricular validity inconsistently, and different judges have found different forms of evidence persuasive to establish what opportunities to learn have been provided to students. While the judges in *Debra P.* at least looked to examinations of what actually transpired in some classrooms, Judge Prado simply assumed in *GI Forum* that teachers' practices conformed to curricular goals, tests, and curricular materials without much evidence directly addressing this issue. Furthermore, clearly more comfortable with legal requirements than conflicting expert testimony, judges in both cases both looked to legal requirements to help determine what was transpiring at the classroom level. But as discussed in Chapter Two, teachers' practices can be quite variable and unaligned with curricular goals and mandates codified into law, despite the presence of standards, tests, and theoretically aligned curriculum materials. Judicial analyses of opportunities to learn through the lens of high-stakes testing law accordingly appear insufficient to consistently produce reliable findings about the opportunities actually available to students.

Judges similarly considered the more general concept of validity differently across high-stakes testing cases and inconsistently looked to the *AERA Standards* to help them address this issue. Indeed, perhaps the most consistent aspect of the high-stakes cases, besides the inequitable effects of the testing practices in question, is the presence of conflicting and technical expert testimony about the validity of testing practices. Given the difficulties that the courts have historically faced when engaging with technical educational matters, scientific uncertainty about core issues in high-stakes testing cases, and the vague legal requirements that guide judicial consideration of these issues, there is little reason to expect courts in high-stakes testing litigation to consistently focus on many of the major problems facing modern standards-based accountability policies.

Other characteristics of high-stakes testing litigation limit its potential to enable courts to effectively address modern standards-based accountability policies as well. As Judge Prado emphasized in *GI Forum*, the scope of judicial analysis in high-stakes testing cases is very narrow—instead of focusing on the underlying causes of poor or inequitable performance on tests, judicial analysis focuses on whether a test fairly measures what students know and have been taught. Several courts have emphasized their reluctance to broaden the scope of their analysis in such cases by repeatedly discussing the deference due to states' education policies. As a result of this narrow analysis, judicial decisions that are favorable to plaintiffs generally require states to stop their testing practices until they can establish that their testing practices are sufficiently valid; these judicial decisions generally do not result in orders that directly affect the causes of low and inequitable performance, or the failure of states' policies to effectively address these causes.[75]

The focus of high-stakes testing litigation on protecting individual students against the unfairness of testing practices also limits the applicability of this litigation to modern standards-based accountability policies. While protecting individual minority students is clearly important, especially given the potentially negative effects of modern testing practices on these students, standards-based reform and accountability policies involve an array of other concerns as well. These polices are aimed at boosting the level of education for all students by leveraging structural changes in the U.S. education system. High-stakes testing litigation can address these structural-level problems to a certain extent—as discussed above, these frameworks can focus a court's attention on alignment between different policy elements. But this litigation can ultimately do little to address various structural problems facing the implementation of standards-based reforms, such as building the knowledge needed to change teachers' practices in the classroom and to implement well-functioning data management systems, and increasing financial and physical resources. Moreover, this litigation can do little to address certain political problems, such as ensuring that standards enacted in states are high quality. As a result, high-stakes testing litigation appears to have limited potential to help leverage the fundamental changes entailed by standards-based reform and accountability policies, or to mitigate its inequitable effects.

Given the highly contested nature of the implications of modern standards-based accountability systems for educational equity, it is also unclear whether many potential reformers would consider high-stakes testing litigation to influence these policies. While some have labeled these systems, such as those implemented to satisfy NCLB mandates, as extremely harmful to minority groups, others have labeled these systems as central in the ongoing fight for civil rights because they are aimed at improving schools and the performance of all students.[76] For example, MALDEF, the organization spearheading the *GI Forum* litigation for the plaintiffs, has emerged as a supporter of NCLB in certain respects.[77] Furthermore, absent novel and untested legal theories that modern accountability systems focused on schools and districts violate the requirements of high-stakes testing law, the type of litigation discussed in this chapter can only be brought in the states that employ testing practices involving high-stakes decisions for students. Given the roots of the legal frameworks governing high-stakes testing in the civil rights movement, this host of limitations makes much sense—high-stakes testing litigation is ultimately a creature of its history and can only be stretched so far as the education policy environment changes through time.

In short, high-stakes testing litigation has historically enabled the courts to protect the rights of minority students in the context of high-stakes testing systems that have resulted in certain undesirable effects on these students. However, the legal frameworks employed in these cases have taxed the capacities of the courts to make decisions in an area characterized by scientific uncertainty and where the line between educational and legal standards has become blurred. This litigation has also become increasingly less viable and does not well position courts to deal with several major problems that modern standards-based accountability policies have faced. As a result, high-stakes testing litigation, which has traditionally constituted the flagship type of litigation for addressing educational problems involving large-scale educational testing practices, appears to poorly position the courts to effectively influence the development and implementation of modern standards-based reforms and accountability policies.

CHAPTER FOUR

No Child Left Behind Litigation

In addition to addressing standards-based reform and accountability policies in the context of litigation aimed at high-stakes testing practices, courts have begun to address issues related to such polices in the context of claims brought directly to influence the implementation of No Child Left Behind (NCLB). As discussed in Chapter Two, NCLB was signed into law in 2002 and reauthorized the Elementary and Secondary Education Act (ESEA). With its passage, NCLB altered the legal landscape governing standards-based reform and accountability policies across the country—in exchange for Title I funds, states were required to develop standards and assessments, and hold schools and districts accountable for their performance on these assessments. If schools and districts failed to meet their performance goals, a variety of administrative sanctions were prescribed. In contrast to the ways in which the Goals 2000: Educate America Act (Goals 2000) and the Improving America's Schools Act (IASA) were enforced by the U.S. Department of Education (ED), NCLB provisions have been enforced by ED rather strictly.

NCLB has accordingly been at the center of protracted and often heated disagreements. While some have praised NCLB as the remedy to the problems that plague the U.S. education system, others have attacked NCLB as too demanding. Critics have complained that states, districts, and schools possessed little capacity to comply with NCLB provisions regarding standards, testing, and accountability, and that schools simply could not meet their performance goals. Critics have also complained that the institution of NCLB has resulted in undesirable consequences in the classroom, such as "teaching to the test," and has inequitably affected certain groups of schools and students more than others. In addition, some have argued that NCLB was simply poorly designed to yield valid interpretations about the performance of students and schools. As a result of such increased and inequitably distributed pressures on students, schools, districts, and states, NCLB has begun to face a variety of legal challenges across the U.S.

This chapter examines the litigation generated directly in response to NCLB and focuses on the ways in which courts have addressed NCLB-related claims. As Title I of NCLB laid out requirements that governed the development and implementation of standards-based reform and accountability policies around the country, NCLB has been one of the primary sources of law that has regulated these policies. Cases directly aimed at the design and implementation of NCLB thus constitute one of the most important groups of cases for understanding how the courts have addressed these polices. These cases have varied significantly in several respects. Entities such as private individuals, nonprofit organizations, teachers' unions, and school districts have all brought suit to influence NCLB's design and implementation. These entities have focused on a range of issues, including the implementation of NCLB accountability sanctions, the justifiability of student and school performance determinations, and the underlying capacities possessed by various entities to respond to NCLB mandates, and they have also employed a range of different legal theories to achieve their goals.

Despite the array of concerns raised by plaintiffs, the courts generally have not been willing to order changes in NCLB's implementation. The legal frameworks employed by courts to analyze NCLB's implementation were generally not structured in ways that easily enabled courts to order changes in standards-based reform and accountability policies—due to various legal issues, such as the unavailability of a "Section 1983" action, plaintiffs have faced substantial difficulties crafting viable legal theories.[1] NCLB-related litigation has also poorly framed many of the problems facing standards-based reform and accountability policies. For example, in some cases, litigation targeted bare noncompliance with the law instead of more fundamental factors, such as a lack of financial or technical capacities, underlying this noncompliance. As a result, several key issues surrounding NCLB's design and implementation have largely remained hidden from judicial analysis. And some of the major problems facing NCLB that have arisen in the course of litigation have involved issues that the courts are generally not well positioned to address, such as extremely technical aspects of testing systems.

In order to examine how the courts have addressed NCLB, this chapter primarily includes case studies of NCLB-related litigation in the three major areas in which such litigation has occurred: cases focusing on the implementation of NCLB accountability sanctions, cases focusing on the justifiability of student and school performance determinations, and cases focusing on the underlying capacities possessed by various entities to respond to NCLB requirements. While this chapter includes detailed examinations of most of the cases that have focused on NCLB, this chapter does not include examinations of all the cases because of their relative importance. Unlike the previous chapter, this chapter also does not include a more general description of the relevant legal frameworks—in part because NCLB is so recent, there is no coherent and well-established body of precedent to guide judicial decision making in this litigation. Indeed, plaintiffs' legal theories have differed significantly, and many of the cases discussed in this chapter were based on novel legal theories. Because NCLB is still being implemented and litigation is in progress as this book is being completed, this book does not include an examination of litigation that was initiated after March 2007.

Finally, it is important to note that, although NCLB-related litigation has not consistently focused on major problems facing standards-based reform and accountability policies, much of this litigation has more directly involved the major problems that these policies have recently faced than high-stakes testing litigation. Unlike high-stakes testing litigation, NCLB-related litigation was originally generated in direct response to issues facing modern, standards-based accountability polices. As such, this litigation offers a useful window into the potential of courts focused on these issues to effectively influence the course of standards-based reform and accountability policies. To be sure, the analyses conducted in this chapter may not completely apply to the standards-based reform and accountability policies that are implemented in 2008 and beyond. As this book is being completed in early 2008, the U.S. Congress has notably begun to consider the reauthorization of NCLB, and the final shape of the law is thus far unclear. However, as discussed in Chapter Two, current indications are that that NCLB will change in some key respects but that its fundamental policy logic will remain in place. To the extent that the core features of the law remain in place, this chapter offers an important window into the precise ways in which the courts can effectively address standards-based reform in the modern policy landscape. To the extent that the law is changed, this chapter still offers key insight into how the courts have previously addressed modern standards-based reform with a significant focus on accountability and the various factors underlying the courts' treatment of these policies.

The Implementation of Accountability Sanctions

As discussed in Chapter Two, the failure of states, districts, and schools to effectively implement accountability sanctions has constituted a major NCLB implementation problem and has been the object of much political criticism. This failure took center stage in *ACORN v. New York City Department of Education*

(*ACORN*).[2] In this case, the Albany and New York City school districts, two urban districts in New York, allegedly failed to fully implement NCLB provisions regarding public school choice, supplemental services, and parental notice about the failure of schools to make adequate yearly progress (AYP). The plaintiffs sued to ensure that these accountability sanctions were effectively implemented.

New York City and Albany were struggling to make AYP as early as the first year of NCLB's implementation.[3] For the 2002–2003 school year, 487 schools in New York failed to meet AYP. New York City contained 331 of these schools with approximately 282,000 students. Albany, a much smaller district, contained three of these schools with approximately 2,000 students. In this respect, the problems facing New York City and Albany reflected problems occurring around the country—as discussed in Chapter Two, the AYP provisions of NCLB have disproportionately affected urban schools due to various issues, such as inequitably distributed opportunities to learn, capacities to change instructional practices, and the inclusion of several student groups that needed to make AYP in a given year.

Once the schools in New York City and Albany were identified as having failed to make AYP, several problems implementing the required accountability sanctions quickly emerged. Although the New York State Education Department (NYSED) was required to release the list of failing schools to the public before the beginning of the following school year so that parents could take advantage of any public school choice or supplemental services options available to them, the NYSED released the list shortly after the following school year started—the NYSED released this list on September 4, 2002 for New York City and on September 9, 2002 for the rest of the state. The NYSED also failed to make many parents of children in schools that had failed to make AYP aware of their schools' status. Parents involved in the *ACORN* litigation submitted that they had never received any information about their rights under NCLB.[4] Indeed, although 94 percent of parents with children in these schools indicated in a survey that they would have likely requested transfers to a different school, 75 percent of these parents were unaware of their schools' status.[5] Many parents also indicated that they received misleading information about their right to transfer. For example, one parent learned from a list printed in a newspaper that her child qualified for a transfer, but when she inquired about taking advantage of this option, she was told that she was months too late.[6] Other parents were allegedly told that, due to a lack of capacity, stemming from issues such as requirements for class size reduction, not all transfer requests could be accommodated.[7] New York City allegedly denied most transfer requests outright. According to the plaintiffs, nearly 5,000 of 6,400 such requests were rejected.[8] The situation was quite similar in Albany. Many parents indicated that they never received notification about the status of their schools or rights to transfer, and press releases and letters sent to parents in Albany did not explain the meaning of failure to make AYP and the transfer options available to parents.[9]

Virtually identical issues surrounded the implementation of supplemental educational services provisions in New York City and Albany. The Executive Director for Advocates for Children, a nonprofit organization in New York, indicated that no parents she talked to were aware of their rights to request supplemental services for their children.[10] In some parts of New York City, schools allegedly promoted their own programs over the programs of supplemental services providers.[11] The parents that had read the supplemental services providers list found this list difficult to understand, and many parents had also been told that supplemental services were not available for their children. In Albany, parents experienced similar difficulties taking advantage of their supplemental services options.[12]

In order to address these issues, the Association of Community Organizations for Reform Now (ACORN), a nonprofit community organization largely comprised of low- and middle-income families and focused on social justice issues, brought a class action suit in federal court against the New York City and Albany school districts on behalf of the parents who were denied their "rights" for public school choice and supplemental services under NCLB. The case was assigned to Judge John G. Koeltl of the Southern District of New York. ACORN asked Judge Koeltl to order the districts to immediately provide parental notification that complied with NCLB and to provide the required opportunities to transfer and use supplemental services to all appropriate students in the two districts that had failed to make AYP. But in one of the most important decisions regarding the implementation of standards-based reform and accountability policies, Judge Koeltl refused to take any action and dismissed the case. The primary reason underlying Judge Koeltl's decision conspicuously was not the lack of evidence that the districts had in fact failed to comply with NCLB requirements; the primary reason was in the ability of the plaintiffs to enforce the provisions of NCLB.

USING SECTION 1983 TO ENFORCE FEDERAL LAW

In order to enforce the parental notice provisions, public school choice provisions, and supplemental services provisions of NCLB, the plaintiffs in *ACORN* brought a "Section 1983" action. Generally, private plaintiffs cannot bring a successful claim against a governmental entity by simply proving that the entity has failed to comply with the requirements of a federal statute. Private plaintiffs first need to establish a cause of action that allows them to bring such a claim. Private plaintiffs have generally found a cause of action to enforce the provisions of a federal statute from three primary sources: an express private cause of action, an implied private cause of action, and a Section 1983 action. An express private cause of action is available where a federal statute contains a provision explicitly specifying that private citizens or entities can sue the government to enforce other provisions of the statute. NCLB (along with most other federal statutes) does not contain an express private cause of action. An implied private cause of action is available where a federal statute evinces a congressional intent to allow private plaintiffs a cause of action.[13] However, under recent Supreme Court jurisprudence, the rules regarding implied private causes of action have largely collapsed into those regarding Section 1983 actions.[14] Thus, bringing a Section 1983 action appears at first glance to be a logical move for plaintiffs wishing to enforce NCLB requirements, and this was the strategy employed by the plaintiffs in *ACORN*. To help the reader understand the reasoning of Judge Koeltl's decision, a brief overview of the history of Section 1983 is in order.

As it was originally enacted, Section 1983 constituted the first section of the Ku Klux Klan Act of 1871. This law was passed by Congress in the aftermath of the Civil War and permits U.S. citizens to bring lawsuits against the government in response to actions that deprive them of their "rights, privileges, or immunities secured by the Constitution and laws."[15] For over a century after its passage, the Supreme Court only allowed plaintiffs to sue under Section 1983 for violations of constitutional rights.[16] However, in the past few decades, the Supreme Court has interpreted Section 1983 as capable of supporting claims to enforce the provisions of a federal law.

Although the Supreme Court has historically articulated the requirements governing Section 1983 actions in a seemingly haphazard fashion, recent Supreme Court jurisprudence has yielded a somewhat clear test focusing on congressional intent to determine whether plaintiffs can use Section 1983 to enforce the provisions of a federal law. In *Blessing v. Freestone*, the Supreme Court stated that plaintiffs have a right to sue under Section 1983 to enforce the provisions of a federal law where (1) plaintiffs are the "intended beneficiaries of the legislation," (2) the right must not be "so 'vague and amorphous' that its enforcement would strain judicial competence," and (3) the statutory language "clearly bind(s) the states with an obligation to comply."[17] In *Gonzaga University v. Doe*, the Supreme Court cemented the *Blessing* approach by focusing on whether a federal law includes "rights-creating language" instead of an emphasis on "institutional policy and practice."[18] This test has made it very difficult for private plaintiffs to use Section 1983 to enforce the provisions of a federal law and has consequently faced much criticism.[19]

The jurisprudential history of Section 1983 and current difficulty of brining a Section 1983 action played a central role in the *ACORN* court's decision. The plaintiffs in *ACORN* brought suit under Section 1983 specifically to enforce the NCLB provisions governing parental notice, school choice, and supplemental services—the plaintiffs argued that the districts' failure to notify parents and provide transfer and supplemental services options violated the express requirements of NCLB. Applying the Supreme Court jurisprudence governing Section 1983 for the first time since the Supreme Court had decided *Gonzaga*, Judge Koeltl found that NCLB did not manifest the requisite congressional intent to allow a Section 1983 action.[20]

First, Judge Koeltl examined the sections of NCLB providing for the creation of state plans, the development and implementation of systems of standards and assessments, and the requirements for schools to make AYP, and concluded that these provisions had only an aggregate focus and were not concerned with the needs of individuals; thus, the provisions did not contain the requisite rights-creating language. Judge Koetl next examined the parental notification, choice, and supplemental services provisions in considerable detail—his opinion quoted six provisions governing school transfer, five provisions governing supplemental services, and one provision governing parental notification—and Judge Koetl again concluded that these NCLB provisions did not contain the requisite rights-creating language. After examining these provisions that pertained directly to the plaintiffs' arguments, the judge analyzed the "Penalties" section of NCLB and focused heavily on the enforcement mechanisms—Judge Koetl here concluded that NCLB vested sole authority to enforce violations of NCLB in the U.S. Secretary of Education and did not contemplate enforcement by private plaintiffs. Accordingly, Judge Koetl dismissed *ACORN* and declined to enforce the parental notification, school choice, and supplemental services provisions of NCLB.

ACORN is a very revealing and important case for understanding how the courts have addressed standards-based reforms and accountability policies in the context of cases aimed at directly influencing NCLB's implementation. As mentioned above, *ACORN* highlights some of the major issues surrounding standards-based reform and accountability policies—as urban districts facing the first wave of sanctions for failure to make AYP, the New York City and Albany school districts were by no means alone in the problems they were facing, and these problems were sufficiently important to the plaintiffs to merit costly litigation. *ACORN* also highlights the different interpretations that various groups can have of NCLB's sanctions—while many groups have protested the impact of these sanctions, the plaintiffs in *ACORN* sued to ensure that these sanctions were effectively implemented. In this respect, *ACORN* demonstrates the difficulty of determining the "right" way for reformers and governmental entities to address modern, standards-based accountability policies.

But perhaps most importantly, *ACORN* well demonstrates the significant legal barriers to any judicial action to directly influence NCLB's implementation. In the absence of an express private cause of action, Section 1983 constitutes one of the primary tools that private plaintiffs can use to enforce the provisions of a federal statute in the courts. But even in cases such as *ACORN*, where it clearly appears that a governmental entity has failed to comply with NCLB requirements, using Section 1983 does not constitute a viable option. Indeed, citing *ACORN*, other federal judges in *Fresh Start Academy v. Toledo Board of Education* and *Alliance for Children v. City of Detroit Public Schools* engaged in similar analyses with regard to private plaintiffs' rights to sue to enforce the supplemental services provisions of NCLB, and the judges in this cases reached the same conclusions about the rights of these plaintiffs as Judge Koeltl.[21]

Moreover, even if NCLB were judicially enforceable through Section 1983, the type of litigation in *ACORN* would not have well positioned Judge Koeltl to address the problems cited by the plaintiffs—the litigation in *ACORN* focused on bare noncompliance with NCLB and not the factors underlying this noncompliance, such as the likely lack of technical and financial capacities possessed by the school districts to effectively implement the sanctions for school failure to make AYP. Simply ordering states and districts to change their behavior without detailed attention to the underlying problems likely would not have been an effective response to the problems. So, while *ACORN* highlights major problems that NCLB has faced and reinforces the importance of these problems to interested and disproportionately affected groups, it also demonstrates the substantial difficulty of using the courts to directly influence the implementation of particular NCLB requirements.

The Justifiability of Student and School Performance Determinations

Although the plaintiffs in *ACORN* attempted to ensure that the accountability sanctions for failure to make AYP were faithfully implemented, other plaintiffs reacted very differently to the threat of these sanctions. As discussed in Chapter Two, the implementation of these sanctions has proven quite costly and difficult, and has been viewed as a punishment for failure to help students perform at a certain level. Given these implications of school failure to make AYP, several plaintiffs have brought suit to ensure that student and school performance determinations were justifiable, and under the theory that they were not, to have determinations of school failure to make AYP rescinded.

READING SCHOOL DISTRICT v. PENNSYLVANIA DEPARTMENT OF EDUCATION

A series of three related cases, all titled *Reading School District v. Pennsylvania Department of Education*, focused on the justifiability of student and school performance determinations. Two of these cases stemmed from the same event—the failure of schools in the Reading, Pennsylvania school district to make AYP. As discussed in Chapter Two, the lack of various types of assistance that schools have received to help them make AYP has constituted a critical problem highlighted by entities evaluating NCLB's implementation and a quite visible political issue. The ways in which states determine whether schools make AYP have also constituted important and high-profile issues for NCLB's implementation. Both the assistance that schools received and the methods of measuring student and school performance were framed as issues that impacted the justifiability of AYP determinations in the *Reading* cases.

The major event that triggered the *Reading* litigation occurred in January 2003 when the Pennsylvania Department of Education (PDE) informed Reading that 13 of its 19 schools had failed to make AYP. Six of these 13 schools received Title I funds, and seven of them did not. Because the timelines for making AYP differed with regard to Title I schools and non-Title I schools, the six Title I schools were identified for school improvement. The remaining seven schools were placed on a "warning list" that did not involve any sort of formal sanctions.

The characteristics of the Reading school district made it especially likely that it would be strongly impacted by NCLB's requirements. Reading is an urban district and during the 2003–2004 school year, 64 percent percent of the student population in the Reading school district was Hispanic.[22] Fifteen percent of Reading's student population was classified as having limited English proficiency (LEP), ranking Reading in the 99th percentile statewide in this category. Poverty in the community that Reading served was ranked in the 98th percentile statewide, and both the student dropout and student mobility rate ranked in the 100th percentile statewide. The student/teacher ratio ranked in the 93rd percentile statewide, and the student/administrator ratio ranked in the 99th percentile statewide. School funding in Reading was also very low. The annual expenditure per student in Reading was $8,369, compared to the countywide average of $10,262 and the statewide average of $10,643 at the time. In short, Reading was a poor school district with a relatively high percentage of Spanish-speaking LEP students, and the district accordingly exemplified the type of district that has most often become the object of NCLB accountability sanctions. It was primarily because of the performance of these students that the 13 Reading schools were identified as failing to make AYP.

Before the Reading school district brought its grievances before a court, it first asked the state to reconsider its AYP determinations. Upon learning that PDE had identified 13 of its schools for failure to make AYP, Reading appealed these identifications to PDE. PDE reviewed Reading's appeal on two separate occasions. Both of these reviews occurred without a formal hearing and resulted in denials of Reading's claims. In October 2003, PDE reviewed Reading's appeal for the final time. At this time, PDE conducted a formal administrative hearing before a hearing officer who gathered evidence, heard witnesses, and submitted information to the Pennsylvania Secretary of Education, Vicki L. Phillips, for a final determination. The four witnesses at this hearing provided information largely about the makeup of Reading students, the technical and financial assistance provided by PDE to Reading, how PDE arrived at its number specifying minimum subgroup size for making AYP determinations, and the steps PDE was taking to provide native language assessments to its Spanish-speaking students.[23] Two of the witnesses at the hearing were employees of PDE, and the two other witnesses were employees of Reading. The information elicited from the witnesses at the administrative hearing generally constituted the basis for the factual deter-minations made by both PDE and ultimately the courts that considered issues related to this case. However, upon reviewing the evidence and testi-mony from the hearing, Secretary Phillips again denied Reading's appeal.

In the first of the *Reading* cases (*Reading I*), the Reading school district appealed Secretary Phillips' decision to the Commonwealth Court of Pennsylvania, a court able to hear appeals from final orders of certain state agencies, and sought to have PDE's AYP determinations rescinded.[24] The case was assigned to a panel of three judges, composed of Judge James Colins, Judge Rochelle Friedman, and Judge Charles Mirarchi, Jr. Reading based its case on three separate arguments: First, Reading argued that PDE had failed to provide the district with sufficient financial and technical assistance to meet NCLB's requirements. Second, Reading argued that PDE had failed to provide native language testing to Spanish-speaking LEP students and thereby failed to assess Reading's student population accurately. Third, Reading argued that PDE had failed to use sound statistical methodology to determine the minimum number of students that could constitute an assessable subgroup for NCLB purposes.

Reading's first argument about the lack of financial and technical assistance focused on one of the most important and high-profile problems associated with NCLB—the lack of various capacities needed to meet NCLB's requirements. However, instead of framing the lack of assistance as a legally recognizable problem in itself, Reading expressly tied this problem to AYP determinations. At the time of the trial, PDE had only provided Reading with five one-day workshops and had posted information on its web site to help schools in school improvement, which constituted insufficient technical support according to Reading. Reading also claimed that PDE did not provide the district with sufficient funds to pay for the school improvement measures flowing from failure to make AYP—in the year before *Reading I* was brought, Reading had received a little over $6 million in Title I funds and had thus begun to implement only some of the school improvement requirements, such as offering limited public school choice. Bringing almost identical claims against PDE in *Reading II*, Reading specifically detailed the difference between the amount of funds that district officials believed were needed to implement NCLB sanctions effectively and the funds that were actually received—while Reading officials believed that they needed $26 million to implement NCLB sanctions during the 2003–2004 school year, the district only received $8 million for this purpose from PDE.[25] Reading claimed that, as a result, all the AYP determinations were unjustifiable.

Reading's second argument focused on the method of making AYP determinations. Reading argued that, despite its high proportion of LEP students, PDE did not provide any native language tests to Reading for the assessment of these students. Indeed, PDE did not announce plans to administer native language tests in Spanish until a few years after *Reading I* was filed.[26] Reading consequently claimed that its students were inaccurately assessed and that AYP decisions made on the basis of student performance on NCLB tests were unjustifiable. Given the high proportion of LEP students in Reading, PDE's testing practices at the time that *Reading I* was brought appear to raise significant psychometric concerns. As noted in Chapter Two, it is very difficult to make valid interpretations about the knowledge and skills of LEP students, even when test administrators use accommodations.

Reading's third argument similarly targeted the method of making AYP determinations but focused on the statistical methodology underlying these determinations. NCLB required states not only to assess entire schools but also different types of subgroups, such as LEP students within schools, to determine whether schools made AYP. Under NCLB, subgroups were required to be of a certain minimum size in order to trigger AYP requirements. Reading specifically argued that PDE had failed to use sound statistical methodology to determine this minimum number of students necessary to constitute an assessable NCLB subgroup, which was referred to in *Reading I* as the "N" number.[27] Evidence in the case indicated that the N number was set after a series of computer runs and bargaining with ED.[28] According to an employee of PDE, PDE had originally proposed 75 as the N number because of its statistical significance; as the employee indicated, a higher N number would yield more valid and reliable results. ED, however, did not accept 75 as the N number. Instead, ED entered into negotiations with PDE, and the number 40 was the result of these negotiations. According to the PDE employee, ED did not want PDE to set the N number as high as 75 because fewer schools would be forced to measure AYP with regard to LEP students and some schools would unjustifiably avoid NCLB's requirements. Like Reading's other two claims, this claim reflects serious problems that critics of NCLB accountability mechanisms have cited—an insufficient number of students in a subgroup can cause volatility in school-level AYP determinations and preclude valid interpretations of school performance.[29]

Appealing Administrative Decisions to Challenge Aspects of NCLB Implementation

The legal strategy employed by Reading to address the issues of assistance and measurement was quite different than the strategy employed by the *ACORN* plaintiffs. A Section 1983 action clearly appeared unavailable to Reading. In addition to the difficulties of bringing a Section 1983 action to enforce NCLB, as demonstrated by the *ACORN* court's decision, Section 1983 actions are simply unavailable to governmental entities (including school districts).[30] As a result, Reading was forced to pursue a different sort of legal strategy to allow a court to review PDE's implementation of NCLB— Reading brought suit under a state administrative law which allowed governmental entities to appeal final determinations, such as AYP determinations, made by state administrative agencies.

When a plaintiff wishes to challenge decisions made by administrative entities in court, there are several requirements that the plaintiff generally must fulfill. One of the major requirements is that a plaintiff first must exhaust all its administrative remedies by appealing the agency's initial decision (the AYP determinations, in this case) to the agency itself. After a plaintiff exhausts all possible appeals within the administrative agency, the plaintiff can then challenge the agency's final determination in a court. This is precisely the process that Reading followed. Reading first challenged PDE's AYP determinations by appealing to PDE. After Reading exhausted all of its administrative appeals within PDE and was ultimately unsuccessful at persuading Secretary Phillips that the AYP determinations should be rescinded, Reading appealed PDE's final order to the Commonwealth Court of Pennsylvania.

Writing for the panel of judges assigned the case, President Judge Colins crafted an opinion in *Reading I* describing the panel's reasoning and ultimately dismissing all of Reading's claims. In accordance with statutory requirements and state precedent regarding administrative appeals, the panel reviewed PDE's determinations in *Reading I* to see if they were supported by "substantial evidence." The judges conducted this review using a standard for substantial evidence that was earlier defined by the Pennsylvania Supreme Court:

> Substantial evidence has been defined as such relevant evidence that a reasonable mind might accept as adequate to support a conclusion . . .
> The Court must simply determine whether, upon consideration of the evidence as a whole, [the administrative agency's] findings have the requisite measure of support in the record.[31]

So, due to the nature of the administrative appeal process, the *Reading I* court was required to treat the AYP decisions of PDE with a good deal of deference—so long as PDE could prove that its determinations were supported by substantial evidence, the reviewing court would be required to defer to the decisions of the agency.

After discussing the applicability of the substantial evidence standard in the *Reading I* opinion, Judge Colins turned to Reading's arguments about PDE's AYP determinations. As discussed above, Reading argued that PDE failed to comply with three express requirements contained in NCLB. Judge Colins first discussed PDE's determination that PDE had complied with the NCLB provisions regarding the financial and technical assistance that states were required to provide to schools and districts. Under NCLB, states were to establish a system of "intensive and sustained support and improvement" for Title I schools and districts, create school support teams to devise additional approaches to provide assistance, and designate and use "Distinguished Educators" to help improve student achievement.[32] In addition, under both

NCLB and its regulations, states were required to provide districts identified for school improvement with technical assistance if requested.[33] As noted above, PDE had only provided Reading with five one-day workshops, and had posted information on its web site to help schools in school improvement. Indeed, as discussed in Chapter Two, the support provided to schools under these provisions to help their students perform well has varied dramatically.

Nevertheless, Judge Colins wrote that such assistance was sufficient to satisfy NCLB requirements. The court found that PDE was still in the process of implementing its program of technical assistance required under NCLB and that the technical assistance required by the statute and regulations had no effect on the analysis of whether the AYP determinations were justifiable—as the court stated, much of the technical assistance required by NCLB and its regulations is a *consequence* of failure to make AYP, not a "condition precedent."[34] In other words, because NCLB did not condition the justifiability of AYP decisions upon the actual receipt of technical assistance, the court refused to find that the decision to identify a school for school improvement was unjustifiable on technical assistance grounds. The court also found that Reading cited no NCLB language requiring states to pay for school improvement measures. Because of the precise way in which NCLB's assistance provisions were drafted, the panel simply had little grounds to address any of Reading's problems stemming from the lack of financial and technical assistance.

The precise language of NCLB also constituted a major factor preventing the *Reading* court from finding that PDE's failure to provide native language tests was grounds to overturn the AYP determinations. NCLB required states to provide native language tests "to the extent practicable."[35] According to the testimony of a PDE employee, the costs of providing native language tests were very high—such tests would cost more than $15 per student, and each native language test would have had to be developed from scratch to be valid.[36] Due to the time required to develop test items, field test the items, and analyze the results of the field testing, it would take at least two to three years to develop a valid native language test. After examining the time and money needed to administer native language tests, the panel let stand PDE's determination that such tests were not practicable.[37] As the court's opinion highlights, the "practicable" standard contained in the native language testing provision was very deferential to a state and made it very difficult for a court to regulate the behavior of a state in regard to native language tests. Even where the failure to provide such tests may result in inaccurate determinations about what students know and can do, the deferential language of

NCLB provided the *Reading I* court with little basis to find that agencies have acted improperly.

The language of NCLB and its regulations similarly constituted a major factor preventing the court from finding that the low N number set by PDE was grounds to overturn the AYP determinations. Under NCLB, states were not allowed to evaluate a subgroup separately if "the number of students in a category is insufficient to yield statistically reliable information."[38] NCLB regulations contained similar requirements.[39] As discussed above, the N number chosen by PDE was the product of bargaining with ED and may have been low enough to lead to statistically unjustifiable AYP determinations. The court, however, found that the N number was sufficient to yield statistically reliable information—citing its own incompetence to evaluate technical matters of education policy and employing the substantial evidence standard, the court refused to delve too deeply into PDE's decision-making process. Accordingly, despite the problems cited by Reading, which reflected serious problems school districts were facing around the U.S., the precise language of NCLB, the deferential character of the administrative review process, and the court's own concerns about its limited technical capacities constituted an insurmountable hurdle for judicial action in the context of the *Reading I* litigation.

Revisiting Reading

Although Reading met with little success in its first attempt to use the courts to have its AYP determinations rescinded, Reading returned to the courts twice more shortly after *Reading I* was decided. In the second case (*Reading II*), the Commonwealth Court of Pennsylvania faced almost exactly the same issues that were present in the first case.[40] In *Reading II*, Reading attempted to re-litigate the three claims that it had litigated in *Reading I*. The primary difference between the two cases was the amount of evidence that Reading submitted regarding the lack of funds that Reading received to implement NCLB—as mentioned above, Reading detailed in *Reading II* the precise difference between federal funds received and the federal funds that school officials believed were needed to implement NCLB. Because these issues had previously been litigated in *Reading I*, the court issued a very short opinion dismissing *Reading II* under the doctrine of *collateral estoppel*—a legal concept that prevents a plaintiff from re-litigating issues previously determined against that party. Thus, while *Reading II* again highlighted major implementation problems faced by many other school districts' entities implementing NCLB, the *Reading II* court was presented with very little legal basis in this case to find that PDE had acted improperly.

In *Reading III*, however, the Commonwealth Court of Pennsylvania was willing to order a change in the way that PDE was implementing NCLB. In this case, Reading attacked not the assistance provided by PDE, the quality of tests, or the statistical methodology underlying AYP determinations, but PDE's policy regarding appeals in the case of NCLB. PDE's appeal policy prohibited all appeals of AYP determinations unless these determinations related to (1) statistical error, (2) growth in academic performance, or (3) unforeseen circumstances beyond a district's control that prevented the district from making AYP.[41] According to Reading, such a policy unconstitutionally violated Reading's due process rights—PDE had too narrowly limited the range of appeals to which schools are constitutionally entitled.[42] A panel of judges, including Judge Colins, agreed with Reading and ordered PDE to hear a wider range of appeals. So, although Pennsylvania courts refused to overturn PDE's AYP determinations on the grounds of inadequate assistance or improper measurement, one court was willing to overturn an NCLB appeal policy.

Together, the three *Reading* cases illustrate several important issues regarding the ways in which courts have addressed standards-based reforms in the context of NCLB. First, like *ACORN*, these cases underscore some of the major issues surrounding standards-based reform and accountability policies discussed in Chapter Two—technical problems regarding the justifiability of student and school performance determinations have plagued the implementation of NCLB, and the *Reading* cases concretely illustrate how these problems have emerged. Moreover, although the legal arguments in the cases ultimately revolved around the justifiability of AYP determinations, the plaintiffs highlighted the lack of sustained support they were given to help develop their capacities to increase student and school performance—another serious problem several entities implementing NCLB have faced. And the *Reading* cases starkly highlight the inequitable effects of NCLB on schools with large populations of minority students and LEP students who have likely received comparatively limited opportunities to learn.

In addition, the *Reading* cases demonstrate the significant barriers to judicial action where plaintiffs attempt to influence NCLB implementation through the appeal of administrative decision making instead of through a Section 1983 action. Despite the pervasiveness of the problems highlighted in *Reading I* and *II*, the courts had little legal basis on which they could order any changes to NCLB's implementation. *ACORN* had demonstrated the ineffectiveness of a legal approach built on Section 1983, and as a school district, Reading could not use Section 1983 in any case. But the strategy employed by Reading—the appeal of PDE's administrative AYP decisions—involves its own share of limitations. The deferential character of administrative appeals made it very difficult for courts to overturn agency determinations, and in regard to the particular problems targeted by Reading, the actual language of NCLB gave the courts little grounds for deciding that PDE had acted improperly. Compounding these difficulties, the *Reading* cases involved very technical implementation problems, and the courts were loath to question the decisions of what they considered to be educational experts. If the courts had overturned PDE's decisions on the grounds that PDE did not implement valid testing practices or use sound statistical methodology, the courts accordingly would have decided in a field where they have historically faced significant difficulties.

Still, the *Reading* cases at least framed the problems facing modern standards-based accountability systems in a way that well matches some of the major problems these systems have actually faced. Unlike *ACORN*, which focused on bare noncompliance with NCLB provisions, the *Reading* litigation focused on fundamental issues impacting various entities' implementation of NCLB. While the litigation ultimately did not well position the courts to effectively address standards-based reform and accountability policies, it well serves as a window into the ways in which such problems can impact schools and districts to the extent that litigation becomes an appealing solution.

CENTER FOR LAW AND EDUCATION v. UNITED STATES DEPARTMENT OF EDUCATION

In two related cases, both entitled *Center for Law and Education v. United States Department of Education* (*CLE I* and *CLE II*), courts also focused on the justifiability of student and school performance determinations.[43] In these cases, nonprofit organizations and parents sued ED soon after NCLB was passed to change two sets of regulations that ED had proposed and adopted regarding NCLB testing practices. In *CLE I*, the plaintiffs sued before the final regulations had been passed, and in *CLE II*, the plaintiffs sued after the final regulations had been passed. In both cases, the plaintiffs argued that the regulations did not ensure that students would be accurately assessed by NCLB assessments.

Although NCLB gave states much latitude to design their own standards and assessments, the regulations considered and ultimately adopted by ED set broad limits on the types of assessments that states could administer for NCLB purposes. One set of regulations allowed states to use "augmented" norm-referenced assessments rather than criterion-referenced assessments.[44] Generally, norm-referenced tests measure a student's performance against other students' performance, while criterion-referenced tests measure a student's performance against mastery of identifiable skills or knowledge. "Augmented" norm-referenced tests are norm-referenced tests that incorporate additional items written specifically to assess student performance against content standards. The second regulation required state assessments to involve "multiple up-to-date measures of student academic achievement."[45] The plaintiffs sought a court order for ED to change the first regulation to require states to use criterion-referenced assessments and to clarify the second regulation—the plaintiffs wanted ED to make clear that the phrase "multiple up-to-date measures" referred to multiple ways of assessing the same proficiencies. Officials in ED, however, did not want to make the clarifications because they wanted the phrase "multiple measures" to mean either measures that differed in format or in the type of knowledge tested and did not wish to restrict the meaning in the narrow fashion sought by the plaintiffs.[46]

As discussed in Chapters Two and Three, education researchers have emphasized that valid testing practices are an essential element of well-functioning standards-based reform and accountability systems. While the psychometric community has indicated that many different factors should contribute to any evaluation of whether particular testing practices are valid, researchers from this community have highlighted certain factors as particularly useful and important for making such an evaluation. The use of multiple measures and criterion-referenced tests to measure student academic achievement are two of these factors. In 2004, when *CLE II* was decided, the plaintiffs' concerns reflected the state of the NCLB testing landscape—during this year, eight states did not use criterion-referenced assessments at all, while 21 states used norm-referenced tests and 12 states used augmented norm-referenced tests.[47] States continued to implement similar testing practices in the following years, as five states did not use criterion-referenced tests in 2007, while 18 states continued to use norm-referenced tests and 10 states continued to use augmented norm-referenced tests.

Despite the validity concerns raised in *CLE I* and *II*, neither court ruled in favor of the plaintiffs for a variety of legal reasons. In both cases, the plaintiffs sued ED to invalidate the regulations based on ED's selection of participants in the "negotiated rulemaking process" that contributed to the text of the regulations. NCLB provided that, prior to issuing regulations regarding standards and assessments, ED must obtain the advice and recommendations of various groups, such as administrators, parents, and teachers, in accordance with the requirements of the Negotiated Rulemaking Act (NRA).[48] In order to comply with NCLB and the NRA, ED was required to convene representatives from these groups into a committee that would then submit recommendations to ED. ED began the process for forming this committee, just 10 days after NCLB was passed, with the publication of a notice in the Federal Register soliciting participants for the committee.[49] The selected participants in the committee included six representatives of state administrators, four representatives of local administrators, three representatives of principals and teachers, one representative of business interests, two representatives from ED, and seven representatives of students. Of these final seven representatives, two were characterized as parents, one was characterized as a teacher, and four were state or local education officials.

Several problems ensued due to the makeup of the committee. At the first committee meeting, Paul Weckstein, Co-Director of the Center for Law and Education, a nonprofit organization that became the lead plaintiff in both cases, petitioned ED to be included in the committee.[50] Weckstein argued that the committee makeup, as described in the Federal Register and later convened by ED, did not adequately represent the needs of parents and students, and that the inclusion of his organization would contribute to a more equitable balance between representatives of parents and education officials. Weckstein also presented a petition from Designs for Change, a nonprofit group based in Chicago, Illinois. This petition argued for similar reasons that Designs for Change should be included in the committee. Upon a vote of the committee, neither group was allowed to participate formally. All committee members, except for the two parent representatives, appeared to indicate that parents' and students' interests were already represented on the committee—a number of committee members explained that they could "wear multiple hats," and represent the interests of their organizations and parents simultaneously. Weckstein, however, was allowed to attend the meetings as an "elbow advisor" to Minnie Pearce, one of the parent representatives.

The discussions at the meetings dealt with a number of rather technical issues. Various elements of test validity and reliability, alignment between tests and curricula, and use of tests for multiple purposes were central topics of discussion. According to a brief submitted by one of the plaintiffs, the parents generally remained silent while the committee was discussing these types of technical issues. Indeed, both parent representatives indicated that they remained silent because they felt that they did not have adequate representation and did not understand the technical issues discussed at the meetings.[51]

The Negotiated Rulemaking Act and Standing

Because both *CLE I* and *CLE II* involve quite similar legal and factual issues and were heard by the same judge, this section discusses both cases together.

In both cases, the plaintiffs sued ED in a U.S. district court in Washington, D.C. and argued their claims before Judge John D. Bates. As mentioned above, *CLE I* was filed after the committee met but before the final regulations were passed, and *CLE II* was filed after the final regulations were passed. The plaintiffs generally argued that the events surrounding the makeup of the committee should invalidate the regulations and that the regulations themselves would lead to an incorrect evaluation of students' abilities and knowledge. In both cases, Judge Bates cited several reasons why the plaintiffs' arguments were unpersuasive and dismissed the cases—in both cases, Judge Bates conducted a detailed examination of the precise language of the NRA and found that it expressly precluded judicial review of the process of a negotiated rulemaking committee. Thus, he found that the makeup of the committee was shielded from judicial scrutiny and ruled that the regulations should not be rescinded on the grounds that the committee was improperly constituted.

In addition to focusing on the language of the NRA, Judge Bates highlighted a perhaps even more important legal issue in *CLE II*—that neither the nonprofit organizations nor the parents could maintain "standing," a requirement that all plaintiffs generally must meet in order to litigate a case successfully. In order to determine whether an entity has standing to sue, the Supreme Court has articulated a three-part test: A plaintiff must show (1) that he has suffered an "injury in fact" that is "concrete" rather than "conjectural or hypothetical," (2) that the facts reveal a "causal connection between the injury and the conduct complained of," and (3) that it is "likely" and not merely "speculative" that the injury complained of will be "redressed by a favorable decision."[52] Applying the standing test to the claims of the plaintiffs, Judge Bates determined that there must exist "an adequate causal chain . . . [that] must contain at least two links: one connecting to alleged imbalance of the committee to the rule promulgated, and another connecting the rule to the plaintiffs' particularized injury."[53] Judge Bates then found that, under the basic design of NCLB, no such injury was traceable to the federal government. As NCLB devolves significant discretion to state and local authorities for the development and implementation of standards and assessments, *states* are more properly thought of as the causal source for any injuries suffered from the inaccurate assessment of students. Thus, Judge Bates found that all the plaintiffs in *CLE II* lacked standing (in addition to finding the plaintiffs' argument about the NRA unpersuasive).

Judge Bates was not alone in his treatment of standing in the context of NCLB. In *Board of Education of Ottawa Township v. U.S. Department of Education* (*Ottawa*), local school boards, special education students, and the students' parents sued ED to halt the implementation of NCLB consequences with regard to special education students.[54] In response, the *Ottawa* court expressed standing concerns similar to those voiced by Judge Bates. The *Ottawa* court stated that school districts have much flexibility under NCLB and accordingly refused to find that the plaintiffs could maintain standing. The *Reading III* court expressed a similar sentiment, indicating that standing issues would prevent a district from suing the federal government over AYP determinations—because AYP is a matter for each state to determine, the federal government is not properly thought of as the source of school failure to make AYP.[55]

Both *CLE I* and *CLE II* accordingly illustrate several important issues regarding the ways in which courts have addressed standards-based reforms in the context of NCLB. Like *ACORN* and the *Reading* cases, the *CLE* cases reflect concerns about the ways in which these policies were being implemented under NCLB. Getting states to implement valid testing practices to satisfy NCLB mandates has proven quite difficult, and these cases highlight at least some factors underlying this problem—both the regulations promulgated by ED and the latitude given to states under NCLB's statutory scheme, in addition to the technical and financial difficulties of constructing and adopting new assessments, appear very influential in shaping states' testing practices. Indeed, the types of validity problems highlighted in the *CLE* cases also emerged in the high-stakes testing context, and the *CLE* cases highlight the presence that technical issues concerning the validity of testing practices with a significant focus on accountability continue to maintain in the courts.

Moreover, these cases highlight important additional barriers to judicial action to directly influence the implementation of standards-based accountability policies at the federal level. First, these cases highlight the legal barriers to specifically using the NRA to force ED to reconsider regulations passed via the negotiated rulemaking process. But as the NRA generally applies to the construction of negotiated rulemaking committees, the problems associated with judicial interpretations of the NRA appear to be somewhat isolated—the litigation generated in response to NCLB has not been consistently grouped around regulations developed by such committees, and given the limited range of issues that could be included in such litigation, it does not appear that such litigation will be prevalent in the future. However, the legal barriers to judicial action stemming from standing are much more applicable to a range of litigation. Due to the ways in which NCLB devolves decision-making authority to states, it is quite difficult for plaintiffs targeting NCLB problems to establish standing against the federal government, despite the variety of ways in which the federal government has shaped and will likely continue to shape standards-based reform and accountability policies. Given the interaction demonstrated by cases such as *CLE II* between the well-established legal doctrine of standing and the structure of modern standards-based reform and accountability policies, courts have faced and will likely continue to face significant barriers influencing the course of such policies in lawsuits focusing on the federal government.

Capacities to Respond to Federal Requirements

In addition to focusing on compliance with NCLB accountability require-ments and the justifiability of determinations of school and student perform-ance, courts have had the opportunity to address the various capacities possessed by governmental entities to respond to federal requirements. While courts examined the legal requirements governing some of these capacities in the *Reading* cases (e.g., by looking at NCLB provisions governing the support provided to schools), courts in these cases did not focus on what capacities were needed to implement NCLB from a broad standpoint—the cases did not focus in depth on pressing issues such as the amount of funding it takes to enable students to perform at a level specified by standards and to enable states and districts to construct the administrative infrastructure required by NCLB. However, in two similar cases, *Pontiac v. Spellings* (*Pontiac*) and *State of Connecticut v. Spellings* (*Connecticut*), litigation focused precisely on these issues.[56]

Reflecting the political attention devoted to the capacities needed to implement NCLB, *Pontiac* and *Connecticut* have proven to be perhaps the most high-profile cases directly aimed at NCLB. As discussed in Chapter Two, NCLB funding levels have been repeatedly attacked—in addition to receiving criticism from various politicians during and after the passage of NCLB, formal participants in congressional hearings have attacked these funding levels.[57] The President of the National Education Association (NEA), Reg Weaver, called NCLB "the granddaddy of all underfunded federal mandates."[58] And 21 civil rights and education groups, including the NEA and NAACP, issued a joint statement calling for higher NCLB funding levels.[59] In the midst of this focus on funding, many schools around the country failed to make AYP shortly after NCLB began to be implemented. Two years into the implementation of NCLB, state departments of education had identified about one-fourth of schools in the U.S. (21,350 schools) and 1,675 districts as failing to make AYP.[60] At this time, 10,992 of these schools had failed to make AYP for at least two years and were thus already subject to NCLB accountability sanctions. Many of these schools included a disproportionately high number of minority students, poor students, and LEP students. The plaintiffs in both *Pontiac* and *Connecticut* decided to bring cases against ED in federal courts primarily in response to such issues.

In *Pontiac*, the NEA sued ED in a federal court in the Eastern District of Michigan in April 2005 and focused almost exclusively on the financial capacities provided by ED to states to implement NCLB.[61] The NEA is the country's largest teachers' union with over 2.7 million members nationwide, and it filed suit on behalf of school districts in Pontiac, Michigan; Laredo, Texas; south-central Vermont; 10 state affiliates of the NEA, and itself.[62] According to the NEA, these co-plaintiffs represented a cross section of the schools and students that NCLB was harming—while most of the Pontiac school district's students were African-American, most of the Laredo school district's students were Hispanic. The school districts in Vermont were primarily rural. Despite the inclusion of these school districts, the NEA was the driving force behind the lawsuit. The NEA announced its intention to file a lawsuit over a year and a half before *Pontiac* was filed, and it had been discussing the possibility of a lawsuit with various districts and states since that time. The case was assigned to Judge Bernard A. Friedman.

The NEA primarily argued that the U.S. Secretary of Education, Margaret Spellings, was implementing NCLB in violation of its "Unfunded Mandates Provision." This provision states that an "officer or employee of the Federal Government" cannot require states or districts to "spend any funds or incur any costs not paid for under this Act."[63] The NEA also argued that Secretary Spellings was violating the Spending Clause of the U.S. Constitution—a clause governing the conditions under which the federal government can provide funding to state-level governmental entities. Under established precedent, states generally must have clear notice of the conditions of receiving federal funds through laws, such as NCLB, that are enacted under Congress' Spending Clause powers.[64] According to the NEA, Secretary Spellings' violation of the Unfunded Mandates Provision also constituted a violation of the Spending Clause because she changed "one of the conditions pursuant to which states and school districts accepted federal funds under the NCLB"— that states and school districts would not be required to spend any funds or incur costs not paid for under NCLB. The NEA accordingly asked Judge Friedman to issue an order that states and districts are not required to comply with NCLB requirements.

In order to prove that ED violated the Unfunded Mandates Provision, the NEA submitted evidence about several types of costs that it claimed were not sufficiently funded by ED.[65] The NEA particularly cited several school districts that had determined that they would need more funds in order to comply with the AYP requirements. For example, the NEA cited a district in Jordan, Utah, that determined it would likely cost more than $182 million to comply with the NCLB mandate to have all students achieving at state proficiency levels by 2014. According to the NEA, the district needed $59 million more to reach this funding floor.

The NEA also cited several "cost studies" completed for various state departments of education that estimated how much funding it would take to comply with the NCLB mandate of all students reaching proficiency by 2014.[66] For example, a study conducted for the Illinois Department of Education estimated that this compliance would cost $1.8 billion per year, which represented over three times the amount of NCLB Title I funds provided to Illinois when *Pontiac* was filed. In order to confirm the results of the cost studies conducted for various states, the NEA cited a report conducted by the bipartisan National Conference of State Legislatures, which found that the federal government has provided "minimal or nonexistent new federal resources to allow schools to offer the remediation services and enhanced learning opportunities necessary to meet the ambitious proficiency goals of the NCLB."[67] The NEA also cited studies completed by recognized school finance experts. For example, a study completed by San Diego State University professor Jennifer Imazeki and University of Wisconsin-Madison professor Andrew Reschovsky estimated that the amount of money needed to help students in Texas reach proficiency would cost over $10 billion, which represented approximately ten times the total amount of NCLB Title I funds provided when *Pontiac* was filed.[68]

In addition, the NEA devoted significant attention to the amount of funding needed to comply with the procedural requirements of NCLB, such as the implementation of the testing and data collection requirements and the institution of accountability sanctions. Based on such evidence, the NEA argued that states and school districts have been and will be required to spend substantial amounts of non-NCLB funds in order to comply with NCLB mandates (which would in turn divert scarce resources from local educational priorities), that a large number of schools would in turn unjustifiably fail to make AYP, and that schools and districts would thereby suffer harm to their reputations and legal status.

Connecticut raised similar issues in its lawsuit but focused on the particular costs associated with NCLB in Connecticut.[69] The state had been implementing a testing scheme since 1985 that assessed student performance in grades four, six, and eight, and it had been annually profiling and publishing school and district performance since before NCLB was passed. The state had also tested its LEP students during most of the time in which the testing scheme was being implemented. While student performance of students in Connecticut consistently ranked above the national average on the NAEP, the achievement gap in Connecticut was one of the worst in the U.S.[70] Prior to bringing a lawsuit, Connecticut had attempted a less adversarial strategy to influence NCLB's implementation—state officials had requested waivers from NCLB provisions governing testing on at least three separate occasions, and all its requests had been denied by ED.[71] In these waiver requests, state officials had particularly asked ED to waive annual testing requirements so that the state could administer annual tests in alternate grades and conduct formative testing in the other grades. The state had also asked for the option to conduct growth analyses instead of statutorily prescribed AYP analyses, for the option to assess special education students at their instructional level rather than at their grade level, and for LEP students to be permitted three years in U.S. school systems to learn English rather than one year before taking the tests. Moreover, Connecticut had filed requests for amendments to their Title I plan regarding the testing of LEP students. ED denied the requests for plan amendments as well. Notably, ED never held a formal administrative hearing to flesh out the relevant factual and legal issues related to the waiver requests and amendment requests. Despite these requests, Connecticut stayed in compliance with NCLB testing and accountability requirements since the law's passage.

After this strategy proved unsuccessful, the state turned to litigation. With the support of the governor and state legislature, Connecticut Attorney General Richard Blumenthal announced his intention to sue ED. When the state filed suit against Secretary Spellings in a federal court in Connecticut in August 2005, the case was assigned to Judge Mark R. Kravitz. Like the NEA, Blumenthal argued that Secretary Spellings was violating the Unfunded Mandates Provision of NCLB and the Spending Clause of the Constitution. Blumenthal also argued that Secretary Spellings had acted "arbitrarily and capriciously" by denying Connecticut's requests for waivers from NCLB accountability provisions and by denying the state's request for plan amendments without an adequate hearing. Unlike the NEA's arguments before Judge Friedman, Blumenthal's arguments were almost entirely legal. That is, Blumenthal almost exclusively focused on the statutory, constitutional, and case law supporting his arguments, and devoted much less attention to proving that ED had provided insufficient funding to Connecticut to implement NCLB—Blumenthal primarily pointed to a study conducted by the General Accounting Office indicating that states would need to spend approximately

$3.9 billion to $5.3 billion simply for developing and administering the assessments required by NCLB and that federal funds would cover only 59 percent of Connecticut's estimated expenses for complying with NCLB testing requirements. Blumenthal accordingly asked Judge Kravitz for an order specifying that Connecticut and its districts would not be required to spend non-NCLB funds and would not be punished for any resulting noncompliance with NCLB.

INTERPRETING THE UNFUNDED MANDATES PROVISION

Although the arguments made by the plaintiffs in *Pontiac* and *Connecticut* were similar in several ways, the judges ruling in these cases considered these arguments quite differently. In *Pontiac*, Judge Friedman (the district court judge assigned to the case) directly addressed the meaning of the Unfunded Mandates Provision. Judge Friedman found that the Unfunded Mandates Provision did not actually prevent Congress from imposing "unfunded mandates."[72] According to the judge, the inclusion of the words "an officer or employee of" in NCLB indicates that Congress clearly meant to prohibit *federal officers and employees* from imposing additional, unfunded requirements, beyond those provided for in the statute; if Congress generally intended to prohibit unfunded mandates, Congress instead would have stated that the "Federal Government" will reimburse states for all costs incurred in complying with NCLB.[73] Accordingly, without commenting on the merits of the evidence submitted by the plaintiffs, Judge Friedman found that Congress "has appropriated significant funding for NCLB requirements" and that Congress did not intend for NCLB requirements "to be paid for *solely* by the federal appropriations."[74] Because the NEA's Spending Clause claim was so dependent on the meaning of the Unfunded Mandates Provision, Judge Friedman also found that the Spending Clause claim was unpersuasive and accordingly dismissed the lawsuit.

In response to the dismissal, the NEA promptly appealed. In January 2008, a three-judge panel of the Sixth Circuit Court of Appeals issued a ruling that reversed Judge Friedman's decision.[75] In this ruling, two of three judges conducted a detailed analysis of NCLB's statutory language and structure (including the Unfunded Mandates Provision) and the law's legislative history, and found that NCLB did not provide clear notice to states that they would be required to pay for the costs of implementing NCLB that were not paid for by the federal government. In other words, the court found that a state official could reasonably look to the Unfunded Mandates Provision and conclude that states would not be held responsible for complying with federal requirements for which federal funding falls short. The majority then applied the requirement from Spending Clause jurisprudence that federal laws must present clear notice of states' obligations to NCLB and concluded that Judge Friedman's interpretation of the Unfunded Mandates Provision was incorrect—the majority found that the language of NCLB and the Unfunded Mandates Provision was unclear and that Secretary Spellings' interpretation of the Unfunded Mandates Provision violated the Spending Clause. The one dissenting judge conducted a similar analysis as the majority, but in light of NCLB's general statutory scheme, specific provisions like the Unfunded Mandates Provision, and legislative history, found that the law provided sufficient notice to states about their obligations.

As this book is being completed in early 2008, the ultimate effects of this decision are unclear. The case was remanded to Judge Friedman, who must complete a detailed examination of the evidence in the case. So, NCLB may in fact be reauthorized with new language before Judge Friedman (or the Sixth Circuit, in the case of an appeal) issues a ruling. President George W. Bush and Secretary Spellings have also left open the possibility that they could appeal the case to the Supreme Court, which could delay any effects of the case even longer or eliminate any impact of the case at all.[76] Moreover, the appellate court left at least one key question unanswered: Does the Unfunded Mandates Provision apply only to NCLB funds spent to implement the administrative requirements of the law, or does it apply to funds spent to boost student achievement up to certain proficiency levels as well? This question is critical because, as discussed further in Chaper Five, determining how much money it takes to enable students to perform at various proficiency levels is an incredibly difficult and technical task that most courts are not well positioned to address. Indeed, without precise language in NCLB directly addressing this issue, courts would be left with little guidance to address the extent to which NCLB is underfunded.

In contrast to the reasoning of the judges in *Pontiac*, Judge Kravitz did not directly address the meaning of the Unfunded Mandates Provision when considering Connecticut's case. Judge Kravitz focused on the fact that ED had not yet taken any enforcement action against Connecticut—as mentioned above, Connecticut was complying with NCLB, even though state officials believed NCLB was illegally underfunded, and ED was never given reason to do anything but negotiate with the state. Indeed, the judge emphasized that determining whether the Unfunded Mandates Provision was correctly interpreted and implemented by Secretary Spellings in the specific case of Connecticut would involve an analysis of NCLB and a factual and technical assessment of the state's claims. Because this particular type of analysis—reviewing the costs and efficacy of implementing NCLB—is one that "falls squarely within the expertise of the Secretary," Judge Kravitz was unwilling to craft a ruling about the costs of NCLB without more detailed factual evidence developed by governmental entities that theoretically had a greater competency in education.[77] Without any enforcement action by ED and a formal hearing to develop such evidence, Judge Kravitz found that the court had no jurisdiction to hear this claim and dismissed it.[78] Like Judge Friedman, Judge Kravitz found that Connecticut's Spending Clause claim was so paired with the Unfunded Mandates Provision claim that the same reasoning applied to this claim as well.

Judge Kravitz also found that Connecticut's claim that ED had arbitrarily and capriciously denied the state's requests for waivers from NCLB accountability provisions was not reviewable. According to the judge, Congress did not provide any standards that a court could use to analyze ED's reasons for denying the waivers. Emphasizing the lack of such standards, Judge Kravitz stated:

> Would it be unlawful to deny a waiver if a state could prove that its request would better educate its students? Or, would it be unlawful to deny a waiver so long as a state could show that its request would not inflict harm and might, if tried, do some good? Or, would it be unlawful to deny a waiver if the state could show its request would be equally effective but less costly, thereby allowing scarce resources to be spent on other educational programs?[79]

Judge Kravitz thereby emphasized the need for ED, an agency with significantly more educational expertise than the court, to make such decisions in the absence of relevant standards, found that the court also lacked jurisdiction to rule on this claim, and dismissed it.

The judge, however, did not dismiss the final claim that ED acted arbitrarily and capriciously by denying Connecticut's request for plan amendments. Here, Secretary Spellings did not argue that the court lacked jurisdiction but instead that the courts should reject the state's claim as a matter of law—Secretary Spellings argued that she was bound by law to reject the state's plan amendments. Judge Kravitz found that the court was not in any position to reach a decision on the validity of this claim until the court conducts a detailed analysis of the plan amendments in question, the requirements of NCLB regarding amendments, and Secretary Spellings' reasons for rejecting the amendments. According to the judge, this analysis would require a compilation of an administrative record to flesh out the relevant legal and factual issues. Judge Kravitz accordingly ruled that the parties needed to file a joint report with the court outlining their plan for proceeding with the complication of such a record. As of this writing, the parties have begun to create such a record, and Judge Kravitz has not yet issued a second ruling.

In short, *Pontiac* and *Connecticut* focused on some of the most important and high-profile issues facing the implementation of modern standards-based accountability systems—that of resources. Reflecting several critiques of NCLB, these cases focused on the funding needed to implement the administrative infrastructure required by NCLB, especially as schools increasingly failed to make AYP, and the funding needed to help students learn the knowledge and skills specified in state standards. At the trial court level, the structure of this form of litigation failed to well support effective judicial involvement in these issues. Legal hurdles grouped around the nature of the administrative process and the precise language of the Unfunded Mandates Provision made it very difficult for plaintiffs to successfully argue that a court should deeply analyze the funding provided to states and districts under NCLB. While one claim in *Connecticut v. Spellings* remained alive after Judge Kravitz's initial decision, this claim only involved requested plan amendments and was not central to the issue of the sufficiency of funding. The plaintiffs' victory at the appellate level in *Pontiac* was striking because it potentially represents a successful use of the courts to influence NCLB's implementation on the basis of insufficient resources. However, the ultimate effects of this opinion are unclear, the effects will likely be long delayed as the case winds through the litigation process, and NCLB may be reauthorized in a way that avoids such problems before a court issues a final ruling in this case.

Moreover, although the plaintiffs in *Pontiac* presented a substantial amount of evidence regarding the sufficiency of funding, the quality of much of this evidence may have been questionable—as some legal scholars have highlighted, the quality of cost studies (especially those aimed at measuring the funding it takes to help students reach proficiency on standardized tests) is quite varied.[80] Furthermore, given courts' limited capacities to engage with complex and technical educational evidence, it is uncertain whether courts could effectively interpret such evidence even if they had attempted to do so in *Pontiac* and *Connecticut*, and it is unclear how Judge Friedman will interpret this evidence if he gets the opportunity to do so in the future—as Judge Kravitz emphasized in his discussion of waivers in *Connecticut*, the text of NCLB gives courts little in the way of precise standards to address the issue of resource allocation. Indeed, Judge Kravitz repeatedly emphasized the greater expertise of ED and the Secretary of Education to address technical matters of education policy. So, while the Sixth Circuit's decision in *Pontiac* left open the possibility of using the courts to halt NCLB's implementation (or at least give schools and districts the option of noncompliance with NCLB) with regard to the implementation of "unfunded" provisions, the structure of the litigation in both of these cases failed to frame the important problem of NCLB funding in a way that was directly and easily addressable by courts.

Other Litigation Involving No Child Left Behind

To be sure, the cases discussed above are not the only ones in which courts have addressed issues related to NCLB. In *Californians for Justice Education Fund v. California State Board of Education* (*CJE*), community organizations brought a lawsuit against the California State Board of Education in response to the definition of a highly qualified teacher (HQT) that the Board adopted pursuant to NCLB—the definition of an HQT adopted by California included teachers certified on an emergency or provisional basis and therefore clearly did not comply with NCLB requirements.[81] But because California had already begun the process of adopting a new and compliant definition by the time *CJE* was decided, the *CJE* court found that the plaintiffs' claim was *moot*, or already resolved, and dismissed the case. In *Kegerreis v. United States*, a *pro se* plaintiff claimed that NCLB is unconstitutional.[82] Because the case rested on no ostensible legal grounds, the *Kegerreis* court dismissed the case in an extremely short and unpublished opinion. The implementation of public school choice under NCLB has also brought some districts into conflict with the requirements of judicially required desegregation plans.[83] Because such conflicts do not involve issues central to the design and implementation of standards-based reform and accountability policies, this chapter does not examine these cases in detail. In *Fresh Start Academy v. Toledo Board of Education*, a case briefly mentioned above, a supplemental services provider sued a school district for its failure to secure a contract to provide supplemental services to students in that district. In *Alliance for Children v. City of Detroit Public Schools*, a supplemental services provider similarly sued a school district for its refusal to include the provider on an approved list of supplemental services providers.[84] But both the *Fresh Start* and *Alliance for Children* courts dismissed the cases because the supplemental services providers had no Section 1983 or private right of action available to them.

As mentioned above, this chapter is not meant to cover in detail the specifics of every single instance in which a court has addressed issues related to NCLB. The cases discussed in depth are the most important ones for understanding the major educational and legal issues surrounding the implementation of NCLB. While the cases mentioned in this section are important for charting the response to NCLB, they are less important for understanding how well the courts are positioned to influence the implementation of NCLB, especially given the limited scope of the legal and educational issues litigated in these cases.

Discussion and Conclusion

Since it was passed, NCLB has constituted the most important law governing standards-based reform and accountability policies in the U.S. In receipt for Title I funds, NCLB required states to implement systems of standards and accountability. If schools and districts failed to make AYP, they were required to implement prescribed administrative consequences. Outside of the litigation context, NCLB (in conjunction with earlier federal laws, such as Goals 2000 and the IASA) appears to have strongly influenced the development of standards-based reforms and related accountability systems. Currently, all states have systems of standards and accountability in place. Moreover, ED appears to have enforced NCLB more strictly than it has enforced Title I in the past. As a result, NCLB and likely the subsequent reauthorization of the ESEA appear as if they will continue to have a strong influence on the implementation of standards-based reforms and accountability mechanisms in the states. Nonetheless, states have faced serious problems implementing NCLB requirements regarding standards-based reform and accountability systems. In response to such problems, NCLB has come under heavy criticism and has increasingly constituted the object of a significant amount of litigation.

Like much educational litigation of the past 50 years, several lawsuits aimed directly at NCLB have been generated by the perceived effects of education policy on various underserved groups, such as students in urban (and usually high-poverty) schools or on minority students and LEP students. Many of these groups have perceived such effects as undesirable and have driven litigation efforts to alter or halt the implementation of NCLB. Schools and districts threatened by NCLB sanctions, such as Reading, have strongly fought against the application of NCLB. Other groups that represent the interests of historically underrepresented groups, such as the Education Law Center, a nonprofit legal advocacy organization that has fought for the rights of minority students, LEP students, and students with disabilities, filed an *amicus curiae* brief in *Reading I*. Given their focus in the *CLE* cases on the validity of testing practices that could especially harm LEP students or students with disabilities, the Center for Law and Education also constitutes such a group. Although the Center for Law and Education did not litigate issues regarding validity through legal frameworks traditionally used to address such issues (such as the high-stakes testing frameworks discussed in Chapter Three), this group still focused on a basic type of harm long targeted in civil rights lawsuits. In this respect, several groups focusing on the potentially harmful effects of NCLB have used the courts in a fairly traditional manner.

However, to those who support the idea of strong accountability for the performance of these student groups and the basic theory of action underlying NCLB, such effects were precisely the point of NCLB—the law was aimed at helping all students perform well and was aimed at exposing schools that did not meet performance goals to sanctions, thereby providing incentives and instituting the needed changes for these schools to improve the performance of various subgroups. Indeed, some groups that have historically defended minority rights, such as the Lawyers' Committee for Civil Rights Under Law, have publicly expressed support for the basic design of NCLB.[85] Similarly, ACORN, a community organization largely comprised of low- and moderate-income families working for social justice, used litigation in an attempt to enforce NCLB sanctions for school failure to make AYP.

Still, some litigation seems to have been generated by yet another type of concern—the more diffuse burden that NCLB has put upon states, districts, schools, and educational personnel. The parties present in *Pontiac* reflect this broad type of opposition—the parties ranged from rural districts to urban districts and were spread across the country. Because NCLB has entailed significant costs, required significant changes, and instituted pressure at a number of levels, ranging from the state level to the classroom level, many perceived the new requirements as unnecessary and undesirable, especially in the context of a limited capacity to change. Thus, the litigation directly aimed at NCLB not only reflects various problems in its implementation but also reflects divided opinions about its desirability and effectiveness and reveals a much changed landscape of educational litigation—one that is structured around defending the rights of underrepresented students while also being highly attentive to the more general performance of the U.S. education system and the burdens of reforming this system, and is in some cases supportive of large-scale institutional reform efforts aimed at improving its performance through standards-based accountability policies.

Despite this new landscape of educational litigation, attempts at using the courts to influence NCLB's implementation have largely failed. Due to hurdles such as the unavailability of a Section 1983 action, the limitations of administrative appeals, standing problems related to NCLB's design (which places certain decision-making powers at the state level), and the language of specific provisions (such as those governing native language testing), the courts have not ordered any substantive changes in NCLB's implementation. These hurdles have prevented plaintiffs from winning lawsuits against various entities, including school districts and state- and federal-level governmental entities. To be sure, the Sixth Circuit's decision in *Pontiac* represents a significant instance in which plaintiffs were successful at overcoming such legal hurdles—this ruling potentially provides the basis for allowing schools and districts not to comply with "unfunded" NCLB provisions without triggering major consequences. However, upon this writing in early 2008, this case still has many more hurdles to overcome before it is ultimately resolved. Even if the legal hurdles that courts have faced were not so insurmountable, it still appears that the courts would not have been well positioned to influence many important aspects of standards-based accountability systems through such litigation. This litigation has sometimes focused on surface problems facing the implementation of NCLB, such as mere compliance with accountability provisions, rather than more systemic problems, such as the reasons underlying this noncompliance.

And even where this litigation has focused on major underlying problems, such as the financial capacities necessary to implement NCLB effectively, it still appears that the courts would have been ill-positioned to effectively address such issues. The text of NCLB itself simply did not contain much detail about the capacities that states, districts, and schools needed to comply with NCLB requirements. As discussed in Chapter Two, NCLB expressly required ED to provide states with assistance developing standards and assessments and creating state plans, required states to provide various types of technical supports, and authorized ED to award grants to states for the implementation of school improvement and corrective action measures. But the minimum funding that the federal government was required to provide to states under some of these provisions was low, and these provisions were quite vague about the amount and type of resources that ultimately needed to be provided.

Pontiac highlights the failure of NCLB to provide courts with solid grounds to effectively address NCLB implementation problems related to capacity. Unlike most other provisions in NCLB, the Unfunded Mandates Provision at the very least demonstrated a congressional concern that states, schools, and districts would not have the financial capacities to fully implement NCLB requirements. Indeed, this provision was the major legal hook in NCLB that addressed such capacities. The Unfunded Mandates Provision, however, was very limited in terms of scope—the provision only addressed financial capacities that state entities may possess, and not any other kind of capacity, such as technical skill or knowledge. Moreover, the provision did not indicate any way of determining whether the funds provided to schools are sufficient for boosting students' proficiency levels, or even if such issues should be considered at all in the course of determining whether NCLB includes unfunded mandates. So, even if the plaintiffs ultimately win in *Pontiac*, the courts will have very little in the way of precise legal standards for structuring their analyses of NCLB and determining appropriate remedies. Without more explicit attention to the various capacities needed by states, schools, and districts in the text of NCLB itself, the courts likely cannot effectively address the implementation of modern, standards-based accountability systems in the context of litigation aimed directly against NCLB. Given the courts' lack of capacities to sort through technical educational issues, judicial action in such an area appears as if it could result in a range of interpretations, some of which do not well reflect policy knowledge on these issues.

Reflecting upon the way in which the ESEA and the federal role in education have developed over time, it makes much sense that NCLB did not include specific requirements governing many of the problems that the law has faced. As the federal role in education has traditionally been small, NCLB devolved much authority to states and localities even as it put demands upon them in relation to the implementation of accountability mechanisms. The ESEA has long specified that ED is not permitted to direct the instructional program of a school or state, and similar specifications have been written into the charter of ED since its enactment in 1979.[86] While NCLB was certainly more prescriptive than previous iterations of the ESEA about the educational duties that states and schools must undertake to receive Title I funds, the law is still grounded in its history.

Even if NCLB were not grounded in this history, it would still have been very difficult for Congress to have included detailed provisions in NCLB that could support judicial intervention in some of the fundamental problems facing standards-based reforms. As discussed in Chapter Two, we simply have limited knowledge about the types of instructional programs (and related policies such as professional development) needed to facilitate standards-based reform and boost student achievement in relation to standards. Without this type of knowledge, there would be little reason for Congress to have crafted provisions specifying the types of legally acceptable instructional approaches.[87] Indeed, this lack of knowledge is partly what NCLB is designed to overcome—the law was largely built to employ pressure to achieve results instead of precisely directing educational inputs.

So, just as NCLB represents a significant change in the direction of federal education policy, the litigation aimed directly at NCLB represents a significant change in traditional patterns of educational litigation. Groups that have traditionally had similar interests in education have become involved in a variety of cases aimed at influencing NCLB in a variety of ways. While some groups still appear to have been almost exclusively focused on protecting the rights of underrepresented student groups, litigants have also exhibited stronger concerns with the performance of the U.S. education system in general and accordingly with the tools used to boost such performance. But especially given the structure and language of NCLB, the litigation aimed directly at the law has not well positioned courts to achieve these goals. As a result, the courts have proven to be an ineffective venue in the context of litigation aimed directly at NCLB's implementation to protect the rights of underrepresented students against the potentially undesirable consequences of modern standards-based accountability systems and to ensure that such systems are implemented more effectively and leverage desired changes in educational practice at all levels of the U.S. education system.

CHAPTER FIVE

School Finance Reform Litigation

Although courts addressing standards-based reforms in the context of high-stakes testing cases and in cases aimed directly at No Child Left Behind (NCLB) were often poorly positioned or unwilling to influence the course of these reforms, other courts have assumed a more active role. State courts hearing school finance reform cases have begun to consider several issues related to standards-based reform and accountability policies, and these issues have played a significant role in determining the outcomes of these cases. Until recently, legal issues related to standards, testing, and accountability rarely appeared in the context of school finance reform litigation. School finance reform cases (as their label indicates) traditionally concentrated on the funds available to schools and localities for education—much of the litigation focused on funding disparities and legal mandates regarding equality and adequacy that could potentially remedy these financial problems. Due to ways in which the litigants' arguments regarding school finance reform and judicial consideration of these arguments have evolved, however, some of these cases have also begun to involve active judicial analyses of laws and evidence regarding standards, testing, and accountability.

Since school finance reform litigation emerged in the late 1960s and early 1970s, it has constituted one of the most important and visible areas of education reform. As of 2005, plaintiffs had brought some form of school finance reform litigation in 45 states.[1] As discussed in the Introduction, school finance reform litigation has experienced some success. School finance reform cases have generally reduced the inequality of per pupil expenditures across districts and have resulted in increased funding for many low-funded schools and districts.[2] However, school finance reform litigation has also faced certain pervasive and recurring problems. Due to the familiar problems facing courts in education cases, such as vague legal language and doctrine, empirical uncertainty about key factual issues, and a political climate hostile to educational change, the overall effectiveness of school finance reform has been somewhat limited. Even in cases where courts ruled for plaintiffs, equalization of education spending within states often did not improve states' overall education spending.[3] Additionally (and perhaps more importantly), student test scores showed little or no gains in many cases where school finance reform litigation increased educational spending.[4] Litigants and courts have increasingly begun to focus on issues related to standards-based reform and accountability policies in the context of school finance reform litigation as a means of responding to these persistent problems.

Thus far, issues related to standards-based reforms have emerged in school finance reform litigation in three major ways. First, legislatures have responded to court orders that their education systems are not constitutionally adequate by building systems of standards and accountability—according to these legislatures, the institution of standards-based reforms and related accountability systems, in addition to altering their education funding systems, constitutes their chosen method for providing students with a legally adequate education. Second, plaintiffs have argued that content standards and data from standards-based assessments should be used to determine whether states have actually provided students with an "adequate" education, and some courts have looked favorably upon such arguments. A state's duty to provide students with an adequate education generally stems from the state's constitution. Because state constitutions are vague about what constitutes a legally adequate education, some courts have used state standards and assessments to more precisely articulate constitutional adequacy standards and to examine the sufficiency of a state's education policies against these standards. Third, some courts have begun to order states to implement standards-based reform and accountability systems as a means of providing students with a legally adequate education. Courts addressing standards-based reforms in this fashion have generally considered the institution of these policies as a potential answer to the concern that simply ordering states to provide students with an adequate education cannot alone boost student performance. In short, especially with regard to crafting remedial orders, some courts have begun to treat standards-based reforms as tools that are well suited to respond to important problems that courts around the country have persistently faced in school finance reform cases.

The convergence between standards-based reforms and school finance reform litigation is an extremely important, and perhaps revolutionary, trend in education law. This convergence represents the increasing involvement of the courts in technical matters of education policy, the forging of potentially new relationships between the courts and other governmental branches in education, and the synthesis of two major types of education reforms. In order to help the reader understand the complicated legal issues at play in this field, this chapter first provides a brief overview of the history of school finance reform litigation. This overview particularly focuses on the problems courts have faced in school finance reform cases and the factors driving the active judicial consideration of standards-based reform and accountability policies in this field. Second, this chapter includes case studies of how issues regarding standards-based reform and accountability policies have emerged in five recent school finance reform lawsuits. This second section focuses on cases in North Carolina, New York, Ohio, Massachusetts, and California because these cases well represent the range of ways in which standards-based reform and school finance reform litigation have begun to converge, and the ways in which various courts have differently considered issues central to this convergence.

Based on this examination, previous discussions of the institutional characteristics of courts, and previous analyses of standards-based reform and accountability policies, this chapter concludes that a more active stance taken by courts toward standards-based reforms in the context of school finance litigation may serve as a useful foundation to help courts and litigants address the persistent problems facing these reforms. As some commentators have noted, the convergence of these two areas of law entails many dangers. But at the same time, this convergence holds great potential to address many of the problems that both the courts and standards-based reforms have faced—while the ways in which courts have addressed standards-based reforms in this context are clearly not perfect, they are largely rooted in judicial awareness of the familiar problems courts have persistently faced in education policy and reflect an approach towards standards-based reforms that leans more heavily on the other governmental branches. Moreover, this approach appears to have effectively focused courts on fundamental problems facing the implementation of standards-based reforms, such as the lack of penetration of these reforms across administrative levels and a lack of attention to students' opportunities to learn. As such, some major and recent instances of school finance reform litigation appear to contain a basic structure that may better position the courts to address standards-based reform and accountability policies as they move forward.

A Brief Overview of School Finance Reform Litigation

Since the late 1960s, school finance reform litigation has appeared in almost every state and has exhibited a good deal of durability as a means employed by reformers to effect educational change. Because local wealth or property value has traditionally constituted one of the primary determinants of school and district funding, there are often dramatic per pupil spending differences across districts within states. School finance reform litigation has targeted this funding structure by aiming at the equalization and augmentation of education funding. Because certain classes of legal arguments have proven more successful in court than others, plaintiffs have shifted their legal strategies over time. Where the legal arguments of early school finance reform plaintiffs primarily relied on the Equal Protection Clause of the federal Constitution or equal protection clauses of state constitutions, plaintiffs have more recently begun to adopt arguments based on "education clauses" of state constitutions.[5]

Due to the shifting nature of the arguments employed by plaintiffs in school finance suits, legal scholars have characterized school finance litigation as appearing in three different waves.[6] Legal arguments employed by plaintiffs in the first wave of school finance litigation closely paralleled the type of argument that had proven successful in *Brown v. Board of Education*. Like the plaintiffs in *Brown*, plaintiffs bringing first wave school finance cases relied on the U.S. Equal Protection Clause. These plaintiffs generally argued that education is a right that must be provided equally to all students and that the government cannot discriminate between students on the basis of wealth. When the Supreme Court considered this argument in the 1973 landmark case *San Antonio Independent School District v. Rodriguez*, the Supreme Court found that local control of education is a rational and justifiable reason for the unequal funding of schools.[7] Thus, the Supreme Court found that the U.S. Equal Protection Clause does not constitute a viable basis for equalizing differences in education funding.

In the second wave of school finance cases, plaintiffs continued to rely on arguments based on the idea of equality, but they shifted both the venue and legal basis for their arguments. Plaintiffs now relied on equal protection clauses contained in state constitutions, which often look very similar to the federal Equal Protection Clause.[8] A small number of plaintiffs also relied on "education clauses" contained in state constitutions. Every state constitution contains an education clause, and these clauses generally indicate that states have a duty to provide students with a "thorough and efficient" education or some similar kind of education.[9] Basing their arguments on a state equal protection clause or education clause, or both of these clauses taken together, plaintiffs generally argued that states have a legal duty to equalize funding or educational opportunities across schools and districts.[10]

Although second wave suits were more successful than first wave suits, their effectiveness was also quite limited.[11] Equality is a vague concept that can be defined in several different ways in the context of school finance reform. One can view equality in terms of tax capacity, per pupil expenditures, the goods or services bought with funds, or even student performance, and it is unclear which construction should be used. Moreover, each of these constructions suffers from particular problems. While a construction such as per pupil expenditures can be easily quantified, the causal links between expenditures and educational opportunities are often opaque, and some courts have focused on the lack of clear causal links.[12] Similarly, while a construction such as goods or services offered is more closely related to actual educational opportunities, this construction resists easy quantification and would require courts to delve more deeply into the details of education policy and the inner workings of schools than they have generally felt competent or justified to do.[13] Given that successful equality arguments have often required the shift of limited resources from wealthier districts to poorer school districts, these arguments have also faced heated political opposition and have been portrayed as destroying local control of education.[14] Indeed, the rhetoric of equality has proven politically problematic in legislative responses to successful second wave suits—given the difficulties of defining equal educational opportunities and concerns about the legal justifiability of crafting more specific orders involving detailed policy matters, courts often crafted vague remedial orders, and legislatures under court order to equalize educational funding often failed to fulfill their obligations.[15] As a result of these sorts of familiar doctrinal, political, and competency-related issues, courts dismissed several second wave school finance cases, and judicial findings of unconstitutional funding structures repeatedly failed to produce intended results.

THE MOVE FROM EQUALITY TO ADEQUACY AND THE ENTRANCE OF STANDARDS-BASED REFORMS

In response to the problems faced in second wave school finance suits, many plaintiffs shifted the focus of their arguments from educational equality to educational adequacy. In the third wave, plaintiffs generally based their claims on the education clauses of state constitutions. But instead of arguing that the education clauses require states to equalize spending, plaintiffs generally argued that these clauses require states to provide a sufficient level of funds to meet the constitutional guarantee of a "thorough and efficient" education, or whatever type of education is guaranteed by the constitution in question. So, instead of focusing on equality between students, many third wave school finance arguments focused on the substantive opportunities available to students.

Widely considered one of the landmark cases in the third wave, *Rose v. Council for Better Education* provided a model for many subsequent school finance reform decisions and resulted in one of the first appearances of standards-based reform and accountability policies in the school finance reform context.[16] *Rose* was filed in Kentucky in response to what appeared to be horrible educational conditions.[17] Given the state of education in Kentucky, arguments addressing adequacy and not just equality seemed to make sense. The plaintiffs thus argued that Kentucky had failed to provide students with an adequate education as required by the education clause in the Kentucky constitution: "The General Assembly shall, by appropriate legislation, provide for an efficient system of common schools throughout the State." Because the Kentucky education clause is rather vague about exactly what level of education is constitutionally required, the *Rose* court needed to articulate a more precise standard. After a detailed examination of expert testimony and state constitutional history, the Kentucky Supreme Court famously defined a constitutionally adequate education—the court listed seven substantive capacities, such as knowledge of economic, social, and political systems to enable informed choices, that Kentucky must provide students with a sufficient opportunity to obtain.[18]

In order to determine whether Kentucky met this standard, the court not only examined the financial inequities present across districts; the court also examined curricula, facilities, student-teacher ratios, and achievement test scores. Based on these kinds of evidence, the court ruled that Kentucky's system of public schools was not adequate to produce the kind of student required by the state constitution and ordered the state legislature to remedy this deficiency. With this expansive ruling, the Kentucky Supreme Court had done something remarkably important: It had attempted to give precise substantive content to an education clause, and had focused on both inputs and outputs to determine whether the state was providing students with a substantive set of skills and knowledge.

The response of the Kentucky legislature to the *Rose* court's order seized upon the possibilities offered by this sort of legal reasoning. In 1990, less than a year after *Rose* was decided, the state legislature enacted the Kentucky Education Reform Act (KERA).[19] On one level, KERA looked much like legislation that other states had enacted in response to school finance decisions. KERA provided for many changes in the state funding system to equalize and increase education funding.[20] On another level, KERA mandated major education reform in the areas of curriculum and school governance. KERA required Kentucky to develop learning standards, a model curriculum framework based on these standards, assessments of student progress in relation to the standards, and accountability measures triggered by student performance on the assessments.[21] KERA particularly provided that the state must develop a performance-based assessment for students in grades four, eight, and twelve, and must group student scores on the assessment into the categories of novice, apprentice, proficient, and distinguished.[22] Moreover, KERA provided that schools must be held accountable for the performance of their students—KERA required an "accountability index" to be created for each school.[23] If a school's accountability index failed to exceed its performance requirement in any given year, a host of administrative sanctions, such as replacement of school management, was to follow.[24] Modeled on Kentucky's school finance reform experience, other state supreme courts, such as Massachusetts', have similarly defined adequacy and prompted a legislative response involving the institution of standards-based reform and accountability policies.[25]

Based on the type of reasoning present in *Rose*, adequacy arguments have generally fared better than the equality arguments employed in the first and second waves. According to one report, 27 states have faced adequacy suits, and plaintiffs have prevailed in 20 state supreme courts' decisions and unappealled trial court decisions from 1989 to 2006.[26] Several factors appear to have contributed to the greater success of adequacy arguments in school finance cases.[27] First, adequacy arguments are not as politically explosive as equality arguments. The rhetoric of ensuring that all students have adequate educational opportunities does not directly threaten wealthy districts and undermine local control to the same extent as equality arguments. One court has expressly noted that the concept of educational adequacy does not "translate into equal educational opportunity."[28]

Second, courts do not necessarily need to define educational adequacy with specificity in order to find that students are not receiving required educational opportunities. In many school finance cases, the evidence depicts educational conditions that are quite poor by almost any standard. Third, unlike in the case of equality arguments, courts have legal sources that they can use to more specifically define educational adequacy. As discussed above, some of the courts ruling on adequacy arguments have examined the constitutional history of education clauses to determine the content of an adequate education. However, sources such as constitutional history rarely, if ever, indicate what the constitutional framers considered to be an equal education. Thus, adequacy arguments generally appear much more efficacious than equality arguments as school finance reform litigation moves forward.

LIMITATIONS OF ADEQUACY ARGUMENTS

Despite the comparative success of adequacy arguments, plaintiffs bringing adequacy claims have still faced several pervasive and recurring problems. For our purposes, these problems are quite important to keep in mind—the judicial consideration of standards-based reform and accountability policies in school finance reform cases emerged largely in response to such problems, and these problems will likely continue to shape the courts' treatment of standards-based reforms as school finance litigation moves forward. One of the greatest problems faced by courts in school finance suits is defining what constitutes adequate educational opportunities. Even with the use of constitutional history and expert testimony, adequacy clauses are still quite ambiguous as to the specific type of education that is constitutionally required. In light of such ambiguity, several courts have questioned their institutional competencies and the constitutional justifiability of defining adequacy with any precision, and some have accordingly dismissed third wave cases.[29]

In some lawsuits, courts used a detailed legal doctrine to animate their concerns about their institutional competencies and legal powers. According to the *non-justiciable political question* doctrine, only a legislative body may decide certain types of issues. The Supreme Court specified six criteria to determine whether a case involves a non-justiciable political question.[30] In school finance cases, the criterion that often determines whether a case involves a non-justiciable political question is whether judges must discuss standards that are neither judicially discoverable nor manageable. *Committee for Educational Rights v. Edgar*, a school finance reform case decided in 1996 by the Illinois Supreme Court, provides a colorful example of an invocation of this doctrine. In this case, Justice Nickels focused on the unmanageability of defining an adequate education and the state legislature's superior position for this task. Quoting the dissent of a judge in a Washington school finance case, Justice Nickels wrote:

> I would be surprised to learn that the people of this state are willing to turn over to a tribunal against which they have little if any recourse, a matter of such grave concern to them and upon which they hold so many strong, though conflicting views. If their legislators pass laws with which they disagree or refuse to act when the people think they should, they can make their dissatisfaction known at the polls. They can write to their representatives or appear before them and let their protests be heard. The court, however, is not so easy to reach nor is it so easy to persuade that its judgment ought to be revised. A legislature may be a hard horse to harness, but it is not quite the stubborn mule that a court can be. Most importantly, the court is not designed or equipped to make public policy decisions, as this case so forcibly demonstrates.[31]

Focusing on the vagueness of an education clause and the legal powers and institutional competencies of courts, the court, led by Judge Nickels, dismissed the plaintiffs' adequacy claim as a non-justiciable political question.

Even in cases where a court found that a state's funding policy violated the state constitution, problems flowing from the vagueness of constitutional language and tension between legislative and judicial responsibility to decide educational questions have hindered the effectiveness of judicial action. Courts have particularly faced problems when attempting to craft effective remedies. In many cases, courts simply pointed out that a state had failed to fulfill its constitutional duty and, without further defining the state's responsibilities, let the state determine how it would meet this duty. For example, although *Rose* is sometimes held as an instance in which a court delved too deeply into education policymaking (because the court specified seven capacities that constitute an adequate education), the court in this case largely let Kentucky decide how it would respond to a finding of inadequacy. Indicating their belief that other governmental branches are better positioned to specify effective remedies, several other courts finding violations of a state's adequacy clause have followed a similar path.[32]

But left to their own devices, states have faced many difficulties devising and implementing effective responses to courts' orders. Some states have simply been unable to overcome the political barriers to passing comprehensive education legislation in response to a school finance decision. For example, although members of both the New Hampshire legislative and executive branches publicly stated that the implementation of a standards-based accountability system (in addition to changes in the state funding system) constituted the appropriate response to a judicial finding of inadequacy, the legislature failed to pass such legislation after years of attempts.[33] Similarly, the New Jersey legislature and judiciary engaged in a 30-year struggle over school finance reform in the state.[34] And as mentioned above, even in cases where states actively reacted to judicial findings of inadequacy, student test scores showed little or no gains. In short, while adequacy arguments entail a number of advantages over equality arguments, the familiar problems plaguing judicial action in education reform have persisted, and the ultimate effectiveness of adequacy arguments has been somewhat mixed. It is precisely in response to these sorts of issues that the active judicial consideration of standards-based reforms in school finance reform litigation has emerged.

The Emergence of Standards-Based Reforms in School Finance Reform Litigation

As courts around the country continued to rule in school finance reform cases, these courts increasingly began to consider arguments about the role of standards-based reform and accountability policies in defining, measuring, and ensuring educational adequacy. Based on such considerations, courts also began to craft rulings directly addressing the relationship between these policies and educational adequacy. Given the goals of these policies, the history of school finance litigation, and the problems courts ruling in this area had historically faced, the active judicial consideration of standards-based reforms in school finance reform litigation appears somewhat natural. The ultimate goals of standards-based reforms and adequacy litigation are quite similar. Both methods of reform aim at providing students with the educational opportunities they need to learn substantive skills and knowledge. Where standards-based reforms aim at providing students with the education embodied in content standards, adequacy lawsuits aim at providing students with the education embodied in the education clauses of state constitutions.

Moreover, adequacy arguments and standards-based reforms emerged on the educational landscape at approximately the same time. As discussed above, some states in the late 1980s and early 1990s, such as Kentucky, voluntarily enacted standards-based reform and accountability policies in response to school finance decisions. At the same time, however, other states began to enact such policies without judicial orders from school finance suits. Under the federal Improving America's Schools Act passed in 1994, every state was required to enact standards-based reform and accountability policies as a condition of receiving Title I funds, and NCLB maintained these requirements.[35] By 1999, such policies were pervasive, and all but one state had content standards in place in reading and mathematics.[36]

As discussed in the previous section, several fundamental problems, such as vagueness in the language of education clauses, the resulting doctrinal ambiguity, and judicial reluctance or incapacity to make decisions in education policy without precise guidelines, greatly limited the effectiveness of school finance litigation. With its detailed explication of the seven capacities entailed by an adequate education, the *Rose* court had certainly begun to address these problems—in response to vague constitutional standards and the difficulty of evaluating state education policies against these standards, the court drew on different sources to define educational adequacy with more specificity. Facing precisely the same problems, other courts copied the reasoning of *Rose*. Still, many questions remained: Although the concept of adequacy may be linked to the creation of democratically and economically capable citizens, precisely what level and type of education is necessary or sufficient to create such citizens? What output measures, if any, are relevant to determining whether a state has provided students with sufficient opportunities to receive an adequate education? What inputs, in addition to funding, are relevant to an adequacy analysis? Are courts competent or legally justified to make such determinations? As some courts and litigants found, standards-based reform and accountability policies offered answers to many of these questions.

Grounded in the previous analysis of the history and problems of adequacy arguments, this section closely examines the increasingly active stance that courts have begun to take toward standards-based reforms in school finance reform litigation. This section particularly traces the convergence of school finance reform litigation and standards-based reform and accountability policies in five lawsuits in North Carolina, New York, Ohio, Massachusetts, and California. These cases are among the most important that have thus far been decided for understanding this convergence, and they well illustrate the commonalities and differences among the various cases in this area.

NORTH CAROLINA: *LEANDRO v. STATE OF NORTH CAROLINA*

In *Leandro v. State of North Carolina*, five poor rural school districts sued North Carolina in May 1994 for failing to provide students with equal and adequate educational opportunities.[37] When *Leandro* was filed, school funding was fairly low and unequal across the state. The per pupil expenditures of Hoke County (one of the plaintiffs) were $467 annually, while the per pupil expenditures of Dare County (a wealthy country in North Carolina) were $2,410 annually.[38] The plaintiffs argued that, as a result, the state funding system was not sufficient to enable them to purchase various kinds of school materials (such as laboratory equipment and textbooks) and that poorer schools were therefore not capable of providing students with the required educational opportunities. Student performance in North Carolina at the time was low as well—only 37.3 percent of high school students in the state scored at or above the proficient level on end-of-grade tests in core courses.[39] In October 1994, six high-wealth urban school districts filed a complaint against North Carolina and became plaintiff-intervenors in the lawsuit (and were thus effectively treated as plaintiffs for certain purposes in the lawsuit). Unlike the five rural counties, the plaintiff-intervenors did not focus on inter-district funding disparities; instead, the plaintiff-intervenors focused on the issue of funding for and educational opportunities available to "at-risk" students.

As with many other school finance cases, *Leandro* wound its way through the state court system until it was eventually heard by the state supreme court. In February 1995, a state trial court denied the state's motion to dismiss.[40] In March 1995, a state appeals court found that the state constitution only grants students the right of equal access to public schools and reversed the trial court's decision.[41] However, in July 1997, the North Carolina Supreme Court reversed the appeals court.[42] In this decision, the state supreme court rejected the plaintiffs' arguments regarding the equalization of educational resources, but the court found the adequacy claim more persuasive. In considering the adequacy argument, the court directly addressed the relationship between financial resources and student performance in relation to state standards for one of the first times in the history of school finance reform litigation.

Following in the footsteps of *Rose*, the North Carolina Supreme Court began its adequacy analysis by asking precisely what the education clause means. The court first found that the state constitution requires North Carolina to provide students with a "sound basic education" (or an adequate education).[43] The court then continued that a sound basic education must provide students with the opportunity to receive four of the seven basic competencies specified in *Rose*. However, even as the court began to define a sound basic education, it also expressed a strong awareness of the familiar concerns about defining this type of education more fully:

> We have announced that definition with some trepidation. We recognize that judges are not experts in education and are not particularly able to identify in detail those curricula best designed to ensure that a child receives a sound basic education . . . We acknowledge that the legislative process provides a better forum than the courts for discussing and determining what educational programs and resources are most likely to ensure that each child of the state receives a sound basic education. The members of the General Assembly are popularly elected to represent the public for the purpose of making just such decisions. The legislature, unlike the courts, is not limited to addressing only cases and controversies brought before it by litigants. The legislature can properly conduct public hearings and committee meetings at which it can hear and consider the views of the general public as well as educational experts and permit the full expression of all points of view as to what curricula will best ensure that every child of the state has the opportunity to receive a sound basic education.[44]

Still, the court did not back away from defining adequacy. Mindful of these concerns, the court instead took a new path and looked to other branches of the state government for help.

As *Leandro* was being decided, the North Carolina General Assembly was in the process of adopting a standards-based reform and accountability system—the "ABCs" system. The court considered the development of the ABCs as an opportunity to address some of the serious concerns that it had just raised. The court stated that the "[e]ducational goals and standards adopted by the legislature," the "level of performance of the children of the state and its various districts on standard achievement tests," and "the level of the state's general educational expenditures and per pupil expenditures" are "factors which may be considered on remand to the trial court for its determination as to whether any of the state's children are being denied their right to a sound basic education."[45] The court also expressly stated that it was quite useful to examine the performance of students on achievement tests linked to the standards because such performance may actually be "more reliable than measurements of 'inputs' such as per-pupil funding or general educational funding provided by the state" for determining whether the state was providing students with an adequate education.[46] The court thus encouraged (and perhaps even required) other courts that would hear the case to consider state standards and student performance on tests to determine whether the state's education system was performing adequately.

After articulating the relationship between standards-based reforms and adequacy, the court remanded the case to Wake County Superior Court Judge Howard E. Manning, Jr. for a full decision based on the facts of the case. Because of the different factual issues applicable to rural students and urban students, Judge Manning split *Leandro* into two separate cases. In the case focusing on rural education, newly titled *Hoke County Board of Education v. State of North Carolina*, Judge Manning specifically looked at whether North Carolina students were receiving an adequate education using the criteria articulated in *Leandro*.[47] (Notably, Judge Manning did not launch a second trial because the plaintiff-intervenors were allowed to participate in almost all aspects of *Hoke*, and Judge Manning's ruling in *Hoke* applied to both the plaintiffs and plaintiff-intervenors.) In order to determine whether the state's education system was providing students with adequate educations, Judge Manning was required to sort through a huge volume of technical educational information. During a trial in 1999 that lasted over 20 days, the plaintiffs called 26 witnesses and introduced other testimony by deposition, and the defendants called 17 witnesses. The parties also submitted 670 documentary exhibits. After the trial, Judge Manning issued a series of four opinions over approximately a year and a half, with each opinion focusing on separate, but conceptually related, issues raised during the trial.

In the first opinion, Judge Manning paid close attention to the precise meaning of test scores in conducting an adequacy analysis.[48] Citing the state supreme court's 1997 decision, Judge Manning found that student performance on state exams was "highly probative" of whether students were receiving adequate educations.[49] Judge Manning further determined that achieving a "Level III" proficiency on the state test—the level indicating that students had demonstrated mastery of course subject matter and skills—specifically indicated that students had received adequate educations. According to Judge Manning, "[a]cademic performance below grade level (Level II) is a constitutionally unacceptable minimum standard."[50] So, given the utility of information about test scores linked to state standards, a particular level of performance against state standards, determined by other governmental branches, had begun to define constitutional duties.

In the subsequent opinions, Judge Manning determined that North Carolina was not providing its students with adequate educations. Focusing on the difficulties of educating "at-risk" students, the benefits of early childhood education, and the test scores of at-risk students, Judge Manning found in the second opinion that North Carolina was required to offer free preschool to all at-risk students in the state.[51] In the third opinion, Judge Manning analyzed the characteristics of students in Hoke County (one of the plaintiff districts) and compared Hoke County students to their peers in the rest of the state.[52] In conducting this examination, Judge Manning heavily focused on disaggregated student test score data and its relationship with funding patterns, and other types of evidence, including graduation rates and information about the educational offerings and administration of Hoke County schools. From this analysis, Judge Manning determined that Hoke County schools were not providing students with adequate educations, but not necessarily because of insufficient funding. So, relying heavily on the extensive information provided by the operation of the ABCs, Judge Manning found that schools did not need more funding under the North Carolina constitution; instead, schools needed to use money in a more coordinated and efficient way to help students attain the knowledge and skills embodied in state standards.

In addition to looking at various traditional educational inputs and test scores linked to state standards to determine whether the state was providing students with adequate educations, Judge Manning examined the actual design and implementation of the ABCs. In his first opinion, the judge conducted a broad overview of what he considered to be the major components of North Carolina's education system to determine whether the system's design was constitutional. The bulk of this lengthy (122-page) opinion examined the state's standards, teacher licensure and certification standards, funding delivery system, accountability system, and the statutory provisions for assistance aimed at helping low-performing schools. The judge particularly reviewed the content and goals of state standards in various subjects, and analyzed whether these standards were sufficient to provide students with the opportunities to acquire the four basic capabilities specified by the state supreme court. The judge also reviewed the process used by the state for developing the standards and emphasized the state's periodic revisions of the standards. Based on this information, Judge Manning found that the standards were rigorous and measurable, and focused on important content for students to learn. Thus, the judge found that the standards themselves were constitutional.

Moreover, Judge Manning closely examined the design of the ABCs system. Under the ABCs, North Carolina held individual schools accountable for student performance on tests aligned to state standards. Each year, the state set annual improvement targets for schools. Schools were to receive rewards or sanctions based on their performance. In evaluating the ABCs, Judge Manning looked to the testimony of Jay Robinson, the former chairman of the State Board of Education, who indicated that the implementation of the ABCs "was one of the healthiest things the State has ever done . . . [because it] simply does not make sense to pour billions of dollars into the educational delivery system without having accountability for those dollars on the academic performance side of the ledger."[53] The judge also highlighted positive statements by various educational experts (such as Dr. Eric Hanushek) and national organizations (such as the National Alliance of Business) that the ABCs was one of the strongest accountability systems in the country. Moreover, the judge heard the plaintiffs' criticisms of the ABCs on several grounds, including exemptions of certain subgroups of students from assessments and an undue amount of emphasis placed on multiple-choice items in tests.

In the final analysis, Judge Manning found that, while the ABCs program is "subject to certain criticisms and is not perfect in all respects, it is a giant step in the right direction," and he accordingly did not order any changes in the design of the ABCs.[54] Building on this logic, Judge Manning continued:

> If the ABCs program were not in place, a similar accountability program would, in the Court's opinion, be required so the State, and the public, could have a statewide accountability system to measure educational progress and to assist in measuring whether or not each child is receiving the equal opportunity to obtain a sound basic education as the Constitution requires.[55]

In other words, highlighting the benefits of increased information for governmental decision making, especially in school finance cases, Judge Manning indicated that the implementation of the ABCs did not simply satisfy a legislative mandate; the accountability system also included a constitutional dimension that could subject the accountability system to judicial review.

In the fourth and final opinion, written after holding ten additional days of hearings to elicit various strategies for helping at-risk students, Judge Manning detailed the remedy that North Carolina would need to implement in order for it to fulfill its constitutional duty.[56] In this opinion, Judge Manning reviewed evidence about the effectiveness of several types of educational strategies and programs, including class size reduction, differentiated instruction, extra tutoring, and particular programs (such as Success for All and Reading Recovery), and found that there are certain "essential ingredients" needed to support successful schools: a principal who is an effective, energetic leader, teachers who are competent, certified, and energetic, and an educational program that ensures that all students are provided the opportunities to learn the knowledge and skills embodied in the standards.

Judge Manning accordingly ordered the state to ensure that schools had sufficient personnel and instructional programs in place to provide students with such opportunities. Still, citing his lack of competence in education and the proper role of the courts, Judge Manning did not order the state to provide more funding to schools, stated that there is no single education program that meets the needs of all at-risk students, and consequently left the "nuts and bolts" of implementing this order to the other governmental branches. In short, based on the benefits of increased information, the other governmental branches' efforts at enabling students to meet state standards, and the institutional capacity of the courts, Judge Manning gave the ABCs a constitutional dimension and considered the implementation of various types of educational programs by educational personnel.

Hoke v. State of North Carolina *on Appeal*

On appeal, the North Carolina Supreme Court reviewed Judge Manning's finding that the state had failed to provide its students with adequate educational opportunities, Judge Manning's use of state standards and tests in making this finding, and Judge Manning's remedial orders.[57] Because the state had failed to argue in its brief about the use of a Level III standard to flesh out the definition of a sound basic education, the court specifically upheld Judge Manning's ruling that Level III is the proper standard for demonstrating compliance with *Leandro*. After examining the "output" evidence examined by Judge Manning (such as student test scores, graduation rates, etc.) and the "input" evidence (such as the funding delivery system, state standards, and the accountability system), the court also concluded that Judge Manning's ruling was premised on a clear evidentiary showing. Because Judge Manning also conducted a comprehensive analysis of the state's inactions and actions to provide students with sufficient educations, and linked this analysis with student performance, the court was ultimately persuaded by both Judge Manning's method of determining inadequacy and his finding of inadequacy. Indeed, upon being interviewed, both Judge Manning and Chief Justice Mitchell of the state supreme court indicated that standards and test results made it much easier to rule in *Hoke*.[58]

In short, growing out of the explicit reasoning about the characteristics of the various governmental branches in *Leandro* and spurred by the utility of standards and test data for judicial decision making, a particular level of achievement, originally defined by nonjudicial governmental entities, was becoming associated with constitutional requirements in North Carolina. At the same time, the state's standards-based accountability policy, independently enacted by the state's legislature, took on a constitutional dimension and became subject to scrutiny by judges. Driven by an analysis of the extensive data created under the state's accountability policy, one judge ordered the legislature to implement certain broad changes to ensure that students were learning the skills and knowledge embodied in this policy, and the state supreme court affirmed these particular actions. Even in the context of judicial concern about the appropriate balance of decision-making authority, school finance reform and standards-based accountability policies had begun to converge in a way that integrated the efforts of the courts and other governmental entities at producing education policy change.

NEW YORK: *CAMPAIGN FOR FISCAL EQUITY v. STATE OF NEW YORK*

Around the same time as *Leandro* was being litigated, other state courts hearing school finance cases also began to directly consider issues regarding standards-based reform and accountability policies. In *Campaign for Fiscal Equity v. State of New York (CFE)*, a nonprofit advocacy organization, 14 community school boards, and 23 parents filed a lawsuit against the state of New York in 1993. At the time, New York City spent approximately $3,000 per pupil annually, while other districts spent approximately $3,400 per pupil annually.[59] *CFE* targeted New York's educational funding structure on the basis of several legal theories, including the familiar theories of equality and adequacy, and primarily claimed that New York City was not receiving its constitutionally required level of funding. When the state's highest court (the Court of Appeals) ruled in *CFE* for the first time in 1995, the court dismissed the plaintiffs' equality argument but allowed the adequacy argument to proceed.[60]

Like the North Carolina Supreme Court, the New York Court of Appeals found that the state's education clause required it to provide all students with the opportunity to receive a sound basic education. Somewhat echoing *Rose*, the Court of Appeals also indicated that this education "should consist of the basic literacy calculating, and verbal skills necessary to enable children to eventually function productively as civic participants capable of voting and serving on a jury."[61] After articulating this standard, the Court of Appeals remanded the case to a trial court for a decision based on the facts of the case. In its opinion, the Court of Appeals specifically directed the trial court to examine inputs provided to students (such as the quality of teachers and the condition of facilities) and outputs (such as graduation rates and student performance). The Court of Appeals specifically indicated that the trial court should use test results "cautiously as there are a myriad of factors which have causal bearing on test results."[62] The case was assigned to Judge Leland DeGrasse, who held an incredibly long and complex trial that began in October 1999 and lasted 111 days over a seven-month period. During this time, 72 witnesses took the stand, and over 4,300 documents were submitted into evidence.

The arguments before Judge DeGrasse focused on several aspects of the schooling process. Since *CFE* had been originally filed, education spending in New York had increased dramatically—at the time of Judge DeGrasse's trial, New York City spent $9,623 per pupil, while the state spent $10,317.[63] However, the plaintiffs argued that these expenditures were not adequate— the plaintiffs presented substantial evidence about educational inputs besides funding, such as teacher quality and the poor condition of school facilities, and argued that these inputs were not sufficient to support a sound basic education. The plaintiffs also presented a substantial amount of evidence related to student outputs. The plaintiffs argued that the state's Regents Learning Standards should be used to define adequacy and accordingly presented evidence about the failure of students in New York City to pass the Regents Exams (which were theoretically aligned to state standards) and to receive Regents Diplomas. While students were not required to pass the Regents Exams in order to graduate from high school at the time of the trial, students were required to pass this exam to graduate beginning in 2004. In response, the state argued that the state's education clause only required it to offer minimal educational opportunities, or the basic tools necessary for productive citizenship, and argued that performance on the Regents Exams was not applicable. In addition to arguing about the place of exams tied to state standards in an adequacy analysis, the parties presented a significant amount of evidence about graduation rates and student performance on other tests, such as the Early Childhood Learning Assessment and the Pupil Evaluation Program (measuring achievement in reading and mathematics).

After reviewing the extensive testimony and evidence from the trial, in addition to several post-trial documents submitted by the parties, Judge DeGrasse ultimately sided with the plaintiffs in an opinion released in 2001. Given the significant amount of output data presented by the parties, Judge DeGrasse expressly addressed the definition of a sound basic education. Citing the previous Court of Appeals decision, the judge stressed that "prudence should govern utilization of the Regents' standards as benchmarks of educational adequacy. Proof of noncompliance with one or more of the Regents' . . . standards may not, standing alone, establish a violation of the Education Article."[64] Indeed, Judge DeGrasse indicated that these standards reflected a "state of the art" (and not a sound basic) education and that use of the standards to define an adequate education would "essentially define the ambit of a constitutional right by whatever a state agency says it is."[65] Still, Judge DeGrasse did emphasize the utility of using the standards in such a fashion—the specificity of the standards could help a court analyze the opportunities actually available to students.

Based on this analysis of the applicability of the Regents Learning Standards, Judge DeGrasse proceeded to a detailed examination of the testimony and evidence, including an array of information about inputs, outputs, and the relationship between the two. The analysis of outputs notably included an examination of student performance data from tests aligned to the Regents Learning Standards. After completing this examination, Judge DeGrasse ultimately concluded that New York was failing to provide students with an adequate education and accordingly ordered the state to revise its funding structure. Stressing the "far greater expertise" of the other branches of government in education, Judge DeGrasse indicated that he would defer to the state to decide how the fix this problem.[66] However, Judge DeGrasse did order the state to determine the actual costs of providing a sound basic education in districts across the state. Moreover, Judge DeGrasse ordered the state to ensure a "system of accountability to measure whether the reforms implemented by the legislature actually provide the opportunity for a sound basic education and remedy the disparate impact of the current finance system."[67]

Campaign for Fiscal Equity v. State of New York
on Appeal

The logic employed by Judge DeGrasse did not prove persuasive to the appeals court that later heard the case.[68] Agreeing with the defendants that the Regents Learning Standards embodied too high a level of education to define adequacy, the appeals court stated that the state's education clause only requires "minimally adequate educational opportunity," or the opportunity to learn at an eighth- or ninth-grade level.[69] The appeals court specifically stated that the Regents Learning Standards are merely "aspirational" (however laudable) and not constitutionally required, and that a constitutionally adequate education should only provide students with "the ability to get a job, and support oneself, and thereby not be a charge on the public fisc."[70] In large part based on this determination, the appeals court found that there was no evidence that students were not receiving adequate educational opportunities, reversed Judge DeGrasse's decision, and held that the state was complying with its constitutional duty. Notably, then Governor Pataki, who had originally ordered the appeal, later stated at a public speech, "I totally disagree with the concept that an eighth-grade education is adequate, and it will never be the policy of this state as long as I am the governor of this state."[71]

The Court of Appeals ultimately took the middle road in a high-profile decision in 2003.[72] On one hand, the court expressed theoretical concerns about using the Regents Learning Standards to define adequacy. Despite the suggestions of several parties that had submitted *amicus curiae* briefs in the cases to equate the Regents Learning Standards and educational adequacy, the Court of Appeals agreed with Judge DeGrasse that equating the two would violate the separation of powers. But the court further indicated that it did not need to rule that state standards are aligned with educational adequacy in order for the assessments to constitute powerful evidence; according to the court, student performance on tests that are unaligned with the proper constitutional adequacy standard can still provide information relevant to the educational opportunities that students have received. At the same time, the court expressly found that students require more than an eighth-grade education and that a sound basic education should not be pegged to the eighth- or ninth-grade level.[73] Thus, mindful of the theoretical issues implicated by the convergence of educational adequacy and state standards, but aware of the utility of standards-based reforms in adequacy decisions, the court acted as though state standards were relevant for evaluating adequacy without expressly equating the two.

After discussing the definition of educational adequacy, the court continued to an examination of the evidence and testimony from the trial. The court reviewed a significant amount of evidence about educational inputs and outputs, particularly focusing on student performance on tests. After determining that there were causal links between educational inputs and outputs, the Court of Appeals ultimately ruled that the state school finance system was unconstitutional and found itself in the difficult position of crafting an appropriate and effective remedy. Describing the difficulties of creating such a remedy, the court stated:

> We are, of course mindful—as was the trial court—of the responsibility, underscored by the State, to defer to the Legislature in matters of policymaking, particularly in a matter so vital as education financing, which has as well a core element of local control. We have neither the authority, nor the ability, nor the will, to micromanage education financing. By the same token, in plaintiffs' favor, it is the province of the Judicial branch to define, and safeguard, rights provided by the New York State Constitution, and order redress for violation of them. Surely there is a remedy more promising, and ultimately less entangling for the courts, than simply directing the parties to eliminate the deficiencies, as the State would have us do.[74]

Noting that it wanted to "learn from our national experience and fashion an outcome that will address the constitutional violation instead of inviting decades of litigation," the Court of Appeals crafted what it considered to be a new sort of remedy—one that highlighted particular problems to which the state needed to pay attention but that also gave the state due deference in light of its legal authority and other capacities.[75] The Court of Appeals ordered the state to ascertain the actual cost of providing a sound basic education in New York City, reform the state's system of school funding and management accordingly, and ensure a system of accountability to measure whether the reforms actually provided the opportunity for a sound basic education. The court gave the state until July 30, 2004, to complete these actions. As the Court of Appeals noted, New York already had an accountability system in place under state law that required the state to identify schools in need of improvement and had already begun to implement NCLB and to institute the standards-based accountability measures required by the statute. Still, the court refused to rule that the existing accountability system was sufficient to meet the state's constitutional burden; the court explicitly indicated that the state must determine the extent to which the accountability system was tied to the definition of a sound basic education and modify the system accordingly.

Implementing the Court of Appeals Decision

The case unsurprisingly did not end with the 2003 ruling by the Court of Appeals. Following this decision, three separate cost studies were conducted to ascertain the amount of funding it would take to provide students with the opportunity to receive a sound basic education. Each of these cost studies recommended different levels of educational funding: The Campaign for Fiscal Equity and the New York State School Boards Association contracted with American Institutes for Research and Management Analysis and Planning, Inc. to create a study that ultimately recommended $5.6 billion additional funding annually.[76] The New York Commission on Education Reform, a group appointed by Governor Pataki, contracted with Standard and Poor's to create a study that recommended between $1.9 and $4.7 billion additional funding annually.[77] Finally, The New York State Education Department created a cost study that recommended $5.3 billion additional funding annually.[78]

The cost studies notably employed different methods, which likely contributed in large part to the differences in the cost estimates. The Campaign for Fiscal Equity study used the "professional judgment" method, which relies on educational experts (such as teachers) to determine the resources necessary to produce a specified level of achievement. In this case, the educational experts determined the resources necessary to produce students that could be deemed proficient under the Regents Learning Standards. After determining what resources were needed, the cost of these resources was determined. Both the New York Commission on Education Reform study and the New York State Education Department Study used the "Successful School Districts" method, which looks at the resources deployed in school districts that are deemed successful via various performance measures. Despite this surface similarity, the methodologies underlying these two studies were different in significant ways as well. The New York Commission of Education Reform study focused on districts that had met performance targets under NCLB and had met the "Regents Criteria" (where at least 80 percent of the students demonstrated proficiency on seven Regents examinations) as model districts. The New York State Education Department Study primarily looked at districts that had simply met the Regents Criteria as model districts.

Despite the completion of these studies in early 2004, the state missed the July 2004 deadline mandated by the Court of Appeals to implement the changes. In response, Judge DeGrasse (who had been assigned the case on remand) appointed a panel of three "referees" to hold hearings and make recommendations. In November 2004, the panel released an extensive report, relying heavily on the three cost studies and input from a number of other groups, that ultimately called for the state to provide an additional $5.6 billion annually and to conduct a new cost study every four years to determine the cost of a sound basic education.[79] The report additionally addressed the implementation of the accountability requirements of the 2003 ruling. While the panel concluded that New York's existing accountability system, mandated by both state and federal law, already provided adequate accountability, the panel also suggested several enhancements to the current accountability system. Noting that the parties to the lawsuit had already agreed that the state department of education should develop a comprehensive sound basic education plan that would detail the precise management reforms and instructional initiatives that the state would undertake, the panel stated its belief that such a plan was necessary. In addition, the panel indicated that this plan should be coordinated with a four-year phase-in of the additional funding and that the state department of education should follow through with its plan to create a "Sound Basic Education Report" that would track additional funding ordered in *CFE* and would track student performance and other benchmarks to see how the department uses the additional funding.

In March 2005, Judge DeGrasse ordered New York to comply with the recommendations in the report.[80] An appellate court that was expressly sensitive to the problems of delving too deeply into complex budgetary matters and social problems reviewed Judge DeGrasse's order in March 2006 and ordered New York to increase education funding by an amount between $4.7 billion to $5.6 billion annually—this court dissected the methods of the competing cost studies but expressly gave the state room to modify the state's education funding structure within the range laid out by the cost studies and referee's report.[81] In November 2006, the Court of Appeals reaffirmed its 2003 decision but ordered New York to increase education funding by at least $1.9 billion.[82] In this opinion, the Court of Appeals expressed the need for deference to the education financing decision of other governmental branches and emphasized that Judge DeGrasse erred in confirming the referee's report; according to the Court of Appeals, the role of the courts is not to determine the best way to calculate the cost of a sound basic education, but to determine whether the state's proposed calculation of that cost is rational. Given that the state's cost study recommended a minimum of $1.9 billion additional annual funding, this figure represented the floor for a rational increase in funding.

In January 2007, the then new state governor, Eliot Spitzer, proposed his "Contract for Excellence"—a plan providing for a $1.4 billion increase in school funding for the following year and moving up to $7 billion in additional annual funding after four years.[83] Governor Spitzer also focused on increased accountability—in return for extra funding, Governor Spitzer asked school districts receiving large amounts of funding to develop a comprehensive plan for spending their money to implement effective educational programs.

Governor Spitzer further asked school districts to establish measures of improving performance, and indicated that failing districts would receive additional support from "distinguished educators" and could be required to overhaul their leadership if performance persistently failed to improve. Discussing his plan, Governor Spitzer stated, "The federal No Child Left Behind Act sadly demonstrated that accountability without resources is a false promise. But we also know that resources without accountability are a recipe for waste."[84] In April 2007, the New York legislature passed a bill that largely included Governor Spitzer's proposal, and the state is currently in the process of implementing it.

OHIO: *DEROLPH v. STATE*

In a string of school finance cases in Ohio, a court articulated a vision of standards-based reform in perhaps the most comprehensive fashion yet and deeply delved into the place of cost studies in an adequacy analysis. *DeRolph v. State* was originally filed in December 1991 by a coalition of five Ohio school districts under equality- and adequacy-based theories. When the Ohio Supreme Court heard the case for the first time, it focused primarily on funding, dilapidated facilities, courses offered in schools, and class sizes. In a 1997 decision (*DeRolph I*), the court dismissed the plaintiffs' equality argument but found that Ohio had failed to provide its students with a "thorough and efficient" education, as required by the state's constitution. The court particularly found that the funding formula "has no real relation to what it actually costs to educate a pupil" and that the formula reflects "political and budgetary considerations at least as much as it reflects a judgment as to how much money should be spent on K-12 education."[85] Disagreeing with a dissent arguing that the case addressed a political question, the majority accordingly found that students were being denied adequate educational opportunities. However, the majority declined to specify a precise remedy and largely left it to the state legislature to determine its own course of action.

In response to the ruling in *DeRolph I*, the state passed a law that increased the number of credits students were required to take to graduate, modified state tests, and established performance standards that districts would be evaluated against in "school district report cards." The state also hired a consultant, Dr. John D. Augenblick, to help determine the cost of an adequate education.[86] In order to determine this cost, Dr. Augenblick employed the Successful School Districts method. At the time the study was conducted, Ohio had 18 performance standards in place to determine whether a district was effective. Dr. Augenblick construed an adequately performing school district as one that met at least 17 of these 18 standards. In addition, Dr. Augenblick screened out some districts that had extreme values for property value per pupil and for median household income.[87] After receiving the cost study, the state legislature largely adopted Dr. Augenblick's recommendations but made some slight modifications to the screening procedures used in the study (which appeared to lower the per pupil expenditures).

The plaintiffs believed that the legislature's new funding policy did little to correct, and possibly even worsened, the problems of the previous funding system. The plaintiffs accordingly attempted to enforce what they considered to be the requirements of *DeRolph I*. In *DeRolph II*, ultimately decided by the Ohio Supreme Court in 2000, the court again struck down Ohio's funding system.[88] Almost the entirety of this decision focused on the ways in which the state provided resources to its schools and efforts to improve facilities— the court systematically examined the legislative responses to *DeRolph I* and found that, even though the responses were largely based on the Augenblick study, they were inadequate to remedy the problems that the court had previously cited. This conclusion was again reached in the presence of strong objections voiced by dissenting judges about the proper relationship between the courts and the legislature. However, while funding again constituted the primary focus of the decision in *DeRolph II*, it was not the entire focus. At the end of its decision, the majority launched into a discussion about the importance of implementing standards-based reforms and a related accountability system.

Expressly addressing the place of standards-based reform and accountability policies in helping students receive adequate educational opportunities, the majority wrote, "[W]e clearly state that in order to have a thorough and efficient system of schools, there must be statewide standards that are fully developed, clearly stated, and understood by educators, students, and parents."[89] Clarifying this reasoning and citing a report by Achieve, Inc. (an independent, nonprofit, bipartisan organization created by the nation's governors and business leaders), the court articulated precisely what it believed standards should accomplish—standards should make "crystal clear" the expectations of what students should know and be able to do, should be the basis for aligning "pre-service training for teachers, the curriculum, student assessments, classroom materials, and ongoing professional development," and should be the basis for a statewide accountability system.[90] Demonstrating an even more complete understanding of the underlying theory of standards-based reforms, the court continued that standards-based reforms by themselves cannot produce significant changes; they should drive change in curriculum, instructional practice, and organization, but should also be accompanied by a comprehensive strategy for strengthening the capacity of educators to change their practice and providing sufficient resources to facilitate this change. The court also touched on funding issues in direct relation to standards-based reforms—the court particularly stressed its concerns about instituting accountability measures without adequate funding. The court then allowed the state one year to fix the problems pointed out in this decision.

After *DeRolph II* was handed down, several parties offered additional recommendations regarding the cost of an adequate education.[91] The Ohio General Assembly recalculated the cost of an adequate education using the Augenblick model but slightly changed the screening criteria for districts. Because the state had increased the number of performance standards to 27 in 1999, the legislature also included all districts meeting 20 out of the 27 standards from 1999 and meeting 17 out of the earlier 18 standards in the cost calculations. The Ohio State Board of Education crafted a separate recommendation based on the "Resource and Accountability Model" for determining the cost of an adequate education. This model was similar to the model used by the state legislature insofar as it used districts meeting 20 out of the 27 performance standards as a criterion for labeling districts as having successfully provided students with adequate educations. However, the model also included input criteria that districts had to satisfy in order to be considered successful, including teacher experience, course offerings, and a teacher/student ratio of less than or equal to 1:21.

The Ohio Coalition for Equity and Adequacy, an advocacy organization spearheading the lawsuit on behalf of the districts, also began to develop a "Basket of Essential Learning Resources for the 21st Century"—a list of educational inputs that were arguably crucial for providing students with adequate educations. This model was largely dependent on the recommendations of a large number of educational professionals who were asked to identify the inputs needed to provide students with educations that meet a set level. Under this model, the cost of providing all the inputs would constitute the cost of an adequate education. Ultimately, the state legislature passed several laws that altered the funding system largely in accordance with its modifications of the Augenblick model, addressed the state of school facilities, established standards, and provided assistance (including additional funding) to failing districts.

In 2001, approximately a year after the Supreme Court of Ohio released *DeRolph II*, the court reviewed the state's actions and handed down *DeRolph III*. In this decision, the court reviewed the actions taken by the legislature to comply with *DeRolph II* and found that, although the state had taken significant steps to comply with *DeRolph II*, its actions were still deficient in some very specific respects. The majority particularly delved into the details of the legislature's cost analysis and indicated that Ohio was required to institute cost changes based on districts meeting 20 out of the 27 performance standards without using any of the screening procedures that it had previously employed. Moreover, the majority was very particular about the changes in the funding method that needed to be implemented. But likely influenced by a political climate that had since turned quite hostile to the court's actions in the *DeRolph* litigation, the court stated that it had "no reason to doubt the defendant's good faith" and that there was "no reason to retain jurisdiction" over the case.[92] Despite harsh dissents from several justices, the majority accordingly deemed the state to be in constitutional compliance if it took certain steps to revise the state's funding system.

Slightly more than a year after the court released *DeRolph III*, the court changed course yet again. After Ohio had filed a motion for reconsideration, the state supreme court released *DeRolph IV* and vacated *DeRolph III*.[93] In a very brief decision, Justice Pfeifer indicated that the members of the court were not comfortable with the consensus that they had reached in *DeRolph III* and that the rulings in *DeRolph I* and *DeRolph II* were to be reinstated. Still, the ruling in *DeRolph IV* was fractured—in addition to the majority opinion, there was one separate concurring opinion and there were two dissents. A few months after *DeRolph IV* was handed down, the plaintiffs filed a motion with a trial court for a compliance conference to ensure that the state was proceeding with a process to implement policies that comported with the rulings of the state supreme court. However, the state supreme court found that the trial court did not have jurisdiction to continue and accordingly dismissed the case—the state supreme court emphasized that it was the legislature's duty to create a system that complied with the various *DeRolph* rulings. So, while the state supreme court framed the constitutional requirements for the legislature by delving into cost studies and the place of standards-based reform and accountability policies in an adequacy analysis, in addition to completing more traditional adequacy analyses, the court ultimately left ongoing oversight of education reform and mandated changes in governance to the legislature.

MASSACHUSETTS: *HANCOCK v. DRISCOLL*

While the judges in the school finance cases discussed thus far directly addressed standards-based reform and accountability policies in various ways, these judges generally did not examine the extent to which and ways in which these policies were being implemented. A judge in Massachusetts, however, did conduct such an examination. In *Hancock v. Driscoll*, a group of students from 19 school districts sued Massachusetts to enforce the remedy prescribed by the state's highest court in an earlier school finance case. The original school finance case, *McDuffy v. Secretary of the Executive Office of Education*, was decided by the state's highest court (formally entitled the Supreme Judicial Court of Massachusetts) in 1993.[94] In this case, this court deemed Massachusetts' system of school finance unconstitutional—based on the education clause contained in the state constitution, the *McDuffy* court found that the system of school finance in Massachusetts failed to provide students with adequate educations. In defining an adequate education, the *McDuffy* court copied the language from *Rose* about the seven capacities that students must attain and ordered the Massachusetts legislature to fix the state's education system in accordance with this definition of an adequate education.

In response to this order, the Massachusetts legislature passed the Education Reform Act (ERA), a law that reorganized the state's system of school funding, required the Massachusetts School Board to create standards and curriculum frameworks in major academic subjects, and required the state to administer assessments to measure student performance against these standards. The ERA also required the state to implement a high-stakes graduation test based on these standards, measure the performance of schools based on these standards, review underperforming schools through a "school panel review process," and sanction continually underperforming schools. Still, the plaintiffs in *Hancock* did not believe that the ERA was sufficient to satisfy the state's constitutional obligations and filed suit in 1999 to enforce *McDuffy*. The case was assigned to Judge Margot Botsford of the Massachusetts Superior Court. Because there was such a large number of school districts directly involved in the suit, Judge Botsford focused the case on a smaller number of these districts, and the plaintiffs ultimately selected four of the 19 districts. Even after she focused the suit on four districts, Judge Botsford was ultimately required to deal with a huge amount of technical educational information during the trial—she heard the testimony of 114 witnesses and reviewed over 1,000 exhibits to determine whether the state was complying with its duties under *McDuffy*.

Like the plaintiffs in many of the other cases discussed in this chapter, the plaintiffs in *Hancock* based their adequacy arguments on both educational inputs and outputs. While the plaintiffs particularly emphasized student performance on state tests (theoretically) aligned to the state standards and curriculum frameworks, the state did not offer a specific way to define and measure an adequate education. Given the state's silence on this issue and its representations about the central role played by the standards and curriculum frameworks in the state's education system, Judge Botsford determined that the state would not be permitted during the trial to define a minimal education that was less comprehensive than that provided by the curriculum frameworks. Indeed, the judge underscored that witnesses for both parties had described the curriculum frameworks to be of excellent quality. By making this proclamation, Judge Botsford effectively used the state's standards to define an adequate education for the purposes of the case. Still, the judge also emphasized that the curriculum frameworks were not constitutionally required—they simply represented the specific way in which the state had chosen to fulfill its constitutional duty, and the state could choose to discontinue use of the frameworks in the future. Given the importance of specifically defining an adequate education for making determinations about the sufficiency of state actions, the judge discussed this issue in the beginning of a mammoth 38-page report to the state's highest court.

Based on this consideration of state standards, Judge Botsford proceeded to conduct a detailed examination of the test scores of students in various grades in the focus districts—she closely reviewed test score data in both the aggregate and disaggregated into various categories, such as race and gender, and she compared differences in test performance across the four focus districts.[95] Summarizing the weight of this data in her examination, she wrote:

> In the past ten years the Commonwealth has adopted a standards based approach to public school education. As a result, there is now a set of objective criteria or measures that may be used to assess the quality of education being provided. The department and the board use them, and clearly other observers may as well. I find that the student assessment data just summarized support the findings set out above that the plaintiff students . . . are not receiving an adequate education.[96]

In large part due to the wealth of information available from the operation of the state's standards-based accountability policy and the use of this policy to help define adequacy, Judge Botsford was able to gain increased analytical traction on whether the state was complying with its constitutional duty.

Throughout her report, Judge Botsford conducted a detailed examination of the schools and administrations in the four focus districts on other grounds as well. She examined more "traditional" sorts of inputs, including funding, teacher certification, number of teachers, and whether curriculum materials were up to date. She particularly highlighted the extent to which the standards-based reform components of the ERA were being effectively implemented.

She focused on the extent to which curricula in different grades were aligned with the state curriculum frameworks by looking at the alignment between the content of course offerings and the curriculum frameworks, and the materials teachers received to support implementation of the frameworks. She also examined the extent to which schools had a sufficient number of textbooks aligned with the frameworks and other physical resources needed to effectively implement the frameworks, such as manipulatives for some mathematics courses. She examined the extent to which several other types of policies related to the standards-based reform components of the ERA were being implemented as well, including the amount of professional development received by teachers and the content of the professional development courses. Moreover, Judge Botsford examined the extent to which the state department of education had the financial and administrative capacities to help districts implement the ERA effectively.

Based on this broad examination, Judge Botsford ultimately concluded, "None of the four districts is implementing the Massachusetts curriculum frameworks in a way that can reach all of the children, and none of the districts is equipping all its students with the capabilities outlined in the *McDuffy* decision."[97] Finding that the state had failed to fulfill its constitutional duty to provide students with an adequate education, Judge Botsford then recommended that the state conduct a cost study to determine the cost of fully implementing the curriculum frameworks and other necessary educational programs, and to implement the needed funding and administrative changes.[98] Emphasizing the decade that the legislative and executive branches had since *McDuffy* to implement effective education reform, the lack of political leadership to effect such reform, and the difficulties other courts had historically faced crafting effective remedies in school finance cases, Judge Botsford further recommended that a judge should monitor the remedial process and provide direction where appropriate. In short, responding to the state legislature's enactment of a standards-based accountability policy, which in turn responded to a previous finding of inadequacy, Judge Botsford deeply examined the implementation of this policy and recommended particular changes to fix problems in its implementation.

Hancock v. Driscoll *on Appeal*

On appeal, Massachusetts' highest court did not follow Judge Botsford's recommendations.[99] A plurality of the court expressly upheld the original holding of *McDuffy* but also praised the efforts of Massachusetts' other governmental branches to overhaul the funding and structure of the state's education system. While acknowledging that Judge Botsford had shown that the education system was "far from perfect," the plurality underscored that the state was "evaluating and addressing problems in underperforming schools and districts according to a plan of 'pragmatic gradualism' that employs objective, measurable criteria to gauge progress."[100] The plurality further justified the state's gradual implementation of the ERA by emphasizing the context in which the ERA was being implemented. According to the plurality, fundamental and sweeping change, such as that mandated by the ERA, is seldom easy, especially when directed at a system as complex as that of public education. As a result, education reform is a naturally slow process. Indeed, the plurality found that delays in the full implementation of the ERA did not derive from legislative or departmental inaction; they derived from continued public debate, political opposition (and sometimes protracted litigation) over some provisions of education reform, deliberate phase-in efforts to permit schools and districts time to adjust to new standards, and severe revenue shortfalls. The plurality also rejected Judge Botsford's remedial recommendations because they were rife with policy choices that the courts were arguably not competent to make. The plurality accordingly found that judicial intervention was not required at the time and that it was the responsibility of the state legislature to meet the requirements of the state education clause.

A concurring opinion and dissenting opinions critiqued various facets of the majority opinion. Judge Cowin concurred with the majority because she believed that courts should have a more limited role in public policy debates. According to this judge, even if the education clause does impose a duty on the state, the duty should be "fulfilled by the legislative and executive branches, without oversight or intrusion by the judiciary."[101] In making this point, Judge Cowin emphasized the separation of powers doctrine and its application in previous Massachusetts cases, and the lack of capacity possessed by the courts to craft solutions to complex social and political problems. Based on such reasoning, Judge Cowin even wrote that the original *McDuffy* decision improperly inserted a final layer of judicial review on top of the public policy debate over education.

In a dissenting opinion, however, Judge Greaney argued that Judge Botsford was correct.[102] This judge, who was the only judge on the state's highest court who had also served on the *McDuffy* court, stated that Judge Botsford's extensive findings conclusively established that the mandate of *McDuffy* was not being satisfied because the focus districts were not effectively implementing the curriculum frameworks. Judge Greaney accordingly supported Judge Botsford's recommendation that the state should determine the cost of fully implementing the curriculum frameworks and an effective educational plan to boost student performance. Moreover, Judge Greaney argued that a judge should continue to monitor the remedial process. According to the judge, "The problem is of such magnitude that the collective involvement of all three branches of government is needed."[103] So, while the highest court in Massachusetts ultimately did not order changes in the state's school funding system or in its implementation of standards-based reforms and accountability policies, one judge in *Hancock* deeply delved into the actual implementation of these policies and another began to consider atypical relationships between governmental branches, centered on these policies, as a potential remedy to educational problems.

CALIFORNIA: *WILLIAMS v. STATE OF CALIFORNIA*

Although all the cases discussed above dealt with the problems of establishing or implementing governance systems centered on standards-based reform and accountability policies, and the opportunities students need in relation to state standards, most of these cases did not deeply focus on governance systems directly related to such opportunities. In *Williams v. State of California*, however, litigation in California highlighted such issues as the plaintiffs focused their arguments on the lack of standards describing the opportunities students need to learn and the lack of an oversight system to ensure that the state actually provided students with such opportunities.[104] *Williams* was filed in a California Superior Court on May 17, 2000, the 46th anniversary of *Brown v. Board of Education*, and was assigned to Judge Peter Busch. The plaintiffs included several major legal groups, such as the American Civil Liberties Union (ACLU), Public Advocates, Inc., the Mexican American Legal Defense and Educational Fund (MALDEF), and Morrison & Foerster LLP, a large private law firm. Although the lawsuit was based on several types of legal arguments, the plaintiffs' case primarily relied on equality- and adequacy-based theories, and it ultimately became a class action filed on behalf of students across California.

As discussed in Chapter Two, California was one of the first states to become involved in the standards-based reform movement. Following its early attempts at crafting curriculum frameworks in the mid-1980s, California created formal content standards and aligned textbook and teacher education policies with these standards in the 1990s. In the decades leading up to *Williams*, California also enacted a series of other policies that dramatically affected school governance and financing. In 1978, California voters passed Proposition 13, which limited the use of property taxes at local and district levels to fund schools and ultimately shifted a significant amount of education policy authority to the state level. California also instituted several policies addressing funding for facilities, teacher quality, and textbooks, and the state targeted categorical funds at several areas, including a class-size reduction program and a beginning teacher program. Beginning in 2004, students were required to pass a graduation test aligned to state standards, and prior to this, the state had already begun to calculate and publicize an "Academic Performance Index" (API) for schools using student performance on the state's standards-based test.[105] The authority for administering these policies was broadly allocated among different policy actors in the state, such as the California Department of Education, the state board of education, and the superintendent of public instruction. As a result, some researchers have concluded that California's school governance and financing system was irrational, incoherent, and often nonfunctional.[106]

The plaintiffs accordingly focused on the substantive opportunities available to students and on this governance structure as an underlying problem that needed to be directly remedied. The plaintiffs primarily argued that California did not have enough qualified teachers, sufficient instructional materials, and adequate facilities—without these elements in place, students were deprived of "essential educational opportunities to learn" and, despite the presence of standards-based reform and accountability policies, were not provided with the minimal tools to help them meet state standards.[107] In order to support this argument, the plaintiffs' complaint detailed the failure of several schools across the state to provide students with such opportunities and included statistics about the lack and unequal distribution of educational opportunities generally available to California students.

After detailing the need to enhance these educational opportunities, the plaintiffs highlighted the structure of the state's education governance system as the fundamental problem influencing these opportunities. The plaintiffs argued that the state (and responsible officials) had failed to fulfill their constitutional responsibilities in four major ways: (1) the state had delegated substantial authority to school districts and had failed to establish minimal standards for many aspects of the types of educational personnel, materials, and facilities encountered by students in schools; (2) where such standards existed, they were often insufficient to ensure minimal educational opportunity; (3) the state had not taken effective action to determine whether conditions in California schools violated such standards; and (4) where California officials had been aware of violations, they had failed to effectively remedy such violations. The plaintiffs accordingly sought a remedial order from Judge Busch that the state must establish adequate minimal standards regarding educational personnel, instructional materials, and school facilities, must take steps to determine whether conditions violating those standards exist, and must take steps to prevent and remedy such violations.

Emphasizing the importance of the plaintiffs' focus on governance in relation to substantive educational opportunities, Judge Busch issued an order in the early stages of litigation that framed the principal issues of the case:

> The lawsuit is aimed at ensuring a system that will either prevent or discover such deficiencies going forward. The specific deficiencies that take up so much of the Complaint are evidence of an alleged break-down in the State's management of its oversight responsibilities. . . . This case will deal with the oversight and management systems the State has in place to determine if they are legally adequate and whether they are being properly implemented.[108]

After Judge Busch issued this order, several experts prepared reports for the plaintiffs that detailed the lack and unequal distribution of qualified teachers, sufficient instructional materials, and adequate facilities available to students, and argued that such opportunities are essential for the successful implementation of standards-based reform and accountability policies—without such opportunities in place, standards directly addressing these opportunities, and an oversight and accountability mechanism tied to such standards, California's standards-based reform policies would not work as intended. Several experts also prepared reports for the defendants.[109] These experts largely argued that there was insufficient research to support the plaintiffs' focus on teachers, instructional materials, and facilities as the factors particularly influencing educational opportunities in California, and that it was improper for the state to dictate how localities should spend their funding. Despite all this preparation, Judge Busch never had the opportunity to issue a formal ruling in the case.

The Williams v. State of California *Settlement Agreement*

In August 2004, after over four years of litigation, the parties entered into a historic settlement agreement. This agreement focused on the problems that the plaintiffs had highlighted throughout the litigation and included proposed legislative text for addressing these problems. In September 2004, Governor Arnold Schwarzenegger signed five bills enacting the legislative proposals included in the settlement agreement. Two of these laws established minimum standards for teacher quality, instructional materials, and facilities, along with an oversight and accountability system to enforce these standards.[110] The standards for teacher quality prohibited teacher "misassignments" (including situations where a teacher lacks subject matter competency or other required training) and teacher "vacancies" (including situations where a classroom has no single teacher and only a string of substitutes). The standards for instructional materials required schools to provide each student with a textbook or instructional materials aligned to state standards. The standards for facilities required buildings to be in "good repair" and required "emergency facilities needs" to be addressed immediately.

The laws also required districts to perform evaluations of their compliance with the instructional materials and facilities standards, to perform reviews of their teacher misassignments and vacancies, and to publicize these evaluations and reviews in annual School Accountability Report Cards. In addition, the laws established a Uniform Complaint Process that enabled parents, students, teachers, and other individuals to file complaints if they believed that schools and districts were not meeting these standards. The laws also provided for changes to the school calendar and hundreds of millions of dollars of additional funds for emergency facilities repairs, facilities assessments, new instructional materials, and programs to place qualified teachers in low-performing schools.[111] These funds were largely targeted at schools that ranked in the bottom three deciles on the API.

Notably, before the settlement was reached, the state already had in place a large number of standards that included a description of the resources that must be provided to students to help them learn the skills and knowledge in the standards.[112] For example, 90 out of 104 standards for history-social science required students to have a textbook or other written instructional materials aligned to the content of relevant standards, many standards addressed the technology and physical materials needed in schools, and California teacher credentialing standards emphasized subject matter competence and knowledge of instructional strategies. Moreover, many of these standards arguably implied that students must be taught in facilities that comply with local health and safety regulations and in settings that are conducive to learning.

By mid-2007, some changes appear to have occurred.[113] For example, while county offices of education found that 20 percent of schools in the bottom three deciles of the API had insufficient textbooks and/or instructional materials in the first year of *Williams* implementation, this percentage decreased to 13 percent in the second year of implementation. County offices of education also reported that, on average, there had been one or more "good repair" deficiencies at 62 percent of schools in the first year of *Williams* implementation and that such deficiencies had decreased to 47 percent of schools in the second year of *Williams* implementation. Moreover, the percentage of fully credentialed teachers in schools in the bottom three deciles of the API increased from 90 percent to 92 percent within two years of implementing the settlement agreement. So, although no court issued a decision in *Williams* that ruled on the merits of the plaintiffs' arguments, the *Williams* litigation centered on school governance and essentially on creating and enhancing OTL standards as well. As a result of this litigation, California enacted legislation containing at least broad standards regarding teacher quality, instructional materials, and facilities to complement the state's content and performance standards, and it has begun to implement this legislation in at least a somewhat effective manner.

THE CONVERGENCE OF SCHOOL FINANCE REFORM LITIGATION AND STANDARDS-BASED REFORMS IN OTHER SCHOOL FINANCE CASES

While the five cases discussed above represent a range of different approaches to the convergence of school finance reform litigation and standards-based reforms, they are by no means the only cases in which this convergence has taken place. Courts hearing school finance cases in other states have begun to consider standards-based reforms in quite similar ways. For example, in Montana, a trial court articulated the tightening relationship between adequacy and standards-based reforms in a very focused fashion. Without directly examining data from tests linked to state standards, the court explicitly linked state standards to a particular level of funding: "A discussion of adequacy involves a determination of funding necessary to produce a specific level of student performance . . . The state must assure that districts have sufficient resources available so that they can reasonably be expected to meet the state's standard concerning student performance."[114] Given this logic, the court relied heavily on a study, conducted by Augenblick & Meyers, a nationally recognized school finance consulting firm, that examined whether the state had provided sufficient funding to enable students to meet state standards.[115] Without explicitly addressing the validity of relying on this cost study and further emphasizing the state's failure to conduct its own study to determine the cost of an adequate education, the state supreme court upheld the trial court's decision on appeal.[116] Indeed, recent school finance decisions generally include at least some sort of discussion about the use of state standards to define adequacy, student performance on tests aligned to these standards, and often the role of an accountability system in helping students receive adequate educations.[117] Still, it should be emphasized that the judicial use of standards to define adequacy has largely occurred in lower courts, and few of the highest courts in states have expressly used standards in this way.[118]

As standards-based reforms have become a ubiquitous feature of state education systems, the reliance on cost studies has become increasingly common. As of 2006, more than 30 cost studies had been undertaken in almost 30 states.[119] While these studies were only ordered by courts in five states, they were initiated by state governments in most of these states, and third parties initiated additional cost studies in 16 of these states. Moreover, although four different methodologies for these studies have primarily been used, these methodologies have at least one important element in common—they largely rely on standards to determine the amount and type of resources to produce an adequate education.[120] The prevalence of states undertaking these studies on their own indicates that states are beginning to make conceptual links between the resources they must provide to support an adequate education and standards.

As indicated by the cases discussed above, courts have begun to follow this reasoning as well—courts located in several states have examined cost studies voluntarily undertaken by others to facilitate an adequacy analysis. Still, some courts have also questioned the validity of the various cost studies and their abilities to interpret these studies in the context of competing methodologies.[121] In addition, some researchers have strongly criticized the cost studies as misleading—these researchers have argued that, while the cost studies have an aura of being scientific, it is simply not possible to precisely determine the amount of funding necessary to provide students with adequate educations.[122] Leveling a strong critique against the various cost studies conducted in the *CFE* litigation, Eric Hanushek argued:

> In the end, the big difficulty with the costing-out exercise is that it purports to provide something that cannot currently be provided: a scientific assessment of what spending is needed to bring about dramatic improvements in student performance. By their very nature such studies provide little information about the costs of achieving improvements efficiently. They contain nary a word about changing the reward structure for teachers (other than paying everybody more). They avoid any consideration of an accountability system based on student outcomes. And they lack any appropriate empirical basis.[123]

So, while cost studies have quickly become an important feature of modern school finance litigation and have become increasingly relevant to judicial decision making as standards-based reforms and school finance litigation have begun to converge, their precise value and the courts' abilities to effectively interpret them remain uncertain.

Other features of the cases discussed above are also fairly common in states and school finance cases across the country. As discussed in Chapter Two, every state currently has in place performance and content standards for students, and accountability systems linked to these standards. Moreover, some states have in place some form of input standards that are tied to content and performance standards to varying extents and that can be construed as relevant to adequacy analyses. For example, in a school finance case in Alabama, a trial court considered provisions in the Alabama Education Improvement Act of 1991 as a "meaningful reference point for assessing minimal educational adequacy."[124] This legislation included standards regarding curricula, educational personnel, and instructional materials. In at least one other state, similar legislation expressly required students to be provided with an opportunity to learn the skills and knowledge contained in state standards.[125]

Even when they have not looked to such legislation, courts hearing recent school finance cases have notably begun to consider the value of particular educational programs besides standards-based reform and accountability policies. Courts hearing school finance cases in at least eight states have ordered their states to institute specific education reforms, including class-size reduction, whole school reform programs, and free preschool programs for "at-risk" students.[126] While the highest courts in all these states have not yet considered or upheld lower court decisions in which these orders were crafted, some state supreme courts have looked favorably on these orders, and it appears as if courts hearing school finance cases may increasingly craft and review such orders. Like orders to implement standards-based reform and accountability policies, orders to implement these other educational interventions appear to respond to many problems that have plagued school finance cases in the past—these orders address problems stemming from the vagueness of legal orders, state actors' political resistance to change, and concerns about the extent to which "money matters" by providing states with very specific actions to take. Recent research on cases that involved the preschool remedy, however, has raised concerns about such orders because courts considered this type of program somewhat inconsistently and at least sometimes with disregard for educational ambiguities and complexities involved with designing and implementing preschool programs.[127] Because the research base underlying preschool appears much more extensive than the research bases underlying the other education reforms discussed above, it is likely that judicial orders addressing other types of specific reforms suffer from similar problems.

Given the importance of this new and increasingly tight relationship between standards-based reforms and school finance reform, one would expect

scholars to have thoroughly analyzed this trend. However, this trend has gar-
nered remarkably little attention from the academic community thus far.
The researchers who have examined this trend have generally commented
from perspectives later echoed or already adopted by the courts discussed
above. A handful of researchers have recommended that courts use standards
and assessments to flesh out educational adequacy because such a move helps
them avoid problems of institutional competency and doctrinal ambiguity.[128]
Other researchers have recommended judicial reliance on standards because
such reliance would make school finance decisions more democratically
legitimate.[129] Yet, Aaron Saiger has criticized this new trend on the grounds
that legislatures actually do not want standards to act as proxies for adequacy
and that precise judicial specification of adequacy robs districts of the opportunity for experimentation with new educational strategies.[130] Michael Heise
has criticized this trend because the courts lack competency to conduct
detailed analyses of education policy and to craft effective remedial orders in
such a technically complex field.[131] And James Ryan has criticized this trend
because the focus on standards may narrow the focus of education reform
efforts; the focus on standards may force the courts to overly rely on test
scores in making adequacy determinations, and the use of standards creates
perverse incentives for legislatures to dilute standards and lower expectations
so that less reform is required.[132]

While the points raised by these researchers are certainly important for
highlighting many of the opportunities and pitfalls inherent in the convergence of educational adequacy and standards-based reforms, these points are
somewhat limited in scope. They generally emphasize that the use of standards-
based reforms to define and measure adequacy can address some of the
primary problems that have long plagued school finance reform cases and
that this use raises certain additional concerns as the school finance reform
movement goes forward. These researchers, however, generally have not
focused on the judicial consideration of standards-based reforms from the
perspective of what this trend means for the standards-based reform movement. Thus, for our purposes, these scholars' points are quite useful for
cementing the theoretical minefield in school finance reform cases and
various cautions that courts acting in this field must navigate. But the perspectives of these scholars are not as useful for understanding the judicial
treatment of standards-based reforms per se.

In short, several state courts ruling in school finance reform cases have
recently begun to take an active stance toward standards-based reforms.
Where the courts examined in previous chapters were often unwilling or too
ill positioned to delve into the technical details of standards-based reforms,

some litigants and courts have found that standards-based reforms can constitute useful tools for defining and measuring adequacy. In doing so, courts have been forced to consider several technical educational issues, such as the meaning of competing cost studies. Still, such litigation has also enabled courts to respond to several long-standing problems that courts across the country had repeatedly faced during decades of school finance reform litigation (and in other areas of education policy), and to think more systematically about the resources *and* governance structures needed to help students learn the skills and knowledge in standards.

To be sure, this trend is somewhat new and by no means pervasive. Many of the courts that have leaned expressly on standards to flesh out adequacy claims were lower courts at the state level, and their opinions do not hold the legal power of those issued by the states' highest courts. Moreover, several of the highest courts in states have not considered or affirmed lower courts' use of standards to flesh out adequacy claims, and in many of the cases examined in this section, courts notably did not order any specific changes in the design or implementation of standards-based reform and accountability policies. But many of the courts discussed in this chapter engaged in a novel and extremely important activity nonetheless—they *reconceptualized* standards-based reforms as a form of governance bound to a state's greater constitutional duty to provide students with an adequate education and as an answer to the persistent problems that courts had persistently faced in previous education cases. In the process of doing so, courts hearing school finance cases considered the value and justifiability of new relationships among the governmental branches in relation to education policy, and perhaps laid the groundwork for a new model of court-based reform in this field.

Discussion and Conclusion

In several recent school finance cases, courts have begun to consider issues central to the purposes and implementation of standards-based reform and accountability policies. For much of its history, school finance litigation primarily focused on the equality and adequacy of the funding provided to schools. However, as courts continued to rule in school finance lawsuits around the country, as litigants' legal arguments changed, and as the education policy landscape shifted, courts increasingly began to consider arguments related to standards-based reform and accountability policies. While funding is still the primary focus of school finance litigation, arguments about these policies have begun to play critical roles in school finance cases. Thus far, standards-based reform and accountability policies have emerged in the context of school finance litigation in three major ways. First, legislatures have established such policies in order to ensure that students receive constitutionally adequate educations. Second, some courts have used standards and assessments aligned to these standards to define and measure adequacy. Third, some courts have construed these policies as tools that can help states provide students with opportunities to receive adequate educations. Indeed, the shift in school finance litigation to include an examination of educational outputs and of policies focusing on outputs comports with broader trends in education policy since the 1970s.

These recent school finance cases are similar to the high-stakes testing cases and cases aimed directly at influencing the implementation of NCLB in several major ways. Plaintiffs have generally brought such cases in response to the effects of governmental policies on poor and minority students. As in some of the cases directly aimed at influencing the implementation of NCLB, the recent school finance cases have generally involved the broad, system-wide performance of education systems—although judges and plaintiffs in these school finance cases construed standards-based reform and accountability policies differently, they generally construed such policies as a central part of a state's attempt to increase system-wide performance. In this respect, the recent school finance cases reflect the shifting perceptions of reformers about the relationship between accountability and the equality and adequacy of educational opportunities.

Recent school finance litigation also appears to involve many of the same sorts of problems that emerged in high-stakes testing litigation and in NCLB-related litigation. Like the legal frameworks employed by courts in these other types of litigation, the legal frameworks in school finance litigation are vague in key respects—despite their normative appeal, adequacy and equality are ambiguous concepts that can be defined in a number of ways. Moreover, plaintiffs in many recent school finance cases presented courts with a huge amount of complex and competing scientific arguments about empirically uncertain issues, which constituted important evidence in these cases. In the context of vague legal requirements, judges considered such evidence inconsistently. For example, the judges ruling in *CFE* and *DeRolph* were presented with several cost studies relating levels of resources to state standards and accountability systems, and the courts' interpretations of these studies varied dramatically. Similarly, courts addressed the implementation of standards-based reform and accountability policies in quite different ways. While Judge Botsford deeply examined the implementation of such policies in

Massachusetts, the *DeRolph II* majority construed the purposes and problems of these policies in a very detailed and nuanced fashion but did not deeply examine the implementation of these policies in schools or at other administrative levels. Many other judges simply looked at the legal requirements in place that governed these policies. Notably, in the cases examined in this chapter, a judge never conducted a detailed examination of teachers' actual instructional practices and the alignment of these practices with state standards.

The remedial orders crafted by courts to address constitutional violations were similarly inconsistent. The remedial orders of some courts focused on various elements of standards-based reform and accountability policies, ranging from the financial resources needed to implement these systems or to produce certain levels of achievement, to other remedial orders focused on the implementation of particular educational interventions. Still, other remedial orders broadly focused on the establishment of accountability systems linked to standards. Given the capacities of courts to understand complex educational information, vague legal requirements, and the often stormy political contexts in which these orders were crafted, such variation makes much sense. With so many factors influencing judicial decision making in this area and few precise guidelines, it is likely unrealistic to expect judges to define the role of standards-based reform and accountability policies, to examine these policies, and to address problems that have faced these policies in a more consistent fashion.

Like the legal frameworks employed by courts in the cases examined in the previous chapters, the frameworks employed in recent school finance cases also failed to focus courts on some important problems facing standards-based reform and accountability policies. For example, although the validity of testing practices is an important element of a well-functioning standards-based accountability system, judges ruling in school finance cases have not systematically focused on this issue. Given the state-level focus of school finance litigation, courts involved in this litigation also have not focused on problems implementing standards-based reform and accountability policies that stem from the federal level or that result from the federalist structure of the U.S. education system. And although state standards are of varying quality and sometimes low, courts in these cases generally have not focused on the quality of these standards. The use of standards to define adequacy has constituted one of the primary legal moves shaping the convergence of school finance reform litigation and standards-based reform, and this use of standards has helped courts overcome major problems courts have faced in several previous school finance cases. If judges were to deeply examine and question the quality of state standards, it would become more difficult to justify the use of standards to define educational adequacy. Indeed, although Judge Manning briefly examined the quality of the North Carolina standards, he displayed a great amount of deference to the state when deciding upon the justifiability of the standards.

ADVANTAGES OF ADDRESSING STANDARDS-BASED REFORM THROUGH SCHOOL FINANCE LITIGATION

Viability of Adequacy Litigation

Still, there are several critical differences between the courts' treatment of standards-based reform and accountability policies in school finance litigation and the courts' treatment of these policies in the other forms of litigation examined throughout this book. Despite problems that school finance litigation has persistently faced, recent school finance litigation focusing on adequacy appears increasingly viable. Several courts have recently found plaintiffs' arguments about the adequacy of education systems persuasive—state courts do not appear to have exhausted their reformist impulses in the same ways as federal courts ruling in desegregation and high-stakes testing cases. The emergence of issues regarding standards-based reform and accountability policies in school finance litigation appears to have contributed to the continuing viability of adequacy arguments. While some researchers have pointed out that the use of these policies to support school finance litigation entails certain problems (such as involving the courts in technical matters of education policy and creating perverse incentives for legislatures to lower standards), this use also has helped to eliminate other problems (such as courts struggling to define adequacy by themselves). To the extent that judges understand these policies as ultimately helping states meet their constitutional responsibilities and enhancing the effectiveness of school finance litigation, a form of litigation that has significant normative appeal but has long been inconsistently effective, judges will likely continue to be receptive to arguments about these policies in the context of school finance litigation. So, on balance, this convergence appears to offer much utility for litigation involving standards-based reform and accountability policies. Again, the convergence of standards-based reform and adequacy litigation is still at an early stage and is by no means pervasive. But this convergence appears to have offered courts certain advantages in school finance lawsuits and will likely continue so long as judicial analyses remain grounded in the problems of the past.

State-Level Character of Adequacy Litigation

The state-level character of school finance litigation also enhances its viability as a form of litigation that enables courts to more effectively consider arguments about standards-based reform and accountability policies. While the federal government established several requirements governing standards-based reform and accountability policies with Goals 2000, the IASA, and NCLB, policymakers have structured these laws to devolve significant authority for designing and implementing these policies to states. Despite important problems facing standards-based reform and accountability policies that stem in part from federal requirements (such as the lack of funding to construct the administrative infrastructure for NCLB implementation), the structure of these laws has made it very difficult for courts to address such problems in litigation directed against the federal government. The state-level character of adequacy litigation, however, tightly fits with the structure and political compromises underlying the laws governing standards-based reform and accountability policies. While litigation focusing on the design and implementation of these policies at the state level cannot easily address problems that stem from federal decision making, this form of litigation at least accords well with the ways in which responsibility for administering these policies has been allocated across governmental units as these policies took hold in the U.S.

Fit between Underlying Concepts of Standards-Based Reform and School Finance Reform Litigation

Even more importantly, the shape of the legal concepts underlying adequacy litigation well matches the central principles underlying standards-based reform. The concepts of standards-based reform and adequacy both aim at providing students with the educational opportunities they need to learn substantive skills and knowledge. Where standards-based reform aims at providing students with the education embodied in content standards, adequacy lawsuits aim at providing students with the education embodied in the education clauses of state constitutions. In addition, the notion of aligning policies to substantive skills and knowledge is central to both concepts—enhancing policy coherence is a primary goal of standards-based reform, and courts ruling in school finance suits have repeatedly emphasized the importance of rationally aligning policy decisions, such as those governing funding and curricular materials, to concrete specifications of skills and knowledge. In this way, the major legal concepts underlying adequacy litigation sharply contrast with those underlying high-stakes testing litigation

—while the equality-based concepts underlying much high-stakes testing litigation also hold significant normative appeal, the imperfect fit between these concepts and those underlying standards-based reform policies has ultimately hampered courts' abilities to effectively address these policies in high-stakes testing litigation.

The courts' focus on educational resources in adequacy litigation highlights the tight fit between the conceptual shapes of adequacy and standards-based reforms. Adequacy litigation has long focused on the sufficiency of educational resources to ensure that students receive a certain type and level of education. While the concept of resources in school finance litigation originally centered on funding, this concept has expanded to include various physical resources (such as curricula), educational programs and systems of governance (such as standards-based accountability systems), and educational personnel (such as teachers and administrators). Thus, the notion of resources in school finance litigation has essentially collapsed into the notion of opportunity to learn pervasive in many theories of standards-based reform, and courts and litigants in school finance cases such as *Williams* and *Hoke* have expressly construed resources in such terms. The *DeRolph II* court even expressed concerns about implementing an accountability system without ensuring that such opportunities are in place, and Governor Spitzer echoed similar concerns in the aftermath of *CFE* litigation. While courts ruling in such cases have by no means agreed upon a definition of resources or opportunity to learn, these concepts have clearly played (and will likely continue to play) a central role in adequacy litigation. Indeed, this focus on resources or opportunities to learn, particularly for poor and minority students, also seems to accord with one of the primary advantages of the courts—the courts have long acted as an institution that can protect the rights of such students where the political process fails. By focusing on resources or opportunities to learn, the courts can continue to act in this vein.

The courts' focus on large-scale structural and institutional-level change in adequacy litigation also highlights the tight fit between the conceptual underpinnings of this form of litigation and standards-based reform and accountability policies. Because state constitutions place legal responsibility for providing students with adequate educations at the state level, adequacy litigation naturally focuses on broad-based education reform rooted in governance structures. Most major theories of standards-based reform and accountability systems similarly focus on structural changes in governance structures at the state level, and as discussed above, a substantial amount of authority for designing and implementing these reforms has in fact resided at the state level. The historical convergence of adequacy litigation and these policies reflects this shared focus on deep changes in education governance at the state level. Since *Rose* was decided, both types of reform efforts have become intertwined not just in judicial decisions, but also in legislative responses to these decisions (such as in Kentucky's KERA or Massachusetts' ERA). Recent school finance cases similarly reflect this convergence by construing the structural changes entailed by standards-based reform and accountability policies as issues susceptible to judicial analysis through an adequacy-based legal framework.

In some cases, the institutional reform goals of both reform efforts have become so tightly linked that courts in adequacy suits have framed major problems hindering the fundamental changes entailed by standards-based reform and accountability policies as problems also preventing states from providing students with adequate educations. Instead of examining only classroom and school level inputs to determine students' educational opportunities, judges have also examined educational resources that extend to higher administrative levels, such as governmental capacities to implement standards-based reform and accountability policies and effective educational leadership—Judge Botsford expressly discussed the lack of capacities at the district and state levels in Massachusetts to implement reform strategies, and Judge Manning expressly addressed the value of principals for increasing student achievement in North Carolina in relation to standards. In *DeRolph II*, the Ohio Supreme Court discussed the necessity of ensuring that educational personnel have the necessary capacities to provide students with the opportunities to learn the skills and knowledge in standards. The litigation in both *Hancock* and *Williams* included significant attention to the alignment between instructional materials and state standards. The *CFE* litigation focused on ways to ensure oversight and accountability, and the referee's report (which was fully adopted by Judge DeGrasse) included recommended adjustments to New York's existing accountability system to more closely track the educational opportunities actually available to students.

Although a court did not issue a formal ruling with precedential value in *Williams*, this case vividly demonstrates the increasingly tight linkages between the reforms in governance entailed by standards-based reform and accountability policies and that entailed by adequacy litigation. As Judge Busch stated, this case was primarily about the management and oversight of California's education system—in this litigation, a well-functioning governance and accountability system was construed as crucial for providing students with adequate educations. Moreover, the changes in governance sought by the plaintiffs were tightly linked with the notion of resources or opportunities to learn. The plaintiffs construed the management and oversight system as one that should ensure that students receive the substantive educational opportunities needed to provide them with adequate educations—the plaintiffs specifically pushed for the creation of more standards governing the resources that students need as the heart of this system. Indeed, the focus on tracking the opportunities available to students in the *CFE* litigation parallels the plaintiffs' requests in *Williams*. Certainly, the laws enacted by California after the *Williams* settlement agreement do not necessarily reflect a nuanced or scientific approach to such opportunities to learn; as discussed in Chapter Two, providing students with opportunities to learn is not simply a matter of aligning curricula or assuring that facilities are in decent repair, and the school review and complaint procedures established by these laws do not necessarily constitute an effective accountability system for ensuring that students receive sufficient opportunities to learn. However, *Williams* at the very least demonstrates the extent to which the notions of resources, OTL standards, content standards, and changes in governance have begun to blur into each other in the context of adequacy litigation.

Knowledge of Historical Problems and New Relationships among Governmental Branches

Although some problems that have persistently plagued judicial action in education emerged in recent adequacy-based litigation involving standards-based reform and accountability policies, this litigation also appears to have helped some courts avoid many other major problems that they have persistently faced. As discussed above, courts in recent adequacy cases exhibited difficulties dealing with technical, educational evidence. But expressly cognizant of the value of increased information for decision making in adequacy cases, some judges examined a substantial amount of information from the administration of various tests and standards-based accountability systems. Although student performance data certainly does not point to precise problems facing the design or implementation of standards-based reform and accountability policies, persistently low student performance can help make the case that these policies are not having their desired effects. Such data can accordingly focus courts on specific areas in which the policies are not having the desired effects and frame a deeper examination of policies in these areas.

This is exactly what occurred in *Leandro* and *Hancock* as both Judge Manning and Judge Botsford heavily relied on such data to focus their analyses and give them a sense of the "bottom line" effectiveness of standards-based reform and accountability policies. In light of such data, the judges conducted deeper examinations of the particular problems facing the implementation of these policies. In these cases, both judges engaged the extensive evidence much as a policy analyst would by crafting uncommonly long opinions focused on making sense out of various types of data. Precisely because education policies were moving toward increased collection and dissemination of information, these judges were able to conduct detailed analyses of these policies and avoid one of their greatest problems from a historical standpoint—the lack of information generally available for judicial decision making. As a result, these judges were able to actively address significant problems that they had historically faced.

Given the history of school finance litigation, courts presented with cases relying on legal theories traditionally used in such litigation also appeared especially sensitive to the political problems that have historically acted as barriers to education reform. Judges in several adequacy cases exhibited an awareness of the often weak responses of states' legislative and executive branches to remedial orders in school finance cases, and these judges underscored the likely lack of leadership and political will exhibited by these branches for education reform. As noted above, by highlighting these problems and requiring them to be fixed, the judges exemplified one of the strongest advantages of courts—where the political branches fail to fulfill certain policy goals due to political opposition or lack of political will, the courts can constitute an alternative institution that can consider these policies in a more evenhanded way and boost the effectiveness of actions taken to fulfill these goals.

Given their awareness of and increasing attention to problems that they have persistently faced, courts have additionally begun to engage in new modes of action by forging new relationships with other governmental branches. Recognizing their comparative lack of institutional capacities to decide technical educational issues, some courts looked to other governmental branches to help flesh out the vague constitutional requirements of adequacy. In this sense, these courts relinquished some degree of authority for constitutional decision making to other governmental branches (which clearly concerned some judges in these cases). At the same time, some courts broadly framed the effective implementation of standards-based reform and accountability policies as part of states' constitutional duties, which effectively gave these courts more authority over education policies than they had in the past. Some courts additionally highlighted broad areas that merited particular attention of these other branches, such as opportunities to learn the skills and knowledge in standards, or the capacities of educators to teach in accordance with standards. Still, these courts usually did not offer specific prescriptions for states' failure to implement these policies effectively—they generally put pressure on other governmental branches to determine exactly what a well-functioning governance system would look like and to determine the amount and types of resources necessary to support such a system. In this respect, some courts used their legal and political muscle to broadly frame the reform agenda, highlight educational problems that needed to be addressed, and enforce policies set by other governmental branches, but these courts also leaned on other branches to flesh out and implement specific plans for addressing these problems.

Notably, this type of process did not always occur in the cases discussed above. For example, although Judge Botsford deeply delved into Massachusetts' implementation of standards-based reform and accountability policies and issued broad recommendations for remedial orders, the state's highest court did not follow these suggestions. This court was willing to let the state proceed with its plan of "pragmatic gradualism" and gave a great deal of deference to the state's attempts at education reform. While the Ohio Supreme Court repeatedly reviewed its state's responses to judicial orders, this court refused to retain jurisdiction in *DeRolph III* and ultimately withdrew from the case a couple years later. Nonetheless, both cases present examples of an ongoing dynamic between courts and other governmental branches of broadly crafting, fleshing out, and implementing a reform strategy, as even *Hancock* was brought to address the implementation of the standards-based reform and accountability policies established in response to the broad remedies ordered by Massachusetts' highest court in *McDuffy*.

In short, recent school finance cases have increasingly begun to involve the sorts of problems that litigants and courts have highlighted in the high-stakes testing cases and in cases directly aimed at NCLB. Like *Pontiac v. Spellings* and *Connecticut v. Spellings*, some recent school finance cases have focused on the amount of funding it takes to help students learn the skills and knowledge in standards, and these cases have focused more broadly on the resources needed to provide students with sufficient opportunities to learn such skills and knowledge. These cases have also focused on the alignment of education policies around standards, the changes that such standards entail at various administrative levels, and the importance of an oversight or accountability system to ensure that such changes take place. And even where these cases centered on the concept of adequacy, they largely focused on protecting poor and minority students.

In these cases, courts faced some major problems that they have also faced in high-stakes testing cases and in cases directly aimed at NCLB—in the context of competing scientific arguments and vague legal requirements, these courts often addressed standards-based reform and accountability policies inconsistently and construed the resources students need to learn in various ways. However, recent adequacy cases also involve several critical differences. Due largely to the viability of the applicable legal frameworks, the fit between these frameworks and purposes and problems of standards-based reform and accountability policies, and judicial awareness of historical problems that courts have repeatedly faced, some litigants and courts appear to have avoided many problems that have plagued other cases in this area. Moreover, some courts have used their legal and political power to highlight major problems standards-based reform and accountability policies have faced and to frame reform agendas around remedying such problems. In this way, some courts have begun to form new relationships with other governmental branches. To be sure, the convergence of school finance litigation and standards-based reform and accountability policies is quite recent and still inchoate; the highest courts in states generally have not yet addressed or affirmed the ways in which standards-based reform and adequacy have begun to converge, and it is unclear how courts will continue to rule in future suits that are similarly oriented. This form of litigation, however, appears to hold much promise for judicial engagement with these policies. The following chapter addresses how courts should rule in this area as such litigation moves forward and the implications of using this form of litigation to become more deeply involved with the intricacies of standards-based reform and accountability policies.

CHAPTER SIX

Conclusion

We are now at a critical time for both U.S. education policy and the courts' involvement with this policy. Over the course of the 20th century, the number and complexity of education policies at both state and federal levels greatly increased and significantly changed the education policy landscape. Although many of these policies were transitory and rarely had a lasting impact on the core of what is taught and learned in schools, some of these reforms were longer lasting and directly aimed at changing this core. Standards-based reform appears to be one of the most durable of these policies. Since it emerged in the 1980s, standards-based reform has become significantly blended with accountability polices and has been implemented in every state and at the federal level. Given that standards-based reform and accountability policies are aimed at changing fundamental structures of education governance that have long been in place, they have generated significant attention, including strong praise and strong criticism, from a variety of different sectors.

Although the courts have long been involved in education, their role in education policy has markedly changed and intensified since the mid-20th century as well. As this book is being written in early 2008, the courts have become deeply involved with the details of a variety of education policies, notably including those governing standards-based reform and account-ability systems, and have increasingly considered cases involving the funda-mental institutional structures of the U.S. education system. While judicial action in education policy has effected desirable change in many respects, such as the Supreme Court's mandate in *Brown v. Board of Education* to desegregate public schools, judicial action in this sphere has also faced sig-nificant and recurring pitfalls, and has accordingly generated significant praise and criticism as well.

Independently, standards-based reform and accountability policies and the courts' involvement in education entail several potential challenges and opportunities. Their recent convergence, however, significantly raises the stakes in a field where the stakes are already high. Since the courts started to become involved with these policies, they have arguably become more deeply involved with the intricacies and technical details of education policies that are aimed at influencing instruction than they have at any time in the past. At the same time, the courts have found themselves addressing some of the most fundamental issues and problems that have surrounded these policies since they emerged on the policy landscape. Moreover, in recent cases involving standards-based reform and accountability policies, the courts have found themselves at a crossroads vis-à-vis both their role in policymaking and the purposes of education policy—both the courts and education policymakers have become increasingly focused on the performance of educational institutions and have become less focused on issues of educational equity. How the courts negotiate their historical and contemporary roles and consider the purposes of the U.S. education system more broadly has the potential to ultimately influence the strength and types of learning opportunities available to students. As such, we are at an important historical moment that could dramatically influence the course of modern education policy and perhaps the courts' involvement in social policy more generally.

This final chapter offers concluding thoughts about the courts' involvement with standards-based reform. First, this chapter includes an overview and an analytical summary of the previous chapters to bring together the analyses presented throughout the book. Second, this chapter examines the implications of the analyses in this book against the backdrop of the courts' historical and more recent involvement with public law litigation in other fields. Third, based on these analyses, this chapter recommends an approach for the courts to take moving forward and discusses the limitations of this approach. Finally, this chapter offers a few final words about the importance of attending to the courts' continuing role in education policy.

Overview and Analytical Summary

Since standards-based reform emerged in the U.S., it has become pervasive and has influenced the education policy process in venues ranging from legislatures and courtrooms to classrooms. Standards-based reform entails an increased focus on student achievement, a relocation of decision-making processes in education, and the alignment of education policies with substantive specifications of the skills and knowledge that students are to learn. By focusing on such educational elements, standards-based reform is aimed ultimately at ensuring that more high-quality content and instruction are delivered to students. In its modern incarnations, standards-based reform also entails a significant focus on holding students and schools accountable for their academic performance, which is generally measured by standardized tests. Given the focus on strengthening instruction and content and on accountability for performance, many theories of standards-based reform have included a significant focus on students' opportunities to learn the knowledge and skills described by content standards.

On one hand, standards-based reform and related accountability policies appear to have generated significant changes in the U.S. education system. All states have enacted standards-based reform and accountability policies, and the federal government has become perhaps more involved in education policy than at any other point in its history in its efforts to encourage and shape the development of these policies. Physical resources, such as curricula, have begun to become aligned with state standards, and while classroom instruction has remained somewhat difficult to alter, some alignment between instruction and state standards appears to have occurred. Accountability mechanisms appear to have focused educators on more equitable instruction, and the data from these mechanisms have begun to provide for increased transparency in the educational process.

On the other hand, several serious problems have emerged. Educational personnel at various levels appear to have lacked necessary technical knowledge and skills, such as the administrative knowledge needed to support instructional practices in schools that are aligned to standards. A number of administrative and instructional personnel similarly appear to have lacked the financial and physical resources needed to support the instructional changes in all schools and to support a well-functioning infrastructure for the administration of accountability systems required by No Child Left Behind (NCLB). Without such resources, states have found it particularly difficult to implement valid testing practices. Various political forces have also had a significant impact on standards-based reform and accountability policies. Educators and administrators have sometimes lacked the political will to change their instructional and administrative practices to support student learning in a way that reflects challenging standards, especially in schools in high-poverty areas. Indeed, one of the biggest blows to the standards-based reform movement was arguably a political one—in the context of substantial political pressure, opportunity to learn standards (OTL standards) under the Goals 2000: Educate America Act (Goals 2000) were never created, and several groups of students continue to lack the opportunities they need to learn the skills and knowledge detailed by state standards. While NCLB devoted some attention to students' opportunities to learn with provisions such as those governing highly-qualified teachers and support for low-performing schools, the notion of opportunity to learn has largely faded from the political discourse. Moreover, the federalist legal and political structure of the U.S. governmental system has resulted in state standards of dramatically different quality and in accountability systems that have defined adequate yearly progress (AYP) quite differently.

While states have made significant progress instituting certain elements of standards-based reform and accountability mechanisms required under state and federal law, fundamental features of teachers' instructional practices and students' opportunities to learn have accordingly proven difficult to alter. And while standards-based accountability policies may have exerted some desirable pressure on educational personnel and students to improve and have highlighted inequities in the U.S. education system, these policies also appear to have exerted significantly more pressure on high-poverty and urban schools than other types of schools. Given such pressures, modern standards-based accountability systems, in part required by NCLB, appear to have exacerbated educational inequities in key respects, especially in places where it is unclear whether the capacities are in place to help all students learn the skills and knowledge embodied in standards. Complicating the analysis even further, the complex interaction between these capacities, the requirements of standards-based reform and accountability policies, and the effects of various political forces, has made it quite difficult to determine the effects of these policies on student achievement.

In response to such issues, several groups of plaintiffs have sued various governmental entities and have enabled the courts to address various facets of standards-based reform and accountability policies. In line with the historical use of the courts as a venue where traditionally underrepresented groups can have their claims about education heard, concerns about the inequitable conditions of education and the related effects of standards-based reform and accountability policies drove many of these lawsuits. Some litigation, however, was substantially different—while some lawsuits focused on ensuring that accountability systems were fully implemented, other lawsuits focused on the more diffuse burden placed on educational personnel and institutions by standards-based reform and accountability policies. The litigation involving standards-based reform and accountability policies thus reflects a much changed landscape of educational litigation. Because the ultimate purposes of these policies are focused on increasing the performance of schools and the achievement of all students by fundamentally changing education governance structures and the processes of educational institutions, these policies can mean different things to different groups, and there is much room for rational disagreement about the desirability or efficacy of these policies.

Still, certain common issues repeatedly emerged in these lawsuits—though their analyses were in large part framed by litigants' legal strategies and relevant precedent, courts often focused on students' opportunities to learn, the validity of testing practices, the resources available for instruction and administration, and the theoretical underpinnings of these policies as tools that can boost the educational performance of educational institutions and all students.

In addition to the similarity of the legal issues addressed by the courts, the problems faced by the courts in these lawsuits were similar in several important respects. Much of this litigation revolved around vague legal language and complex educational issues that yielded few clear answers—several cases were characterized by conflicting expert opinions and evidence about "facts" in the educational world. In the context of ambiguous legal requirements and the prominent place of expert testimony and scientific evidence, educational and legal standards often blurred. Given the courts' inherently limited capacities to interpret scientific evidence and limited guidance provided by the legal frameworks applicable to the lawsuits brought by plaintiffs, courts made decisions about such educational issues in a very inconsistent fashion.

For example, in the context of high-stakes testing litigation, various courts construed the concepts of curricular validity and opportunity to learn very differently—these courts looked upon different types of evidence as persuasive for establishing whether students were receiving their required opportunities to learn and for establishing whether testing practices had curricular validity. Similarly, courts in adequacy cases construed the relationship between resources and student achievement in relation to state standards quite differently, especially when presented with competing cost studies, and they inconsistently considered the relationships between different education reforms (e.g., free preschool) and the overall performance of state education systems. In the cases directly aimed at NCLB, the courts similarly had few precise legal frameworks to guide analyses of fundamental problems facing NCLB, such as whether and/or how the law was insufficiently funded. Indeed, where the courts addressed extremely technical educational issues, such as the validity of NCLB testing practices and methods for determining AYP, the courts generally deferred to the decisions of other governmental branches. In some cases, the courts assumed that other governmental entities had discharged their duties by simply instituting laws addressing policy problems and did not deeply examine the extent to which such laws were effectively implemented or effected intended change. Thus, much of the litigation aimed at influencing the course of standards-based reform and accountability policies does not appear to have well positioned courts to address major issues related to these reforms.

In some cases, the types of litigation brought by plaintiffs and the legal frameworks accordingly employed by courts simply did not seem to support judicial intervention at all. In the high-stakes testing context, it has become increasingly difficult for plaintiffs to make out persuasive claims that testing practices with disparate impacts result from intentional discrimination or preserve the effects of prior segregation because much time has passed since the last applicable instances of *de jure* segregation. Given recent Supreme Court rulings, it has also become extremely difficult to enforce Title VI of the Civil Rights Act, and many federal courts seem to have lost their will for continuing involvement in education policy. Together, these legal developments have eviscerated the continuing viability of high-stakes testing litigation, historically the flagship type of educational litigation for addressing problems related to large-scale testing practices. Moreover, while high-stakes testing litigation has produced orders that have focused on the validity of testing practices, it generally has not produced orders that have directly addressed the causes of low and inequitable performance, or the failure of states' policies to effectively address these causes.

In the cases directly aimed at influencing NCLB, an array of factors has similarly limited the efficacy of legal frameworks to support judicial action, including the Supreme Court cases governing Section 1983 actions, the combination of the federalist division of authority underlying NCLB and the doctrine of standing, and the language of the specific NCLB provisions on which plaintiffs have focused their arguments. While the Sixth Circuit's decision in *Pontiac v. Spellings* indicates that some of these legal hurdles may ultimately be surmountable, the efficacy of this form of litigation to address standards-based reform and accountability policies in a holistic and nuanced way appears quite limited.

The types of litigation brought by plaintiffs and legal frameworks accordingly employed by courts to address standards-based reform and accountability policies also have not focused courts consistently on fundamental issues facing these policies. For example, while the high-stakes testing frameworks were very effective at focusing courts on issues related to the validity of testing practices, these frameworks have proven much less attuned to building the various capacities needed to change practices at the classroom and school levels. These frameworks also have shown little potential to address problems stemming from the division of political authority for deciding issues related to standards-based reform and accountability policies, such as the varying quality of state standards and states' varying methods for determining AYP. Litigation aimed directly at NCLB has faced similar problems—much of this litigation has focused on surface problems facing accountability systems (e.g., the bare failure of school districts to fully implement the choice sanctions), and with a few exceptions (e.g., *Pontiac v. Spellings* and *Connecticut v. Spellings*), this litigation has not directly focused on the various capacities needed to implement this policy effectively. Even in such litigation, courts appear to have focused more on the capacitites needed to institute the administrative infrastructure for NCLB rather than the capacities needed to boost students' opportunities to learn. Adequacy litigation has proven insufficient in some of these respects as well. For example, this form of litigation has not focused courts on problems stemming largely from federal action or the quality of state standards.

Still, there were several aspects of litigation involving standards-based reform and accountability policies that appear to have been desirable for enhancing the justifiability and effectiveness of these policies. Both adequacy litigation and high-stakes testing litigation centering on curricular validity have broadly focused courts on key aspects of standards-based reform and accountability policies that have proven extremely difficult to implement. This type of high-stakes testing litigation has directly addressed students' opportunities to learn in relation to the content covered on tests. Adequacy litigation has directly addressed the various resources devoted to enabling students to learn the skills and knowledge in standards. Indeed, courts engaged in adequacy analyses have often construed the resources available to students in terms of students' opportunities to learn. Given this focus on providing students with the opportunities to learn needed in relation to substantive specifications of knowledge and skills, both types of litigation have also focused courts on the alignment of education policies and resources—in order to ensure that students are provided with the necessary opportunities or resources, courts have examined the extent to which policies governing various educational elements, such as textbooks, are aligned with state tests or standards. While litigation focusing on the design and implementation of these policies at the state level cannot easily address problems that stem from federal decision making, this form of litigation at least accords well with the ways in which responsibility for administering these policies has been allocated across governmental units as these policies took hold in the U.S.

Perhaps more importantly, the shape of the legal concepts underlying adequacy litigation well matches the central principles underlying standards-based reform. As discussed in Chapter Five, the concept of adequacy and historical focus on resources naturally dovetail with the notion of opportunity to learn. This focus on resources or opportunities to learn in school finance cases well accords with the historical role of the courts as a protector of the rights of underrepresented groups. Moreover, adequacy litigation has long focused on large-scale structural and institutional change, which is precisely the sort of change entailed by standards-based reform and accountability policies. In some recent adequacy cases, courts directly focused on the administrative changes needed at various levels and the capacities to make such changes, and the institution of standards-based accountability systems, as key to ensuring that students receive adequate educations. Although *Williams v. State of California* did not result in a decision with precedential value, this case vividly highlights the ways in which adequacy litigation has begun to focus on the institutional change needed to ensure that students have opportunities to learn in relation to substantive sets of skills and knowledge.

Given recent developments in adequacy litigation, this form of litigation also appears well suited for helping courts avoid many of the major problems that have plagued previous litigation in education. Due to the operation of standards-based accountability systems, courts have had a significant amount of information available to them in recent adequacy cases. While such data does not point to precise problems facing the institution of standards-based reform and accountability policies, it has focused some courts on specific areas in which the policies have not had their desired effects and has framed a deeper examination of policies in these areas. Some courts hearing adequacy cases have also demonstrated a marked sensitivity to the problems that have historically acted as barriers to education reform. For example, judges in several recent adequacy cases have discussed the often weak responses of other governmental branches to remedial orders in public law cases. Indeed, by focusing on such problems and requiring them to be fixed, the judges exemplified another advantage of the courts—where governmental entities fail to fulfill important policy goals for lack of political will, the courts can constitute an alternative institution that can consider these policies in a more evenhanded way and boost the effectiveness of actions taken to fulfill these goals.

Based on such express statements about other governmental branches and an awareness of their own limitations, some courts in adequacy cases have begun to engage in new modes of action by forging new relationships with other governmental branches. These courts have reallocated the authority for making educational decisions in various ways, such as by relying on other branches to flesh out vague adequacy standards. Moreover, some of these courts have highlighted areas that needed additional attention, such as educational resources needed at various levels, and have examined the extent to which states were complying with their duties under standards-based reform policies that they had already enacted. So, aware of various problems that they had historically faced (e.g., their lack of technical capacity and vague legal standards) but also aware of their particular capacities (e.g., their ability to focus political attention and the utility of aligning the actions of governmental branches to effect deep institutional change), some courts in adequacy cases have begun to engage with standards-based reform and accountability policies in a very nuanced way—these courts have focused political attention on fundamental problems facing these policies and have broadly framed the duties of governmental entities in this area while expressly deferring more precise decisions to other governmental branches. Although this type of litigation is clearly at its nascent stages as of this writing and has not been widely and expressly addressed by states' highest courts, it appears to hold a great deal of promise for positioning the courts to address the major issues, such as the lack of systematic attention to students' opportunities to learn and the penetration of reform across administrative levels, facing standards-based reform and accountability policies moving forward.

Public Law Litigation Outside of Education

Although this book has focused on how the courts have become involved with a particular area of education policy, it is important to situate litigation in this field in the broader context of litigation that has occurred in different domestic policy fields. After *Brown v. Board of Education*, public law litigation emerged around the country in various areas of domestic policy. In these areas, the courts faced problems that were similar in some major ways to those faced by the courts in education. An analysis of the courts' actions in other areas of public law litigation may accordingly yield useful insight into the courts' roles in both education policy and recent public law litigation efforts across the domestic policy spectrum more generally. Moreover, such an analysis can help frame the recommendations for the courts' involvement with standards-based reform in a way that is sensitive to current trends in public law litigation.

Since public law litigation proliferated around the U.S., this form of litigation has exhibited certain strengths and weaknesses, and in partial response to examinations of its effectiveness, has begun to undergo a sort of transformation. While some public law litigation has clearly resulted in desirable effects (such as the Supreme Court's decision that segregation in public schools is unconstitutional), critics have repeatedly attacked this form of litigation as ineffective and unjustifiable. Although this book has extensively dealt with common problems that courts have faced in public law litigation that have limited the courts' effectiveness, this book has dealt much less with theoretical questions of justifiability about such judicial action. Such questions, however, have also plagued this type of litigation since the beginning.[1] Judicial actions in public law litigation do not easily comport with traditional notions of the judicial role or the separation of powers. Moreover, there have been significant doubts that legal modes of analysis are fundamentally suited for restructuring institutions or organizations. As such, the Supreme Court, various appellate courts, and even the U.S. Congress have expressed their concerns and limited the courts' authority in public law litigation.

In light of the problems public law litigation has faced and the criticisms leveled at it, the form of this litigation has recently begun to change in several areas of domestic policy. In an influential article published in 2004, Charles Sabel and William Simon described this shift in great detail.[2] In a range of public law cases in various domestic policy areas, including housing reform, mental health reform, police reform, prison reform, and education reform, courts have begun to move away from the traditional model of public law litigation. Under the traditional model of public law litigation, courts largely identify problems in institutions that affected underrepresented groups and subsequently issue top-down commands to fix such problems. Many desegregation cases and early school finance cases reflect this traditional model—the remedial phases of these cases involved wide-ranging orders from courts and continuing judicial oversight of administrative details. Many affected actors resisted such orders, and courts often responded with increasingly authoritative and fine-grained commands about actors' legal responsibilities. Given the quite visible problems courts have historically faced in such litigation, some courts have begun to change their modes of decision making. Under novel models of public law litigation, courts have begun to move toward a more experimentalist form of intervention that has emphasized ongoing stakeholder negotiation, continuously revised performance measures, and increased transparency of institutional actions. According to Edward Rubin and Malcolm Feeley, this newer form of structural reform litigation represents a significant advance over previous forms—this form of litigation accounts for the administrative and bureaucratic character of the modern state, and the ways that judicial power can influence this state.[3]

Expanding upon the place of courts in this modern state, Sabel and Simon articulated the concept of "destabilization rights"—"claims to unsettle and open up public institutions that have chronically failed to meet their obligations and that are substantially insulated from the normal processes of political accountability."[4] In public law cases involving such rights, courts initially destabilize the parties' prelitigation expectations about the ways in which institutions are supposed to operate and accordingly open up the possibilities for collaboration among the parties and different governmental branches. Regimes of standards and monitoring often emerge from remedial negotiations and allow reform to continue—under this model, courts are necessary to destabilize institutions that have consistently failed to fulfill their duties as defined by minimum standards in a particular policy area. After a finding of liability, judges do not simply exercise their discretion in choosing from a wide range of possible remedies; they instead supervise a process of negotiation among parties and stakeholders, and this process results in periodic revisions of rules in light of ongoing monitoring. Commenting on this trend, Helen Hershkoff indicated that judicial decrees from such litigation establish a structure for institutional reform but do not fix the precise content of reform—such decrees articulate goals and methods of monitoring institutional performance, but not the precise policies to be enacted.[5]

Public law litigation in the field of prison reform is one of the most developed examples of this type of judicial activity and has been discussed in depth by Feeley and Rubin.[6] Beginning as early as the 1930s, reformers highlighted the horrible conditions of many prisons and brought lawsuits to remedy such problems. While such lawsuits were initially unsuccessful, federal courts in the 1960s began to find that prison conditions constituted cruel and unusual punishment in violation of the Eighth Amendment. In these cases, federal courts proceeded to define the problem at hand as not just the treatment of individual prisoners but also as the outdated institutional structure of prisons that allowed, and perhaps even encouraged, such treatment.

For example, in *Holt v. Sarver*, a landmark prison reform case that began in the 1960s, Judge Henley found that the "totality of the conditions" of Arkansas prisons violated the Eighth Amendment.[7] Because Arkansas and its prison officials lacked the will and capacity to address these conditions, the task fell to the court to systematically transform the institutional conception and structure of prisons in the state. Largely based on the ambiguous constitutional prohibition of cruel and unusual punishment under the Eighth Amendment, Judge Henley developed broad goals for Arkansas prisons and deeply involved prison officials in a process to craft detailed plans and implement these plans. As the process of prison reform continued, new problems continually emerged, and these new problems highlighted increasingly fundamental problems, such as the capacities of various entities to change. By the time the case was finally dismissed in 1982, prisons in Arkansas had fundamentally transformed into a public agency or "system" with a commissioner, wardens, and staff who were accountable to rules and regulations like personnel in other public agencies.[8]

Similar patterns of prison reform have emerged around the country, as 48 of the 53 jurisdictions in the U.S. declared prison conditions unconstitutional by the mid-1990s.[9] Throughout these cases, federal courts engaged in long periods of supervision of prisons, and the cases involved very detailed consent decrees that even included issues such as the wattage of light bulbs. However, throughout the litigation process, the courts increasingly relied on highly reputable prison officials and experts to provide guidance for ongoing reform. Moreover, the courts extensively drew from standards already enacted by two highly reputable sources—the American Correctional Association and the U.S. Bureau of Prisons—that were aimed at increasing professionalism in prison administration and ensuring that prisoners were properly treated to articulate a new institutional model for prisons.

According to Feeley and Rubin, the existence of such standards constituted a major incentive for decision makers to define and address the fundamental structural problems of prisons. In the prison reform cases, the courts largely required prison officials to honor the standards already enacted by two authoritative organizations in the prison field. Moreover, administrative entities emerged in several states to monitor prison conditions. As Feeley and Rubin noted, the courts in the prison reform cases were acutely aware of their institutional limitations, and the interaction with and adoption of standards passed by other governmental entities and external organizations with greater expertise in prison reform greatly reduced the disadvantages of judicial action in this field.

Recent prison reform cases also reflect a mode of litigation that involves litigants and emphasizes experimentalist action to a greater extent. For example, in the 2002 case *Sheppard v. Phoenix* that involved use-of-force practices in New York City jails, the parties agreed that the Department of Corrections would develop new policies under the guidance of two experts in the field within broad the broad limits of a "stipulation."[10] The court in this case emphasized the need for a process of ongoing revision and monitoring instead of the precise content of the policies. In the context of this new type of litigation, the Department of Corrections developed detailed policies and monitoring structures and revised their polices as problems emerged, and the court dismissed the stipulation based on improvement in relevant performance measures. In short, some courts have begun to move from a model of reform focusing on individual rights to one focusing on institutional performance, and have experimented with new relationships among litigants and governmental branches, grouped around the concept of standards and monitoring, in order to effect such changes.

According to the limited number of researchers who have deeply considered this new form of public law litigation, it has several advantages over previous types. Some researchers have argued that such litigation in fact fits well within traditional conceptions of the judicial role and the separation of powers.[11] The growth of the administrative state since the New Deal has altered views about the pace and scope of doctrinal intervention, and has recharacterized doctrine as very flexible and continually evolving in response to changing circumstances.[12] In this administrative state, the role of the courts becomes primarily to reinforce accountability structures, which comports well with the notion that the judicial role should be limited. While I do not devote more attention to the theoretical justifiability of such judicial action here, it is worth noting as an area that should continue to receive attention as the judicial role in public law litigation continues to mature and change. Moreover, although this form of litigation has emerged quite recently, it appears more effective than previous forms of public law litigation.[13] For example, the nuanced approach taken by the courts in the prison reform cases, drawing on institutional norms largely generated from within the correctional community and eventually embraced by the various governmental branches, appears to have significantly reformed the institutional structure of prisons and improved the treatment of prisoners.[14]

Such developments across areas of domestic law and policy can shed much light on what has begun to transpire in litigation involving standards-based reform policies. The forms of litigation characterizing high-stakes testing and cases directly aimed at NCLB appear to conform to a fairly traditional litigation model (and not necessarily a public law litigation model). High-stakes testing cases have been largely aimed at protecting students' rights through the normative structure of equality, and many cases aimed at NCLB were similarly focused on protecting underrepresented student groups from the potentially harmful effects of standards-based reforms and accountability policies. While some litigation aimed at NCLB was more sensitive to the notion that these policies have been aimed at reforming the institutional structure of the U.S. education system, the structure of this type of litigation generally has not comported with the new model of public law litigation—this litigation was not focused on establishing a process that involved the litigants and governmental entities to ensure that fundamental structural reform occurred effectively.

Recent adequacy cases, however, comport to a great extent with the new model of public law litigation. Sabel and Simon pointed to recent adequacy litigation as an example of destabilization rights in action, and Liebman and Sabel focused on the value of such litigation for generally restructuring the U.S. education system.[15] So, the basic structure of litigation that has emerged in recent adequacy cases involving standards-based reform appears to be qualitatively different on a fundamental level than much previous education litigation and other major sorts of litigation involving standards-based reform. In addition, such judicial action appears to have been at least somewhat effective in other contexts (like prison reform) and accordingly suggests that such action in education may be more effective than the courts' previous reform efforts in education.

In turn, the developments in adequacy litigation can shed much light on the new model of public law litigation emerging across domestic policy fields. Adequacy litigation is highly dependent on systems of standards and monitoring largely enacted by legislative and executive entities. In their work on prison reform, Feeley and Rubin emphasized the utility for courts of looking to standards created by non-judicial entities and enforcing them instead of focusing on new areas or types of reform. Specifically focusing on this form of litigation in education, Liebman and Sabel looked favorably on Texas' standards-based reform and accountability policies, and underscored the utility of NCLB for helping courts rule more easily in adequacy cases and for coordinating the actions of various governmental branches. However, given the analyses in this book, these assessments of the new model of public law litigation seem incomplete—while the implementation of standards and accountability mechanisms is critical to new forms of public law litigation, this book has highlighted that such policies can entail some very serious problems as well; without significant attention to the problems of standards and accountability, the fundamental tools of the new form of public law litigation may generate new problems just as they are aimed at solving old ones. If courts address only the problems of old institutions without deeply considering and highlighting potential problems of new institutions and of the tools of governance that these new institutions entail, new forms of public law litigation ultimately may not create desirable change across policy fields.

Of course, courts in recent adequacy cases have not simply used standards-based reform and accountability policies to leverage education reform with an uncritical eye. Many of these courts have, to some extent, highlighted specific areas in which these policies needed to be more effectively implemented. For example, the plaintiffs in *Williams* pushed the court to require the creation of new OTL standards and a linked monitoring system in light of the failure of the existing standards-based reform and accountability policies to effect desired changes on the institutional structure of California's education system. In the high-stakes testing cases and cases aimed directly at NCLB, courts also focused on many problems that such policies have faced. So, instead of simply concerning themselves with reforming old educational institutions, some courts have also begun to address the problems of new educational institutions and of new tools of governance. Indeed, the ways in which courts have addressed such new institutional models and governance tools is precisely what this book is all about. While looking to systems of standards, monitoring, and accountability to destabilize certain institutions appears to be a useful strategy for courts to take, courts also need to critically consider the purposes and effects of such systems in the precise contexts in which they are implemented. Because similar issues may be present in several domestic policy areas in which new forms of public litigation have emerged, researchers, litigants, and courts should critically consider the courts' activities in these areas to determine not just if the courts should jumpstart or help speed the reform of old institutions, but should address the problems of new institutional structures and tools of governance as well.

Given the courts' recent attention in adequacy cases to such problems, adequacy cases constitute an important example for understanding how the concept of destabilization rights can be modified. On one hand, recent adequacy cases may simply reflect a mature stage of the new form of public law litigation or of destabilization rights in action; such litigation involves experimentalist action and a process that periodically revises the rules governing education policy (though, recent changes in these policies have largely resulted from legislative action). On the other hand, new adequacy cases may reflect something more appropriately characterized as "meta-destabilization" rights. Under this formulation, some courts in adequacy cases initially looked to systems of standards and accountability to flesh out ambiguous constitutional responsibilities and to reform the traditional institutional structures of states' education systems. But as these courts continued to address standards-based reform and accountability policies and as problems with these reforms emerged, some courts also began to turn their attention to the problems of these policies—problems that were in part grouped around issues of equity, and that remained unresolved and largely unaddressed by legislatures. In other words, some courts ruling in adequacy cases have begun to destabilize policies that were themselves being used to destabilize educational institutions.

Because it is difficult to definitively determine whether standards-based reform and accountability policies can and will produce their desired changes, construing recent adequacy cases as involving meta-destabilization rights appears to be quite useful—this characterization encompasses the notion that standards-based reform and accountability policies can be effective tools of governance for institutional change, but that these policies themselves also need significant attention from the judiciary if desirable change is to occur. In other words, it is not enough for new forms of litigation to predominantly focus on institutional reform; such litigation should also continue to incorporate the courts' historical focus on the rights of underrepresented groups and individuals to ensure that the reform efforts themselves do not harm the groups these reforms are in part aimed at helping. The efforts of courts ruling in adequacy cases to not simply use standards and tests to define and measure adequacy, but also to address problems in standards-based reform and accountability policies themselves, have just begun, and it is unclear how courts will proceed from here. But so long as courts take a nuanced approach to systems of standards and accountability that result from careful consideration of the courts' strengths and weaknesses in the context of particular legal frameworks, court-centered efforts may help speed the type of change needed in both education and other domestic policy institutions as well.

Recommendations for Court-Based Approaches to Standards-Based Reform

Given the analyses in the previous chapters of the courts' involvement with standards-based reform policies, this book now turns to recommendations about how the courts and future litigants should proceed from here. Any recommendation for the courts and future litigants should account for several different types of factors that have influenced the courts' actions in this field, including the institutional characteristics of courts, the types of arguments that litigants bring before the courts and the educational problems highlighted by these arguments, and the legal frameworks and precedent that courts are able to employ to evaluate these arguments. Moreover, any recommendation should attend to the major extant research in education policy. The analyses conducted throughout this book have attended to these various elements, and the recommendations are accordingly sensitive to these elements as well.

One possible course of action entails the withdrawal of the courts from standards-based reform and accountability policies—litigants could stop bringing claims about these policies, and the courts assigned to such cases could refuse to take an active hand in these policies by consistently deferring all major decisions about these policies to other governmental branches. Indeed, courts have ruled that some of the legal frameworks at play in litigation aimed at standards-based reform are insufficient to support judicial action, and courts could well decide that they are not competent or justified to make precise education policy decisions. In light of the courts' institutional strengths and weaknesses, and the array of problems that they have historically faced in education policy, leaving standards-based reform and accountability policies to the legislative and executive branches is perhaps a wise course of action. When major decisions about these policies have been largely left to legislative and executive entities, however, these policies have faced a range of significant issues, fallen short of accomplishing their goals in several respects, and resulted in a range of unintended consequences. Such problems continue to plague the implementation of standards-based reform and accountability polices. If the courts can mitigate such problems while engaging in theoretically justifiable legal action, the courts should take a more active hand.

While the analyses throughout this book suggest that there are several barriers to effective judicial action in this field, there are also several indications that these barriers are not insurmountable. Accordingly, with an extremely careful and nuanced approach that is sensitive to the problems the courts have historically faced in education policy and broader trends in public law litigation, the courts can likely have a positive role to play in the implementation of standards-based reform and accountability policies.

USING ADEQUACY LITIGATION TO STRUCTURE A COURT-BASED APPROACH TO STANDARDS-BASED REFORM

Given the analyses conducted throughout this book, recent school finance reform litigation focusing on adequacy should constitute the foundation for a court-based approach to standards-based reform and accountability policies. In particular, adequacy litigation involving new relationships among and new distributions of educational authority across governmental branches should provide the basis for this new approach. As discussed above, this type of litigation appears able to maximize the strengths and minimize the weaknesses of the courts in the area of standards-based reform (and education policy more generally) to a significant degree. Moreover, this approach would position the courts to engage in a judicial process that accords with the new model of seemingly more effective public law litigation.

As an initial step, litigants should bring an adequacy lawsuit aimed at educational resources or focused exclusively on standards-based reform and accountability policies, and litigants should attempt to establish the connection between adequacy and these policies—litigants should argue that these policies are critical to ensuring that students receive adequate educational opportunities because these policies are states' primary tools for ensuring educational adequacy and are the primary types of policies aligned with the concept of adequacy. In this sense, such litigation would initially look much like that in *Williams*, and to a large extent, many other recent adequacy cases that focused on management and governance structures as critical to ensuring adequate educational opportunities. To be sure, some courts in recent adequacy cases have been reluctant to explicitly equate state standards with constitutional adequacy, and most state supreme courts have not expressly considered this issue. However, such a legal move may not be absolutely necessary; for the practical purpose of addressing problems in states' education systems, several courts have acted as though adequacy and standards are related without expressly equating the two. If faced with arguments directly addressing the relationship between standards-based reform and accountability policies and adequacy, many courts may proceed in this vein.

Once the relationship between adequacy litigation and standards-based reform and accountability policies is established, both courts and litigants should focus the litigation on certain major problems that these policies have faced. Given the problems that these polices have faced, the historical structure of adequacy litigation, and the courts' institutional characteristics, such litigation should particularly focus on the penetration of standards-based reform across administrative levels (and ultimately into the classroom), and on ensuring that all students receive sufficient opportunities to learn in relation to the skills and knowledge embodied in standards.

Focus Litigants and Governmental Branches on the Penetration of Reform

The focus on the penetration of reform across administrative levels should be designed to address at least two major problems that have prevented the more consistent penetration of standards-based reform and coordination of education policy elements—a lack of political will and a lack of various types of capacities to implement reform mandates. The courts can address both of these problems by broadly serving as a forum for fleshing out the needed changes across administrative and instructional levels, the capacities required for such change, and the disconnect between intended change and the change that has actually occurred. Simple judicial attention to such issues may help speed the process of administrative, and ultimately instructional, change— the courts have historically constituted an institution that can legitimize and focus attention on important educational issues, and can provide needed intervention when the actions of other branches have proven unable to overcome political inertia. By using the courts as a venue to address the capacities needed for such change, the courts can expressly direct the attention of the litigants and other branches to ensuring that such capacities are put in place to increase the coordination of policy elements across a range of administrative and instructional levels.

But given the difficulties courts have faced when addressing technical educational issues with only vague legal guidance, the courts must proceed very carefully in this area. Determining precisely what capacities need to be in place at a variety of levels and the resources needed to support the development of these capacities is an extremely difficult and technical task. In order to account for their historical problems in making such determinations, the courts should structure the litigation in a way that reflects a new model of public law litigation—the courts should lean on the litigants and other governmental branches to figure out the substantive details of reform and focus on effectively framing the litigation process (as opposed to running the litigation process in a way that results in the largely independent judicial construction of detailed, top-down remedies). That is, the courts should direct the other governmental branches and litigants to determine precisely what changes are necessary and the capacities needed for such changes, and should use the litigation process as a way to focus all the branches on these changes and ensure that the branches comply with their duties.

In this respect, the litigation process should be a very organic one that draws on the evenhandedness and legal and political muscle of judicial action to cut through political inertia, and that draws on the expertise and capacities to run day-to-day affairs of other branches, to better ensure that reform more effectively penetrates administrative levels in a coordinated fashion. In light of the problems that standards-based reform and accountability policies have faced, such litigation would likely involve consideration of educational elements such as increased financial resources, high-quality professional development, perhaps analogous support for principals, the development and adoption of curricula aligned to state standards, and more consistent and effective support for schools to improve and change their instructional practices in relation to these standards. Again, in light of the problems associated with top-down specification of reform strategies in public law litigation, especially as such specifications draw closer to the classroom level, courts should focus on framing the litigation process and ensuring that other branches flesh out and comply with their duties to effectively implement standards-based reform across administrative levels. If the courts can properly motivate (or provide political cover) for other branches and entities to engage in such activities, the courts will significantly speed the reconstitution of states' education systems in accordance with the principles of standards-based reform.

Focus Litigants and Governmental Branches on Students' Opportunities to Learn

In addition to focusing on the penetration and coordination of reform across administrative levels, litigation aimed at standards-based reform should focus on the opportunities to learn available to students in relation to the skills and knowledge specified by state standards. As discussed throughout this book, standards-based reform and accountability policies appear promising for restructuring the U.S. education system, but these policies also have had undesirable effects on various underrepresented student groups, especially in the absence of concerted attention to these students' opportunities to learn. As such, opportunities to learn have constituted a central focus of litigation involving standards-based reform and accountability policies, especially where policies attach significant consequences to low student or school performance. Because judicial consideration of opportunities to learn has been so inconsistent (in large part due to judicial capacities to deal with complex educational information and ambiguous legal frameworks), judicial consideration of opportunities to learn in the context of adequacy litigation should occur in a highly nuanced way that accounts for the major problems courts have historically faced.

Given the ways in which new relationships among the governmental branches have begun to develop in adequacy litigation, one would hope that states (or the federal government) would have already initiated legislative and administrative processes to determine and precisely articulate the opportunities to learn necessary to support student learning in accordance with state standards—by drawing on such opportunity to learn specifications and using them to flesh out states' duties, courts could avoid some of the problems stemming from their lack of educational expertise and of precise guidance in this area. As discussed in Chapter Five, however, few states have expressly articulated such specifications. A significant part of the reason for states' failure to do so can be traced back to political sources—political resistance to the creation of OTL standards resulted in the deletion of the major legal provisions in Goals 2000 encouraging the development of these standards at both the state and federal level. Judicial action should be undertaken in light of this specific problem.

In particular, courts focused on standards-based reform and accountability policies should push the other branches to develop such OTL standards and frame the process for doing so as integral to providing students with adequate educations (as largely defined by state content standards). Then, the courts should enforce the OTL standards that states themselves have created through an ongoing interaction between the governmental branches and litigants in a way that reflects the new model of public law litigation. This type of action would well accord with the comparative advantages of the courts and the other governmental branches—by focusing the attention of other governmental entities on the development of OTL standards, the courts would draw on their institutional capacity to focus the attention of policymakers on an important area that has received too little attention largely because political will has been historically lacking. At the same time, the courts would place the authority to make precise decisions about the substantive content of OTL standards in the hands of entities with theoretically higher educational expertise and would therefore minimize the problems of deciding such issues themselves with only the barest legal guidance.

In this way, the courts would engage in a form of litigation involving "meta-destabilization" rights—conscious of their institutional strengths and weaknesses, the courts would highlight serious problems in the existing tools of institutional reform and would require these problems to be addressed as institutional reform continues to occur. Moreover, the courts would continue to use standards, backed by governmental authority, as a general tool for institutional reform, and the courts would still focus on making sure that governmental entities comply with duties that they had developed and agreed to themselves. Finally, by focusing on the opportunities to learn of under-represented students in addition to the penetration and coordination of reform across administrative levels, the courts would bridge their historical role as a protector of underserved students with a modern role as a facilitator of institutional reform. Of course, litigants in such a lawsuit would maintain significant influence over the way in which the courts ultimately address standards-based reforms—the litigants would be responsible for raising the array of arguments necessary to support judicial analyses and remedial orders in the way discussed above, and the cooperation of the litigants would be required to engage in a collaborative litigation process. However, the steady hand of judges would be required to oversee the process in a way that protects and enhances the interests of various stakeholders.

THE HISTORICAL SIGNIFICANCE OF COORDINATED GOVERNMENTAL ACTION IN EDUCATION

Although the focus on coordinating the actions of the governmental branches well accords with recent trends in public law litigation across domestic policy areas, such coordination has historically proven effective at leveraging fundamental changes in education governance as well. While desegregation occurred slowly in the years after the Supreme Court decided *Brown v. Board of Education* in 1954, the pace of desegregation rapidly increased in the late 1960s and early 1970s. During this time, the legislative and executive branches stepped up their efforts to desegregate schools—the passage of the Civil Rights Act of 1964, the passage of the Elementary and Secondary Education Act (ESEA) in 1965, and the willingness of the Johnson administration to enforce the Civil Rights Act, in addition to judicial orders to desegregate schools, spurred quicker changes in education governance than perhaps at any other time in U.S. history.[16] Indeed, laws such as the Civil Rights Act and the ESEA were in part constructed to flesh out precise mechanisms for fulfilling the broad goals articulated in the desegregation decisions of federal courts.

The coordination of governmental branches has notably proven effective in the early stages of adequacy litigation and standards-based reform as well. As discussed in Chapter Five, *Rose v. Council for Better Education* resulted in the legislative establishment of one of the country's first standards-based reform and accountability policies in Kentucky. Before *Rose* was decided, the conditions in Kentucky appeared ripe for such reform—given the poor state of education in Kentucky at the time, actors in the non-judicial branches in the state appeared ready for comprehensive education reform, and non-governmental entities, such as business leaders, also supported such reform.[17] After *Rose* was handed down by the Kentucky Supreme Court, the state legislature quickly enacted the Kentucky Education Reform Act, which included a significant focus on standards-based reform and accountability. In this case, the state supreme court appeared to provide a sort of political cover that allowed for the coordination of reform efforts across governmental branches and other policy actors in the state. The convergence of standards-based reform and accountability policies and adequacy litigation in recent cases potentially sets the stage for more of this type of coordinated governmental action.

Given the utility of this type of governmental action in the past and the current development of new patterns of governmental action in adequacy cases, some other researchers have also made recent calls for the adoption of this general sort of strategy. Focusing on the advantages of increased information and transparency in the educational process spurred by NCLB, James Liebman and Charles Sabel have also called for courts to use adequacy litigation to coordinate governmental action.[18] However, in contrast to the recommendations discussed above, Liebman and Sabel largely called for courts to enforce the duties that other governmental branches had already taken upon themselves—not for courts to highlight areas, such as students' opportunities to learn, that require additional attention or to push the other branches to develop standards in these areas.

Michael Rebell, a researcher and practitioner of education law, similarly called for a "colloquy" of governmental branches in the context of adequacy litigation. Rebell, however, did not specify the precise ways in which the branches should coordinate their actions or the functions that should be undertaken by these branches.[19] Instead, Rebell, largely called for researchers to conduct analyses of the comparative institutional strengths and weaknesses of the different branches in various educational contexts in order to determine precisely how such a colloquy should be structured to address educational opportunities. Given this book's focus on the development and implementation of standards-based reform and accountability policies and judicial action in this field, this book represents a partial answer to Rebell's call. This book includes a detailed consideration of how legislative and executive entities have treated these policies, and it includes detailed analyses of how the courts have addressed such policies. Thus, the coordination of the governmental branches appears to be a very useful tool for addressing the problems of standards-based reform and accountability policies through the courts in light of the history of education reform, recent trends in public law litigation, and the institutional structure of the courts more generally.

LIMITATIONS OF THE RECOMMENDATIONS

Of course, in an area as complex and historically difficult as reforming fundamental aspects of the U.S. education system, the recommendations discussed above entail some significant limitations. The complexity of the subject matter of this book requires all intellectually honest recommendations to be tentative—the recommendations are drawn from analyses of very complex and varied data that are in turn drawn from several differently oriented historical, legal, and qualitative sources. Moreover, although this book focuses on the courts, it is impossible to consider the merits and problems of the courts in hermetic isolation from the other branches because their actions have been so intertwined in this field.

Compounding such complexities, the education policy landscape is somewhat of a moving target. As this book is completed in early 2008, the U.S. Congress has begun to consider the reauthorization of NCLB, but the final shape and requirements of the new law are unclear. In light of recent political rumblings, it appears that NCLB will change in some key respects but that its fundamental policy logic will remain in place—while the methods of measuring AYP and the precise shape of the accountability sanctions may be changed, it currently appears that the reauthorization will still include a significant focus on standards-based reform and holding schools accountable for performance, and will devolve a substantial amount of authority to states to make decisions in these areas. To the extent that the law changes in these fundamental respects, the recommendations included above are certainly limited and would need to be tailored to the new education policy landscape. However, assuming that the law does not change in these fundamental respects, the recommendations included above would still apply—the recommendations are largely aimed at increasing the general effectiveness and mitigating the undesirable consequences of standards-based reform. Even if Congress were to change the law to involve significantly weaker requirements for states, the recommendations would still apply to the states that continue to implement standards-based reform with a significant focus on accountability.

The recommended approach may also run into some theoretical hurdles. As mentioned above, the theoretical justifiability of the new model of public law litigation has been attacked as a potential violation of the separation of powers principle and of the traditional judicial role. While some researchers have countered that the new model of public law litigation is in fact theoretically justifiable for reasons such as the modern demands of the administrative state, this issue has not been (and may never be) conclusively resolved. Because the recommendations in this book comport in many respects with a new model of public law litigation, the recommendations may be limited as well—to the extent that courts consider such new models as theoretically unjustifiable in the future, these recommendations will be significantly limited and perhaps inapplicable (though, notably, the new form of public law litigation has fared fairly well thus far). Given the importance of both education reform and public law litigation more generally, constitutional researchers should continue to consider this issue as efforts to restructure institutions through litigation mount.

On a more concrete level, the recommendations would not enable the courts to effectively address certain significant issues that have consistently plagued the implementation of standards-based reform and accountability policies. Because the concept of adequacy is so broad, plaintiffs could theoretically make persuasive arguments that courts ruling in adequacy cases could address an almost limitless range of educational issues. However, as this book highlights throughout, the courts have rarely, if ever, been well positioned to address all the educational problems highlighted by plaintiffs. Given that adequacy litigation forms the basic frame for the recommendations, the recommendations are also limited to the extent that adequacy litigation has been generally limited for addressing standards-based reform. For example, although the courts may be legally justified to address problems such as the validity of testing practices, the structure of AYP determinations, and the content of state standards through an adequacy-based framework, it is difficult and likely unwise for the courts to second-guess legislative and administrative entities on such technical questions. As emphasized above, the courts should especially shy away from overspecifying remedies for problems residing close to or at the classroom level. Moreover, the recommended approach would not well position courts to address problems stemming from the federal level decisions (e.g., lack of federal funding for NCLB implementation or strong NCLB accountability mechanisms) that are arguably poorly designed to yield intended results. These sorts of limitations of adequacy litigation are discussed in detail in Chapter Five.

If the courts and litigants were to adopt the recommended approach, there is also no guarantee that such litigation would effectively coordinate the actions of the governmental branches and other relevant policy actors. For example, in *Rose*, it appears that various policy actors in Kentucky wanted to engage in education reform before the Kentucky Supreme Court's decision was handed down. Such political conditions may not be easily reproducible in many states, and courts' abilities to cut through political inertia may not be strong enough to facilitate coordination if other policy actors are not already committed to reform to at least a certain extent. Even if the governmental branches can manage to work together in a more coordinated fashion, there are other factors that can significantly influence the policy process that are likely beyond the courts' reach. History has shown that the political will of various "street level" implementers (e.g., teachers and principals) and communities at large are critical for implementing policy effectively across administrative levels.[20] While the coordinated actions of governmental branches may have the potential to influence politics at these local levels, it would not obviate the need for political persuasion through channels that are subtler than legal ones. In addition to formal judicial, legislative, or executive action, interested parties respected by local actors would likely need to become more involved and coordinate their actions with governmental entities.[21] For example, the National Education Association could play an integral role in persuading teachers and principals of the value of altering instructional practices. By aligning the spectrum of broader institutional influences on education, including unions, educators' groups, and states, significant reform at local levels would become much more likely than reform driven by governmental actors alone.

The recommended approach is also limited due to the knowledge needed to effectively boost students' opportunities and increase educators' capacities. One theme that has persistently appeared throughout this book is the lack of knowledge currently available about translating resources into specific achievement levels. This problem is by no means restricted to courts; this problem would significantly influence any attempt by any legislative or executive entity to specify OTL standards or the capacities needed by various governmental entities to ensure that reform penetrates consistently across administrative levels. For example, as discussed in Chapter Five, the laws enacted by California under the *Williams* settlement agreement that addressed opportunities to learn required changes involving textbooks, teacher quality, and facilities. Laws enhancing the quality of the rules governing these various educational elements are certainly desirable. But given the significant gaps between these laws and the various problems of standards-based reform discussed throughout Chapter Two, it does not appear that these laws came close to specifying the opportunities to learn that students need in relation to the skills and knowledge specified by California state standards.

The questionable quality of cost studies similarly illustrates the lack of knowledge available to all the governmental branches. These studies offer seemingly objective analyses to governmental entities about translating resources into student learning in accordance with state standards. But where there are competing cost studies that involve different methodologies and assumptions and that often yield quite different conclusions, it is difficult for any governmental entity to craft scientifically justifiable policies regarding educational resources and opportunities on the basis of such studies. Governmental entities face similar problems specifying the capacities they need at higher administrative levels to implement the administrative infrastructure needed to support standards-based reform and accountability polices—there has historically been limited research about the capacities needed at such levels and the precise resources needed to develop such capacities.

In this respect, the limitations of the recommendations underscore the need not just for increased coordination among the governmental branches but also for more educationally justifiable policies that are based on detailed attention to research. The reauthorization of NCLB represents a hugely significant moment for boosting the effectiveness of standards-based reform and accountability policies. If the U.S. Congress and U.S. Department of Education (ED) can enact and implement a new version of the ESEA in a way that addresses many of the problems highlighted in this book and by other educational researchers, the future for the U.S. education system will look rosier. For example, by crafting more justifiable mechanisms to measure AYP, by developing national standards, and by altering the shape of NCLB accountability mechanisms, the federal government may be able to address pervasive problems that standards-based reforms have faced. If state legislatures and administrative entities can similarly enact better policies and implement such policies more effectively, the U.S. education system will only benefit. As this book demonstrates, the courts can have a vital role to play in standards-based reform and accountability policies and in leveraging fundamental changes in the U.S. education governance structure, but the courts cannot come close to completing such changes by themselves. Governmental branches at both state and federal levels must commit not just to working together more effectively and building political momentum for difficult change, but also to increasing the substantive quality of their education policies.

Although increasing the quality of education policies and decision making more generally across governmental branches is very difficult in light of limited knowledge, there are some promising developments that suggest we may be moving in the right direction. Most notably, the federal government has begun to focus on the notion of "scientifically-based research" in education. NCLB included this phrase 111 times to describe the types of programs that must be implemented by schools to help improve student performance.[22] The Reading First program in NCLB has provided grants for reading programs in partial accordance with recommendations that can be traced back to a report from the National Reading Panel, a prestigious, federally appointed panel comprised of educational researchers and practitioners.[23] In addition, the U.S. Congress passed the Education Sciences Reform Act (ESRA) in 2002.[24] This law authorized the creation of the Institute for Education Sciences (IES), the research arm of ED, included legal standards for scientifically-based research in education, and required all research funded by ED grants to comply with such standards. IES also created the "What Works Clearinghouse" in 2002 to review various educational programs and to report on their scientific justifiability.[25]

Since these various developments focusing on the scientific underpinnings of education policies have emerged, many of them have come under heavy attack. For example, charges of bias have riddled the Reading First program, and NCLB has been attacked for failing to specify precisely what constitutes scientifically-based research.[26] The ESRA has also been attacked by several educational researchers for defining scientific research in an overly narrow fashion and for usurping decisions that should be made by the scientific community.[27] The problems such policies have faced are very serious, and policymakers clearly need to do much work to ensure that these policies are better designed and implemented. But these problems should not obscure the broader point that policymakers have begun to make serious efforts to develop more scientifically justifiable policies and to encourage research that can spur such policies. Indeed, if the policies addressing education research are better designed and implemented, they would dovetail well with the above recommendations—such policies could help specify opportunities to learn in a more precise and justifiable fashion, and courts could look to programs and research vetted by such policy mechanisms as relevant and appropriate attempts by other governmental branches to specify these opportunities to learn. Again, policies governing scientifically-based research in education currently leave much to be desired. However, coordination not just among the governmental branches, but also the governmental branches and the research community, is necessary for the development and implementation of policies that can effect desired and fundamental changes in the U.S. education system.

In short, given their various limitations, the courts cannot effectively address standards-based reform and accountability policies by themselves. But if litigants and the courts take a nuanced approach to these policies, the courts appear able to improve the fate of current reform efforts. When looking to the courts to address standards-based reform and accountability policies, litigants should structure their arguments around adequacy claims. In the context of such litigation, courts should frame the reform process by articulating broad constitutional principles and by highlighting areas of reform that need additional attention, such as opportunities to learn. Then, courts should engage in a process that incorporates other branches to ensure that such principles are more specifically fleshed out and, in turn, implemented effectively. By framing and managing such a process in the context of adequacy litigation, the courts would draw on their capacity for evenhanded analysis and ability to overcome political inertia, especially with regard to underrepresented groups, and would employ a legal framework that is well attuned to many of the major problems faced by standards-based reform and accountability policies. In doing so, the courts would initiate and engage in the type of governmental coordination that has proven effective in the past in education and is currently proving effective in other areas of domestic policy. Moreover, if laws governing scientifically-based research in education are better designed and implemented in the future, they should become integrated with the courts' efforts at leveraging reform because they could draw scientific knowledge into a process that has often lacked a robust scientific base. In this way, the courts could help bring about governance changes at fundamental levels of the U.S. education system while better ensuring that all students are well served by such changes, and could thereby bridge their historical role as a protector of equal rights with support of modern policy initiatives aimed at boosting the institutional performance of the U.S. education system.

A Final Word

As many have noted, reforming schools is a very difficult task. Education reforms have come and gone, and have often done very little to influence the institutional structure of schools and ultimately teaching and learning at the classroom level. Despite such problems, standards-based reform and accountability policies have proven very durable. While reasonable minds can differ about whether these types of policies are desirable and can produce the sorts of changes needed to improve the U.S. education system, it is difficult to argue that these reforms have no promise at all or do not appear here to stay for the foreseeable future. To be sure, the institution of such policies is not the only route to education reform—we can implement (and are implementing to some degree) various promising education policies, such as free preschool for all students in certain areas. But standards-based reform and accountability policies constitute an especially important route for change insofar as they aim at fundamental structures underlying the U.S. education system. Given the amount of energy we have already devoted to these policies, we should devote the energy to make these policies as well designed and implemented as we possibly can and see whether they can produce their desired effects.

In order to achieve this goal, we will need much perseverance and a willingness to experiment with new modes of policy change. This book focuses on only one small piece of the debate in this field—the interface between the courts and standards-based reform policies. At times, this interface may appear somewhat abstract or to reside in venues far removed from classrooms. But this interface also appears to be a critical one for the future of standards-based reform policies; although they have only begun to address these policies, the courts appear to constitute a key force for ensuring that these policies are designed and implemented to the best of our limited abilities. Hopefully, this book will help us think more deeply about the role of the courts in leveraging such policy change so we can ultimately provide stronger and more equitable educational opportunities for all students across the country.

FREQUENTLY USED ABBREVIATIONS

AERA Standards	Standards for Educational and Psychological Testing
API	Academic Performance Index
AYP	Adequate Yearly Progress
ED	U.S. Department of Education
ESEA	Elementary and Secondary Education Act
Goals 2000	Goals 2000: Educate America Act
HQT	Highly-Qualified Teacher
IASA	Improving America's Schools Act
KERA	Kentucky Education Reform Act
LEP	Limited English Proficiency
MALDEF	Mexican American Legal Defense and Educational Fund
MCT	Minimum Competency Test
NAEP	National Assessment of Educational Progress
NCLB	No Child Left Behind Act
NCTM Standards	Curriculum and Evaluation Standards for School Mathematics
NEA	National Education Association
NYSED	New York State Education Department
NRA	Negotiated Rulemaking Act
OTL Standards	Opportunity to Learn Standards
PDE	Pennsylvania Department of Education
Title VI	Title VI of the Civil Rights Act of 1964

Chapter One

1 *Brown v. Board of Education*, 347 U.S. 483 (1954).

2 No Child Left Behind Act of 2001, 20 U.S.C. § 6301 et seq. (2002).

3 Susan Fuhrman, "Introduction," in *Redesigning Accountability Systems for Education*, ed. Susan Fuhrman and Richard F. Elmore (New York, NY: Teachers College Press, 2004).

4 For example, in *Debra P. v. Turlington*, 644 F.2d 397 (5th Cir., 1981), a federal court examined the justifiability of a state testing practice that hinged students' ability to graduate from high school on the results of a test. At the time, the state had not yet enacted standards. This case and other cases regarding the judicial examination of testing practices before states enacted standards-based reforms are discussed further in Chapter Three.

5 There are arguably several different types of capacities, such as financial resources and technical knowledge, that entities need to effectively implement standards-based reforms. These capacities are discussed in detail in Chapter Two.

6 Michael Heise, "Equal Educational Opportunity by the Numbers: The Warren Court's Empirical Legacy," *Washington and Lee Law Review* 59 (2002): 1309–42.

7 Ibid.

8 *Bush v. Holmes*, 919 So.2d 392 (Fla., 2006). Under Florida's Opportunity Scholarship Program, a student who attends or is assigned to attend a failing public school may attend a higher performing public school or use a scholarship provided by the state to attend a participating private school.

9 Chad d'Entremont and Luis A. Huerta, "Irreconcilable Differences? Education Vouchers and the Suburban Response," *Educational Policy* 21, no. 1 (2007): 40–72.

10 See Jay P. Heubert, "Introduction," in *Law and School Reform*, ed. Jay P. Heubert (New Haven, CT: Yale University Press, 1999).

11 For example, in 2003, the performance of U.S. fourth-grade students in mathematics lagged behind the performance of students in 11 out of 24 other participating countries on the Trends in International Mathematics and Science Study. For more information on international comparisons between U.S. students and the students of other countries in science and mathematics, see National Center for Education Statistics, "TIMSS 2003 Results," (Washington, D.C.: National Center for Education Statistics, 2005).

12 Peter Enrich, "Leaving Equality Behind: New Directions in School Finance Reform," *Vanderbilt Law Review* 48, no. 1 (1995): 101–94. According to Enrich, Mississippi is the only state that arguably does not contain an education clause.

13 For a thorough exposition of the different types of education clauses, see Molly S. McUsic, "The Use of Education Clauses in School Finance Litigation," *Harvard Journal on Legislation* 28 (1991): 307–40.

14 The Equal Protection Clause provides, "No state shall make or enforce any law which shall abridge the privileges or immunities of citizens of the United States; nor shall any state deprive any person of life, liberty, or property, without due process of law; nor deny to any person within its jurisdiction the equal protection of the laws." U.S. Constitution, Amendment, XIV.

15 Civil Rights Act of 1964, 42 U.S.C. § 2000 et seq. (1964); Education for All Handicapped Children Act, 20 U.S.C. § 1400 et seq. (1975).

16 Elementary and Secondary Education Act, 20 U.S.C. § 6301 et seq. (1965). The ESEA is perhaps the most sweeping piece of education reform legislation in U.S. history. As it was originally passed, the ESEA included five different Titles, each of which funneled federal funds into state educational programs. Title I, the central portion of the ESEA, authorized the appropriation of $1 billion in categorical grants for the compensatory education of economically disadvantaged students. Other Titles provided millions of dollars for instructional materials, educational improvement centers, research and development centers, and efforts to increase coordination within state departments of education.

17 David Tyack and Aaron Benavot, "Courts and Public Schools: Educational Litigation in Historical Perspective," *Law and Society Review* 19, no. 3 (1985): 339–80.

18 Generally speaking, torts are civil wrongs that courts remedy by awarding damages to an injured party.

19 David Tyack and Elisabeth Hansot, *Managers of Virtue: Public School Leadership in America, 1820–1980* (New York, NY: Basic Books, 1982).

20 Tyack and Benavot, "Courts and Public Schools: Educational Litigation in Historical Perspective."

21 David Tyack, "Toward a Social History of Law and Public Education," in *School Days, Rule Days: The Legislation and Regulation of Education*, ed. David L. Kirp and Donald N. Jensen (Philadelphia, PA: Falmer Press, 1985).

22 Tyack and Benavot, "Courts and Public Schools: Educational Litigation in Historical Perspective."

23 *Meyer v. Nebraska*, 262 U.S. 390 (1923).

24 *Pierce v. Society of Sisters*, 268 U.S. 510 (1928).

25 Abram Chayes, "The Role of the Judge in Public Law Litigation," *Harvard Law Review* 89 (1976): 1281–316.

26 Mark A. Chesler, Joseph Sanders, and Debra S. Kalmuss, *Social Science in Court: Mobilizing Experts in the School Desegregation Cases* (Madison, WI: University of Wisconsin Press, 1988).

27 See, e.g., *Cooper v. Aaron*, 358 U.S. 1 (1959); *Green v. County School Board*, 391 U.S. 430 (1968); *Swann v. Charlotte-Mecklenburg Board of Education*, 402 U.S. 1 (1971).

28 *Brown v. Board of Education*, 349 U.S. 294 (1955); *Green v. County School Board*, 391 U.S. 430 (1968). Many scholars have analyzed the way in which the Supreme Court's mandate to desegregate with all deliberate speed enabled states to stop or slow many desegregation reforms. Both public and private resistance contributed to this problem. For more on this point, see Numan B. Bartley, *The Rise of Massive Resistance* (Baton Rouge, LA: Louisiana State University Press, 1969); Jack Greenberg, *Crusaders in the Courts* (New York, NY: Basic Books, 1994).

29 Mark Yudof et al., *Education Policy and the Law* (Belmont, CA: Wadsworth Publishing, 2001).

30 *Grutter v. Bollinger*, 539 U.S. 306 (2003).

31 See, e.g., *Serrano v. Priest*, 487 P.2d 1241 (Cal., 1971).

32 *San Antonio Independent School District v. Rodriguez*, 411 U.S. 1 (1973).

33 James S. Liebman, "Implementing Brown in the Nineties: Political Reconstruction, Liberal Recollection, and Litigatively Enforced Legislative Reform," *Virginia Law Review* 76 (1990): 349–435; Molly S. McUsic, "The Law's Role in the Distribution of Education: The Promises and Pitfalls of School Finance Litigation," in *Law and School Reform*, ed. Jay P. Heubert (1999); McUsic, "The Use of Education Clauses in School Finance Litigation." Chapter Five discusses adequacy arguments and their intersection with standards-based reform in considerable detail.

34 Michael Griffith, "School Finance Litigation and Beyond," http://www.ecs.org/clearinghouse/60/26/6026.htm (accessed August 10, 2006).

35 Civil Rights Act of 1964, 42 U.S.C. § 2000 et seq. (1964).

36 James S. Liebman and Charles F. Sabel, "Changing Schools: A Public Laboratory Dewey Barely Imagined: The Emerging Model of School Governance and Legal Reform," *New York University School of Law Review of Law and Social Change* 28 (2003): 183–304; Gary Orfield, *The Reconstruction of Southern Education: The Schools and the 1964 Civil Rights Act* (New York, NY: John Wiley and Sons, 1969); Michael A. Rebell, "Poverty, 'Meaningful' Educational Opportunity, and the Necessary Role of the Courts," *North Carolina Law Review* 85 (2007): 1467–543.

37 See, e.g., *Lau v. Nichols*, 414 U.S. 563 (1974); *Castaneda v. Pickard*, 648 F. 2d 989 (5th Cir., 1981).

38 See, e.g., *Larry P. v. Riles*, 793 F.2d 969 (9th Cir., 1984); *GI Forum v. Texas Education Agency*, 87 F. Supp. 2d 667 (W.D. Tex., 2000).

39 Section 504 of the Rehabilitation Act, 29 U.S.C. § 794 et seq. (1973).

40 Education for All Handicapped Children Act, 20 U.S.C. § 1400 et seq. (1975).

41 See, e.g., *Hairston v. Drosick*, 423 F. Supp. 180 (S.D. W. Va., 1976); *Daniel R. R. v. State Board of Education*, 874 F.2d 1036 (5th Cir., 1989); *Oberti v. Board of Education*, 995 F.2d 1204 (3rd Cir., 1993).

42 Yudof et al., *Education Policy and the Law.*

43 Michael A. Rebell and Robert L. Hughes, "Efficacy and Engagement: The Remedies Problem Posed by *Sheff v. O'Neill*," *Connecticut Law Review* 29 (1997): 1115–86.

44 Molly Hunter, "All Eyes Forward: Public Engagement and Education Reform in Kentucky," *Journal of Law and Education* 28 (1999): 485–516.

45 Neil Komesar, *Imperfect Alternatives: Choosing Institutions in Law, Economics, and Public Policy* (Chicago, IL: University of Chicago Press, 1994).

46 Michael A. Rebell and Arthur R. Block, *Education Policy Making and the Courts: An Empirical Study of Judicial Activism* (Philadelphia, PA: Temple University Press, 1982).

47 Charles J. Ogletree, *All Deliberate Speed: Reflections on the First Half-Century of Brown v. Board of Education* (New York, NY: W. W. Norton & Co., 2004).

48 Komesar, *Imperfect Alternatives: Choosing Institutions in Law, Economics, and Public Policy.*

49 Ogletree, *All Deliberate Speed: Reflections on the First Half-Century of Brown v. Board of Education.* See also David Mayrowetz and John F. Lapham, "'But We're in a Court of Law. We're Not in a Legislature.' The *Corey H.* Court Trapped in an Identity Crisis between Adjudicator and Policymaker," *Educational Policy* (in press).

50 Michael Heise, "The Courts, Education Policy, and Unintended Consequences," *Cornell Journal of Law and Public Policy* 11 (2002): 636–63.

51 Kevin G. Welner and Haggai Kupermintz, "Rethinking Expert Testimony in Education Rights Litigation," *Educational Evaluation and Policy Analysis* 26, no. 2 (2004): 127–42, 127.

52 Heise, "The Courts, Education Policy, and Unintended Consequences."

53 Michael Kaufman, "Rhetorical Questions Concerning Justice and Equality in Educational Opportunities," *Loyola University of Chicago Law Journal* 36 (2005): 495–511.

54 Nathan Glazer, "Toward an Imperial Judiciary," *The Public Interest* 41 (1975): 104–23.

55 Gerald N. Rosenberg, *The Hollow Hope: Can Courts Bring About Social Change?* (Chicago, IL: University of Chicago Press, 1991), 338.

56 Greenberg, *Crusaders in the Courts.*

57 James S. Liebman, "Desegregating Politics: 'All-Out' School Desegregation Explained," *Columbia Law Review* 90 (1990): 1463–533.

58 Gary Orfield, "Turning Back to Segregation," in *Dismantling Desegregation: The Quiet Reversal of Brown v. Board of Education*, ed. Gary Orfield and Susan E. Eaton (New York, NY: The New Press, 1996).

59 U.S. Department of Education, "High Standards for All Students: A Report from the National Assessment of Title I on Progress and Challenges since the 1994 Reauthorization," (Washington, D.C.: U.S. Government Printing Office, 2001).

60 U.S. Department of Commerce, "Statistical Abstract of the United States: 2000," (Washington, D.C.: U.S. Government Printing Office, 2000).

61 Ogletree, *All Deliberate Speed: Reflections on the First Half-Century of Brown v. Board of Education.*

62 Gary Orfield, "Conservatives and the Rush toward Resegregation," in *Law and School Reform*, ed. Jay P. Heubert (New Haven, CT: Yale University Press, 1999).

63 Michael Heise, "Litigated Learning and the Limits of Law," *Vanderbilt Law Review* 57, no. 2417 (2004): 2417–61.

64 William N. Evans, Sheila E. Murray, and Robert M. Schwab, "The Impact of Court-Mandated Finance Reform," in *Equity and Adequacy in Education Finance: Issues and Perspectives*, ed. Helen F. Ladd, et al. (1999); Bradley W. Joondeph, "The Good, the Bad and the Ugly: An Empirical Analysis of Litigation Prompted School Finance Reform," *Santa Clara Law Review* 35 (1995): 763–824.

65 Patricia F. First and Louis F. Miron, "The Social Construction of Adequacy," *Journal of Law and Education* 20 (1991): 421–44; Joondeph, "The Good, the Bad and the Ugly: An Empirical Analysis of Litigation Prompted School Finance Reform."

66 McUsic, "The Law's Role in the Distribution of Education: The Promises and Pitfalls of School Finance Litigation."

67 Ibid., Heise, "Litigated Learning and the Limits of Law."

68 Thomas Hehir and Sue Gamm, "Special Education: From Legalism to Collaboration," in *Law and School Reform*, ed. Jay P. Heubert (New Haven, CT: Yale University Press, 1999).

69 Mary Wagner et al., "The Transition Experiences of Young People with Disabilities," (Menlo Park: CA: SRI International, 1993).

70 See, e.g., David L. Kirp and David Neal, "The Allure of Legalism Reconsidered: The Case of Special Education," in *School Days, Rule Days*, ed. David L. Kirp and Donald L. Jensen (London: Falmer Press, 1986).

71 The Congressional Record is the official record of the proceedings and debates of the U.S. Congress.

72 To be sure, some legal scholars feel that what the law says does not determine how judges rule. Generally, the scholars known as "legal realists" (who were prevalent in the 1920s through the 1940s) posited that the law is indeterminate and extremely flexible, and that the law entails only minimal restraints on judicial decision-making. Hence, judicial decisions can turn on "what a judge had for breakfast." For more on legal realism, see Michael Steven Green, "Legal Realism as a Theory of Law," *William and Mary Law Review*, no. 46 (2005): 1915–2000. However, many modern legal scholars have focused on ways in which the law can, does, and should matter in the outcome of a case. For perhaps the most famous response to the principles of legal realism, see Herbert Weshcler, "Toward Neutral Principles of Constitutional Law," *Harvard Law Review* 73 (1959): 1–35.

73 It is important to note that the standards-based accountability systems required by NCLB arguably should not be considered high-stakes testing practices as such testing practices are traditionally conceived. High-stakes testing practices generally hold individual students accountable for their performance. NCLB primarily held schools accountable for their performance.

74 *Debra P. v. Turlington*, 654 F.2d 1079 (5th Cir., 1981); *GI Forum v. Texas Education Agency*, 87 F. Supp. 2d 667 (W.D. Tex., 2000).

Chapter Two

1 David Tyack, *The One Best System* (Cambridge, MA: Harvard University Press, 1974).

2 Richard F. Elmore, "Introduction," in *The New Accountability: High Schools and High-Stakes Testing*, ed. Martin Carnoy, Richard F. Elmore, and Leslie Santee Siskin (New York, NY: Routledge Farmer, 2003).

3 Diane Ravitch, "The Search for Order and the Rejection of Conformity: Standards in American Education," in *Learning from the Past: What History Teaches Us about School Reform*, ed. Diane Ravitch and Maris Vinovskis (Baltimore, MD: Johns Hopkins University Press, 1995).

4 Herbert M. Kliebard, *The Struggle for the American Curriculum* (New York, NY: Routledge, 1995).

5 Ravitch, "The Search for Order and the Rejection of Conformity: Standards in American Education."

6 Ibid.

7 Peter B. Dow, *Schoolhouse Politics: Lessons from the Sputnik Era* (Cambridge, MA: Harvard University Press, 1991).

8 Between 1968 and 1982, SAT scores decreased by .3 standard deviations, which represents a substantial decrease in performance on the test. Martin R. West and Paul E. Peterson, "The Politics and Practice of Accountability," in *No Child Left Behind? The Politics and Practice of School Accountability*, ed. Paul E. Peterson and Martin R. West (Washington, D.C.: Brookings Institution Press, 2003).

9 Ibid.

10 James Coleman et al., "Equality of Educational Opportunity Survey," (Washington, D.C.: U.S. Government Printing Office, 1966). The Coleman Report also focused on the background characteristics of students and the social composition of schools, and many researchers have interpreted the report as indicating that such factors account for a significantly greater impact on student achievement than school resources.

11 Frederick M. Hess, "Refining or Retreating? High-Stakes Accountability in the States," in *No Child Left Behind? The Politics and Practice of School Accountability,* ed. Paul E. Peterson and Martin R. West (Washington, D.C.: Brookings Institution Press, 2003).

12 Office of Technology Assessment, U.S. Congress, "Testing in American Schools: Asking the Right Questions," (Washington, D.C.: U.S. Government Printing Office, 1992).

13 Ibid.

14 National Commission on Excellence in Education, *A Nation at Risk: The Imperative for Education Reform* (Washington, D.C.: U.S. Government Printing Office, 1983), 5.

15 For example, citing poor teaching as fundamental educational problem, the Carnegie Forum on Education and the Economy released a report calling for the creation of a board to establish national teacher standards. Carnegie Forum on Education and the Economy, "A Nation Prepared: Teachers for the Twenty-First Century," (Washington, D.C.: Carnegie Forum on Education and the Economy, 1986). Focusing on the lack of attention to results in the U.S., the Education Commission of the States called for higher standards and better measurement of student performance against these standards.

16 Susan. H. Fuhrman, "The Twenty-Year Effort to Reform Education," in *A Nation Reformed?*, ed. David T. Gordon (Cambridge, MA: Harvard Education Press, 2003). Governors in states including Florida, South Carolina, Arkansas, and Tennessee were at the forefront of the excellence movement.

17 Ibid.

18 Margaret E. Goertz, Mark C. Duffy, and Kerstin C. Le Floch, "Assessment and Accountability Systems in the 50 States: 1999–2000," (Philadelphia, PA: Consortium for Policy Research in Education, 2001).

19 See, e.g., Daniel. P. Resnick and Lauren. B. Resnick, "Standards, Curriculum, and Performance: A Historical and Comparative Perspective," *Educational Researcher* 14, no. 4 (1985): 5–20.

20 National Council of Teachers of Mathematics, "Curriculum and Evaluation Standards for School Mathematics," (Reston, VA: National Council of Teachers of Mathematics, 1989).

21 The goals announced by the National Governors Association were: (1) all students must arrive at school ready to learn; (2) the nation's high-school graduation rate must be at least 90 percent; (3) students must be competent in English, history, geography, foreign languages, and the arts; (4) American students must lead the world in math and science; (5) all adults must be literate; and (6) all schools must be drug free. National Governors' Association, "National Education Goals," (Washington, D. C.: National Governors' Association, 1990). The goals described in the governors' report were a modified version of six education goals originally announced by President Bush in his 1990 State of the Union Address. George H. W. Bush, "State of the Union address," (1990).

22 See, e.g., David K. Cohen, "Policy and Organization: The Impact of State and Federal Education Policy on School Governance," *Harvard Educational Review* 52, no. 4 (1982): 474–99.

23 This section on the different definitions of systemic reform draws heavily from Maris A. Vinovskis, "An Analysis of the Concept and Uses of Systemic Education Reform," *American Educational Research Journal* 33, no. 1 (1996): 53–85.

24 See, e.g., Stewart C. Purkey and Marshall S. Smith, "School Reform: The District Policy Implications of the Effective Schools Literature," *The Elementary School Journal* 85, no. 3 (1985): 353–89.

25 Marshall S. Smith and Jennifer A. O'Day, "Systemic School Reform," in *The Politics of Curriculum and Testing: The 1990 Yearbook of the Politics of Education Association*, ed. Susan H. Fuhrman and Betty Malem (London: Falmer Press, 1991).

26 Jennifer A. O'Day and Marshall S. Smith, "Systemic Reform and Educational Opportunity," in *Designing Coherent Education Policy: Improving the System*, ed. Susan Fuhrman (San Francisco, CA: Jossey-Bass, 1993), 251.

27 Smith and O'Day, "Systemic School Reform."

28 O'Day and Smith, "Systemic Reform and Educational Opportunity," 252.

29 Ibid., 270.

30 Ibid., 275.

31 Chester E. Finn, *We Must Take Charge: Our Schools and Our Future* (New

York, NY: Free Press, 1991).

32 William Clune, "Systemic Education Policy: A Conceptual Framework," in *Designing Coherent Education Policy: Improving the System*, ed. Susan Fuhrman (San Francisco, CA: Jossey-Bass, 1993). Clune's components of systemic reform were: (1) research-based goals for changes in educational practice and organization; (2) working models of new practice and professionally accessible knowledge; (3) a change process involving centralized aspects, such as incentives, technical assistance, mandates, and resources, and decentralized aspects, such as schoolwide planning, teacher collaboration, and restructuring; (4) regular assessment of educational inputs, outcomes, and process; (5) a coherent, sustained, change-oriented political process.

33 Gretchen Guiton and Jeannie Oakes, "Opportunity to Learn and Conceptions of Educational Equality," *Educational Evaluation and Policy Analysis* 17, no. 3 (1995): 323–36.

34 Linda Darling-Hammond, "Education Reform through National Standards and Assessment," *American Journal of Education* 102, no. 4 (1994): 478–510; Jeannie Oakes, "What Educational Indicators? The Case for Assessing the School Context," *Educational Evaluation and Policy Analysis* 11, no. 2 (1989): 181–99; Floraline I. Stevens and John Grymes, "Opportunity to Learn: Issues of Equity for Poor and Minority Students," (Washington, D.C.: National Center for Education Statistics, 1993).

35 Vinovskis, "An Analysis of the Concept and Uses of Systemic Education Reform."

36 Guiton and Oakes, "Opportunity to Learn and Conceptions of Educational Equality."

37 Diane Massell, Michael Kirst, and Margaret Hoppe, "Persistence and Change: Standards-Based Systemic Reform in Nine States," (Philadelphia, PA: Consortium for Policy Research in Education, 1997).

38 Ibid.

39 Christopher B. Swanson and David Lee Stevenson, "Standards-Based Reform in Practice: Evidence on State Policy and Classroom Instruction from the NAEP State Assessments," *Educational Evaluation and Policy Analysis* 24, no. 1 (2002): 1–27.

40 Ibid.

41 America 2000: Excellence in Education Act, H.R. 2460, 102nd Congress (1991).

42 U.S. Congress, *Congressional Record* (May 5, 1992). http://www.gpoaccess.gov/bills/index.html (accessed January 5, 2006).

43 Goals 2000: Educate America Act, 20 U.S.C. § 5801 et. seq. (1994).

44 Ibid.

45 Ibid.

46 Ibid.

47 Ibid.

48 To be sure, some legislators did attempt to reauthorize Title I before Goals 2000 had been passed. However, the Clinton administration generally managed to push Goals 2000 ahead of Title I on the federal agenda, and most Congressional consideration of Title I did not occur until after Goals 2000's passage.

49 Improving America's Schools Act, 20 U.S.C. § 6301 et seq. (1994).

50 One should note that a previous version of the ESEA also addressed substantive academic quality, student achievement, and accountability. With the passage of the Hawkins-Stafford Amendments to the ESEA in 1988, Congress changed Title I to require states to define the levels of academic achievement that students in Title I schools should attain. Moreover, Congress required states to identify the schools that were failing to make substantial progress toward their performance goals. Congress also required states to set out the steps that districts and states must take to assist schools that fail to perform adequately – under the law, these steps were required to include the institution of school improvement plans and eventually state intervention in schools that continued to perform inadequately. Hawkins-Stafford Education Amendments of 1988, 20 U.S.C. § 2701 et seq. (1988). However, these requirements were not robustly implemented. Mary Ann Millsap et al., *The Chapter 1 Implementation Study: Interim Report* (Washington, D.C.: U.S. Government Printing Office, 1992).

51 Individuals with Disabilities Education Act, 20 U.S.C. § 1400 et. seq. (1997).

52 See, e.g., Jonathan Riskind, "State Board Turns Away Protesters; Superintendent Says Meeting Room Too Tiny for Crowd," *The Columbus Dispatch*, October 12, 1994. http://www.lexis.com (accessed January 28, 2006).

53 Katharine Seeyle, "G.O.P. Set to Lead Congress on Path Sharply to Right," *New York Times*, January 3, 1995. http://www.lexis.com (accessed January 28, 2006). The bills introduced by members of Congress to repeal or alter Goals 2000 include H.R. 997 (1995), H.R. 1045 (1995), H.R. 1558 (1995), H.R., 3313 (1996), S. 323 (1995), S. 469 (1995), and S. 1301 (1995). Moreover, Beginning in March 1995, at least three bills (S. 617 (1995), H.R. 1158 (1995), and H.R. 1159 (1995)) were proposed in Congress that would drastically cut Goals 2000 spending. H.R. 1158 would cut $874.5 million from federal education programs, including $84 million from Goals 2000.

54 For example, refusing to apply for Goals 2000 funds, Virginia Commissioner of Education Beverly Sgro stated, "We're very cynical. We're concerned that what's 'voluntary' might not be voluntary." Mark Pitsch, "Conservatives Vie to Use Momentum to Push Reform

Agenda," *Education Week*, February 1, 1995. http://www.lexis.com (accessed January 28, 2006).

55 Benjamin M. Superfine, "The Politics of Accountability: The Rise and Fall of Goals: 2000," *American Journal of Education* 112, no. 1 (2005): 10–43.

56 Government Accountability Office, "Goals 2000: Flexible Funding Supports State and Local Education Reform," (Washington, D.C.: U.S. Government Printing Office, 1998).

57 Ibid.

58 U.S. Department of Education, "Promising Results, Continuing Challenges: The Final Report of the National Assessment of Title I," (Washington, D.C.: U.S. Government Printing Office, 1999).

59 Ibid.

60 U.S. Department of Education, "High Standards for All Students: A Report from the National Assessment of Title I on Progress and Challenges since the 1994 Reauthorization," (Washington, D.C.: U.S. Government Printing Office, 2001).

61 American Federation of Teachers, "Making Standards Matter: A Fifty State Progress Report on Efforts to Raise Academic Standards," (Washington, D.C.: American Federation of Teachers, 1999); Chester E. Finn and Michael J. Petrilli, "The State of State Standards 2000," (Washington, D.C.: Fordham Foundation, 2000); Scott Joftus and Ilene Berman, "Great Expectations: Defining and Assessing Rigor in State Standards for Mathematics and English Language Arts," (Washington, D.C.: Council for Basic Education, 1998).

62 Joftus and Berman, "Great Expectations: Defining and Assessing Rigor in State Standards for Mathematics and English Language Arts."

63 Finn and Petrilli, "The State of State Standards 2000."

64 Arthur Woodward, David L. Elliott, and Kathleen Carter Nagel, *Textbooks in School and Society* (New York, NY: Garland Publishing Company, 1988).

65 Ravitch, "The Search for Order and the Rejection of Conformity: Standards in American Education."

66 Diane Ravitch, *The Language Police: How Pressure Groups Restrict What Students Learn* (New York, NY: Alfred A. Knopf, 2003).

67 William H. Clune, "Toward a Theory of Standards-Based Reform: The Case of Nine NSF Statewide Systemic Initiatives," in *From the Capitol to the Classroom: Standards-Based Reform in the States*, ed. Susan H. Fuhrman (Chicago, IL: University of Chicago Press, 2001); William A. Firestone et al., "Pressure and Support," in *The Ambiguity of Teaching to the Test*, ed. William A. Firestone, Roberta Y. Schorr, and Lora F. Monfils (Mahwah, NJ: Lawrence Erlbaum Associates, 2004).

68 Goeretz, Duffy, and Le Floch, "Assessment and Accountability Systems in the 50 States: 1999–2000."

69 Superfine, "The Politics of Accountability: The Rise and Fall of Goals: 2000."

70 U.S. Department of Education, "Reports on Reform from the Field: District and State Survey Results," (Washington, D.C.: U.S. Government Printing Office, 1997).

71 The *AERA Standards* were jointly developed by the American Educational Research Association, American Psychological Association, and National Council on Measurement in Education. The *AERA Standards* are periodically revised, and the most recent edition of the *AERA Standards* (the one referenced by this chapter) was published in 1999. American Educational Research Association, American Psychological Association, and National Council on Measurement in Education, "Standards for Educational and Psychological Testing," (Washington, D.C.: American Educational Research Association, 1999).

72 To be sure, close textual inspection reveals that the *AERA Standards* are rather vague about what is actually required to validate a testing practice. Most of the standards begin with conditional statements like "when" or "if.' For example, Standard 1.6 states, "when the validation rests in part on the appropriateness of test content, the procedures followed in specifying and generating test content should be described and justified in reference to the construct the test is intended to measure or the domain it is intended to represent." Ibid.

73 Margaret Goertz, "Standards-Based Accountability: Horse Trade of Horse Whip?" in *From the Capitol to the Classroom: Standards-Based Accountability in the States*, ed. Susan H. Fuhrman (Chicago, IL: University of Chicago Press, 2001); Andrew C. Porter, "Measuring the Content of Instruction: Uses in Research and Practice," *Educational Researcher* 31, no. 7 (2002): 3–14.

74 Eric A. Hanushek and Margaret E. Raymond, "Lessons About the Design of State Accountability Systems," in *No Child Left Behind? The Politics and Practice of School Accountability*, ed. Paul E. Peterson and Martin R. West (Washington, D.C.: Brookings Institution Press, 2003).

75 Lorrie A. Shepard, "Curricular Coherence in Assessment Design," in *Towards Coherence between Classroom Assessment and Accountability*, ed. Mark Wilson (Chicago, IL: The University of Chicago Press, 2004).

76 Jamal Abedi, "The No Child Left Behind Act and English Language Learners: Assessment and Accountability Issues," *Educational Researcher* 33, no. 1 (2004): 4–14.

77 Criterion-referenced tests generally measure students' skills and knowledge in relation to a set level of performance, while norm-referenced tests generally measure students' skills and knowledge in relation to the skills and knowledge of other students who also took the tests.

78 American Educational Research Association, American Psychological

Association, and National Council on Measurement in Education, "Standards for Educational and Psychological Testing."

79 Abedi, "The No Child Left Behind Act and English Language Learners: Assessment and Accountability Issues."

80 National Research Council, *Education One and All: Students with Disabilities and Standards-based Reform*, ed. Lorraine McDonnell, Milbrey McLaughlin, and Patricia Morison (Washington, D.C.: National Academy Press, 1997).

81 Margaret E. Goertz, Mark C. Duffy, and Kerstin C. Le Floch, "Assessment and Accountability Systems in the 50 States: 1999–2000," (Philadelphia, PA: Consortium for Policy Research in Education, 2001).

82 Ibid.

83 U.S. Department of Education, "One System or Two? Title I Accountability in the Context of High Stakes for Schools in Local Districts and States," (Washington, D.C.: U.S. Government Printing Office, 1999).

84 U.S. Department of Education, "Reports on Reform from the Field: District and State Survey Results."

85 Ibid.

86 Richard F. Elmore, "Accountability and Capacity," in *The New Accountability*, ed. Martin Carnoy, Richard F. Elmore, and Leslie Santee Siskin (New York, NY: Routledge Farmer, 2003).

87 National Staff Development Council, *Standards for Staff Development (Revised)* (Ohio: National Staff Development Council, 2001); Jonathan A. Supovitz, "Translating Teaching Practice into Improved Student Achievement," in *From the Capitol to the Classroom: Standards-Based Reform in the States*, ed. Susan H. Fuhrman (Chicago, IL: University of Chicago Press, 2001).

88 Supovitz, "Translating Teaching Practice into Improved Student Achievement."

89 David K. Cohen and Heather C. Hill, *Learning Policy: When State Education Reform Works* (New Haven, CT: Yale University Press, 2001). The professional development opportunities examined in this study included workshops focused on content that lasted from two to six days and special issues workshops lasting one day. The researchers particularly found that professional development grounded in content and sustained over time was the most effective in changing teachers' practice.

90 See, e.g., Achieve, Inc., "Staying on Course: Standards-Based Reform in America's Schools: Progress and Prospects," (Washington, D.C.: Achieve, Inc., 2002); American Federation of Teachers, "Making Standards Matter," (Washington, D.C.: American Federation of Teachers, 2001).

91 Heather C. Hill, "Professional Development Standards and Practices in Elementary School Mathematics," *Elementary School Journal* 104, no. 3 (2004): 215–31.

92 Andrew C. Porter and John L. Smithson, "Are Content Standards Being Implemented in the Classroom? A Methodology and Some Tentative Answers," in *From the Capitol to the Classroom: Standards-Based Reform in the States*, ed. Susan H. Fuhrman (Chicago, IL: University of Chicago Press, 2001).

93 S. G. Grant, "An Uncertain Lever: The Influence of State-Level Testing in New York on Teaching Social Studies," *Teachers College Record* 103, no. 3 (2001): 398–426.

94 Cohen and Hill, *Learning Policy: When State Education Reform Works*.

95 James P. Spillane and Nancy E. Jennings, "Aligned Instructional Policy and Ambitious Pedagogy: Exploring Instructional Reform from the Classroom Perspective," *Teachers College Record* 98, no. 5 (1997): 449–81. For similar results, see Roberta Y. Schorr et al., "Teaching Mathematics and Science," in *The Ambiguity of Teaching to the Test*, ed. William A. Firestone, Roberta Y. Schorr, and Lora F. Monfils (Mahwah, NJ: Lawrence Erlbaum Associates, 2004).

96 Janine Remillard and Martha Bryans, "Teachers' Orientations toward Mathematics Curriculum Materials: Implications for Teacher Learning," *Journal for Research in Mathematics Education* 35, no. 5 (2004): 352–88.

97 James P. Spillane and John Zeuli, "Reform and Teaching: Exploring Patterns of Practice in the Context of National and State Mathematics Reforms," *Educational Evaluation and Policy Analysis* 21 (1999): 1–28.

98 James P. Spillane, "Challenging Instruction for 'All Students': Policy, Practitioners, and Practice," in *From the Capitol to the Classroom: Standards-Based Reform in the States*, ed. Susan H. Fuhrman (Chicago, IL: The University of Chicago Press, 2001).

99 Charles G. Abelmann and Richard F. Elmore, "When Accountability Knocks, Will Anyone Answer?" (Philadelphia, PA: Consortium for Policy Research in Education, 1999).

100 Richard F. Elmore, "Bridging the Gap between Standards and Achievement," (Washington, D.C.: Albert Shanker Institute, 2002); Richard Lemons, Thomas F. Luschei, and Leslie Santee Siskin, "Leadership and the Demands of Standards-based Accountability," in *The New Accountability*, ed. Martin Carnoy, Richard F. Elmore, and Leslie Santee Siskin (New York, NY: Routledge Farmer, 2003),

101 William A. Firestone et al., "The Principal, Test Preparation, and Education reform," in *The Ambiguity of Teaching to the Test*, ed. William A. Firestone, Roberta Y. Schorr, and Lora F. Monfils (Mahwah, NJ: Lawrence Erlbaum Associates, 2004).

102 James P. Spillane, "School Districts Matter: Local Educational Authorities and State Instructional Policy," *Educational Policy* 10, no. 1 (1996): 63–87.

103 Katrina Bulkley, Janet Fairman, and M. Cecilia Martinez, "The District and Test Preparation," in *The Ambiguity of Teaching to the Test*, ed. William A. Firestone, Roberta Y. Schorr, and Lora F. Monfils (Mahwah, NJ: Lawrence Erlbaum Associates, 2004).

104 Jane Hannaway and Kristi Kimball, "Big Isn't Always Bad: School District Size, Poverty, and Standards-Based Reform," in *From the Capitol to the Classroom: Standards-Based Reform in the States*, ed. Susan H. Fuhrman (Chicago, IL: University of Chicago Press, 2001), Janet Fairman and William A. Firestone, "The District Role in State Assessment Policy: An Exploratory Study," in *From the Capitol to the Classroom: Standards-Based Reform in the States*, ed. Susan H. Fuhrman (Chicago, IL: University of Chicago Press, 2001).

105 Diane Massell et al., "The Press from Above, the Pull from Below: High School Responses to External Accountability," in *Holding High Hopes: How High Schools Respond to State Accountability Policies*, ed. Bethany Gross and Margaret E. Goeretz (Philadelphia, PA: Consortium for Policy Research in Education, 2005).

106 Ibid.

107 Elliot H. Weinbaum, "Stuck in the Middle with You: District Responses to State Accountability," in *Holding High Hopes: How High Schools Respond to State Accountability Policies*, ed. Bethany Gross and Margaret E. Goertz (Philadelphia, PA: Consortium for Policy Research in Education, 2005).

108 Linda Skrla, James Joseph Scheurich, and Joseph F. Jr. Johnson, "Equity-Driven Achievement-Focused School Districts," (Austin, TX: The Charles A. Dana Center, The University of Texas at Austin, 2000).

109 Lora F. Monfils et al., "Teaching to the Test," in *The Ambiguity of Teaching to the Test*, ed. William A. Firestone, Roberta Y. Schorr, and Lora F. Monfils (Mahwah, NJ: Lawrence Erlbaum, 2004).

110 U.S. Department of Education, "High Standards for All Students: A Report from the National Assessment of Title I on Progress and Challenges since the 1994 Reauthorization."

111 Paula White, Adam Gamoran, and John L. Smithson, "Math Innovations and Student Achievement in Seven High Schools in California and New York," (Philadelphia, PA: Consortium for Policy Research in Education, 1995).

112 Cohen and Hill, *Learning Policy: When State Education Reform Works*.

113 Susan H. Fuhrman, "Introduction," in *From the Capitol to the Classroom: Standards-Based Reform in the States*, ed. Susan H. Fuhrman (Chicago, IL: National Society for the Study of Education, 2001).

114 David Grissmer and Ann Flanagan, "Exploring Rapid Achievement Gains in North Carolina and Texas: Lessons from the States," (National Education Goals Panel, 1998).

115 Martin Carnoy and Susanna Loeb, "Does External Accountability Affect Student Outcomes? A Cross-State Analysis," *Educational Evaluation and Policy Analysis* 24, no. 4 (2002): 305–31.

116 Walt Haney, "The Myth of the Texas Miracle in Education," *Education Policy Analysis Archives* 8, no. 41 (2000). http://epaa.asu.edu (accessed July 9, 2006); Stephen P. Klein et al., "What Do Test Scores Tell Us?" *Education Policy Analysis Archives* 8, no. 49 (2000). http://epaa.asu.edu (accessed July 9, 2006).

117 Anthony S. Bryk, "No Child Left Behind, Chicago-Style," in *No Child Left Behind? The Politics and Practice of School Accountability*, ed. Paul E. Peterson and Martin R. West (Washington, D.C.: Brookings Institution Press, 2003); John Q. Easton, Stuart Luppescu, and Todd Rosenkranz, "2006 ISAT Reading and Math Scores in Chicago and the Rest of the State," (Chicago, IL: Consortium on Chicago School Research, 2007); Brian A. Jacob, "A Closer Look at Achievement Gains under High-Stakes Testing in Chicago," in *No Child Left Behind? The Politics and Practice of School Accountability*, ed. Paul E. Peterson and Martin R. West (Washington, D.C.: Brookings Institution Press, 2003); Penny B. Sebring et al., "The Essential Supports for School Improvement," (Chicago, IL: Consortium on Chicago School Research, 2006).

118 Jacob, "A Closer Look at Achievement Gains under High-Stakes Testing in Chicago."

119 Audrey L. Amerin and David C. Berliner, "High-Stakes Testing, Uncertainty, and Student Learning," *Education Policy Analysis Archives* 10, no. 18 (2002). http://epaa.asu.edu (accessed July 9, 2006).

120 No Child Left Behind Act of 2001, 20 U.S.C. § 6301 et seq. (2002).

121 No Child Left Behind Act of 2001, 20 U.S.C. § 6301(6) (2002).

122 No Child Left Behind Act of 2001, 20 U.S.C. § 6311(a)(1) (2002).

123 No Child Left Behind Act of 2001, 20 U.S.C. § 6311(b)(1) (2002).

124 No Child Left Behind Act of 2001, 20 U.S.C. § 6311(b)(3) (2002).

125 No Child Left Behind Act of 2001, 20 U.S.C. § 6311(b)(3)(C)(v)(I) (2002).

126 No Child Left Behind Act of 2001, 20 U.S.C. § 6311(b)(3)(C)(vii) (2002).

127 No Child Left Behind Act of 2001, 20 U.S.C. § 6311(b)(3)(C)(v)(II) (2002).

128 No Child Left Behind Act of 2001, 20 U.S.C. § 6311(b)(2)(C) (2002).

129 No Child Left Behind Act of 2001, 20 U.S.C. § 6311(b)(2)(C)(v) (2002).

130 No Child Left Behind Act of 2001, 20 U.S.C. §§ 6311(b)(C)(ii)–(iii) (2002).

131 No Child Left Behind Act of 2001, 20 U.S.C. § 6316(b)(1)(E)(i) (2002).

132 No Child Left Behind Act of 2001, 20 U.S.C. § 6316(d)(1) (2002).

133 No Child Left Behind Act of 2001, 20 U.S.C. § 6316(d)(5)(E) (2002).

134 No Child Left Behind Act of 2001, 20 U.S.C. § 6316(b)(6) (2002).

135 No Child Left Behind Act of 2001, 20 U.S.C. §§ 6316(b)(7)(C)(i)–(vi) (2002).

136 No Child Left Behind Act of 2001, 20 U.S.C. §§ 6316(b)(8)(B)(i)–(v) (2002).

137 No Child Left Behind Act of 2001, 20 U.S.C. § 6311(j) (2002).

138 No Child Left Behind Act of 2001, 20 U.S.C. § 6303(g)(5)(a) (2002).

139 No Child Left Behind Act of 2001, 20 U.S.C. § 6303(g)(6) (2002)

140 No Child Left Behind provided that a state may defer the commencement or suspend the administration of assessments if grants were less than $370,000,000 for FY 2002, $380,000,000 for FY 2003, $390,000,000 for FY 2004, and $400,000,000 for FY 2005–2007. No Child Left Behind Act of 2001, 20 U.S.C. § 6311(b)(3)(D) (2002).

141 No Child Left Behind Act of 2001, 20 U.S.C. § 6317(a)(1) (2002).

142 No Child Left Behind Act of 2001, 20 U.S.C. § 6317(a)(5) (2002).

143 No Child Left Behind Act of 2001, 20 U.S.C. § 6319 (2002).

144 National Education Association, "Education Funding: By the Numbers," (Washington, D.C.: National Education Association, 2004). http://www.nea.org/esea/eseafunding.html (accessed June 6, 2006).

145 For example, soon after Bush released his initial outline of NCLB, representatives George Miller (D-CA) and Dale Kildee (D-MI) argued that states would not be able to meet NCLB requirements without drastically increased funding. Erik W. Robelen, "Key House Democrat Offers $110 Billion Education Plan," *Education Week*, February 7, 2001. http://www.edweek.org (accessed January 6, 2006). President George W. Bush disagreed with these proposals. In contrast to the large spending increases proposed by the Democratic leaders, Bush proposed a $1.6 billion increase in ESEA spending. "Congressional Quarterly Weekly Report," April 7, 2001. http://www.lexis.com (accessed January 28, 2006).

146 No Child Left Behind Act of 2001, 20 U.S.C. § 7907(a) (2002).

147 National Council of State Legislatures, "Fiscal Storm Shows Signs of Subsiding," (Washington, D.C.: National Council of State Legislatures, 2003).

148 Although NCLB was authorized at $26.4 billion for FY 2002, the Bush administration proposed a $19.1 billion appropriation for NCLB, and Congress actually appropriated $22.2 billion. Although NCLB was authorized at $29.2 billion for FY 2003, the Bush administration proposed a $22.1 billion appropriation, and Congress actually appropriated $23.8 billion. Similarly, although NCLB was authorized at $32 billion for FY 2004, the Bush administration proposed a $22.6 billion appropriation, and Congress actually appropriated $24.5 billion. National Education Association, "Education Funding: By the Numbers."

149 U.S. Government Accountability Office, "Characteristics of Tests Will Influence Expenses; Information Sharing May Help States Realize Efficiencies," (Washington, D.C.: U.S. Government Printing Office, 2003).

150 Center on Education Policy, "From the Capital to the Classroom: Year 4 of the No Child Left Behind Act," (Washington, D.C.: Center on Education Policy, 2006).

151 For an estimate on NCLB costs in a particular state, see Connecticut State Department of Education, "Cost of Implementing No Child Left Behind Act in Connecticut," (Hartford, CT: Connecticut State Department of Education, 2005). For a broader analysis of the NCLB costs, see William J. Mathis, "The Cost of Implementing the Federal No Child Left Behind Act: Different Assumptions, Different Answers," *Peabody Journal of Education* 8, no. 2 (2005): 90–119.

152 Mathis, "The Cost of Implementing the Federal No Child Left Behind Act: Different Assumptions, Different Answers." The important issue of the amount of funding it may take to enable students to reach proficiency on state tests is discussed in detail in Chapter Five.

153 See, e.g., Bess Keller, "NEA Takes Stand against Bush Education Law," *Education Week*, July 7, 2003. http://www.edweek.org (accessed January 9, 2006); George Miller and Edward Kennedy, "Kennedy and Miller Call on Bush to Back Historic Education Spending Increase to Ensure Success of Historic School Reform," (2002); National Education Association et al., "Joint Organizational Statement on 'No Child Left Behind' Act," (Washington, D.C.: National Education Association, 2004).

154 Center on Education Policy, "From the Capital to the Classroom: Year 4 of the No Child Left Behind Act."; Government Accountability Office, "Education Needs to Provide Additional Technical Assistance and Conduct Implementation Studies for School Choice Provision," (Washington, D.C.: U.S. Government Printing Office, 2004).

155 Center on Education Policy, "From the Capital to the Classroom: Year 4 of the No Child Left Behind Act."

156 U.S. Government Accountability Office, "Education Needs to Provide Additional Technical Assistance and Conduct Implementation Studies for School Choice Provision."

157 U.S. Department of Education, "The Secretary's Second Annual Report on Teacher Quality," (Washington, D.C.: U.S. Government Printing Office, 2003).

158 U.S. Government Accountability Office, "More Information Would Help States Determine Which Teachers Are Highly Qualified," (Washington, D.C.: U.S. Government Printing Office, 2003).

159 Christopher O. Tracy and Kate Walsh, "Necessary and Insufficient: Resisting a Full Measure of Teacher Quality," (Washington, D.C.: National Council on Teacher Quality, 2004).

160 Northwest Evaluation Association, "The State of State Standards: Research Investigating Proficiency Levels in Fourteen States," (Lake Oswego, OR: Northwest Evaluation Association, 2004).

161 U.S. Government Accountability Office, "Improvements Needed in Education's Process for Tracking States' Implementation of Key Provisions," (Washington, D.C.: U.S. Government Printing Office, 2004).

162 Caroline M. Hoxby, "Inadequate Yearly Progress: Unlocking the Secrets of NCLB," *Education Next* 5, no. 3 (2005): 46–51; Robert L. Linn, Eva L. Baker, and Damian W. Betebenner, "Accountability Systems: Implications of Requirements of the No Child Left Behind Act of 2001," *Educational Researcher* 31, no. 6 (2002): 3–16.

163 See, e.g., Robert L. Linn, "Conflicting Demands of No Child Left Behind and State Systems: Mixed Messages About School Performance," *Education Policy Analysis Archives* 13, no. 3 (2005). http://epaa.asu.edu (accessed July 9, 2006).

164 Laura S. Hamilton et al., "Standards-Based Accountability under No Child Left Behind: Experiences of Teachers and Administrators in Three States," (Santa Monica, CA: RAND, 2007).

165 U.S. Government Accountability Office, "No Child Left Behind Act: Education Should Clarify Guidance and Address Potential Compliance Issues for Schools in Corrective Action and Restructuring Status," (Washington, D.C.: U.S. Government Printing Office, 2007).

166 Center on Education Policy, "From the Capital to the Classroom: Year 4 of the No Child Left Behind Act."

167 Ibid.

168 U.S. Department of Education, "No Child Left Behind Is Working," (Washington, D.C.: U.S. Government Printing Office, 2006).

169 John Cronin et al., "The Impact of the No Child Left Behind Act on Student Achievement and Growth: 2005 Edition," (Lake Oswego, OR: Northwest Evaluation Association, 2005); Education Trust, "Stalled in Secondary: A Look at Student Achievement since the No Child Left Behind Act," (Washington, D.C.: Education Trust, 2005); Education Week, "Quality Counts at 10: A Decade of Standards-Based Reform," (Washington, D.C.: Education Week, 2006).

170 Cronin et al., "The Impact of the No Child Left Behind Act on Student Achievement and Growth: 2005 Edition."

171 Center on Education Policy, "From the Capital to the Classroom: Year 4 of the No Child Left Behind Act."

172 Ibid.

173 Cronin et al., "The Impact of the No Child Left Behind Act on Student Achievement and Growth: 2005 Edition."

174 Ibid; Jimmy Kim and Gail L. Sunderman, "Large Mandates and Limited Resources: State Response to the No Child Left Behind Act and Implications for Accountability," (Cambridge, MA: The Civil Rights Project, Harvard University, 2004).

175 James McGreevey, Letter to Secretary Roderick Paige, October 10, 2003; Judy Martz and Bill Richardson, Letter to Secretary Roderick Paige, October 6, 2003.

176 National Education Association, "No Child Left Behind: State Legislative Watch List," (Washington, D.C.: National Education Association, 2005); National Education Association, "Urge Congress to Support Bills to Improve NCLB," (National Education Association, 2005).

177 See, e.g., William J. Erpenbach, Ellen Forte-Fast, and Abigail Potts, "Statewide Educational Accountability under NCLB," (Washington, D.C.: Council of Chief State School Officers, 2003); "Title I - Improving the Academic Achievement of the Disadvantaged; Final Rule." *Federal Register* 68: 236 (9 December 2003) pp. 68698–707; U.S. Department of Education, "Press Release: Secretary Paige Issues New Policy for Calculating Participation Rates under No Child Left Behind," (Washington, D.C., U.S. Department of Education: 2004).

178 Since its inception, researchers have highlighted the lax enforcement of Title I and related legal requirements. See, e.g., Ruby Martin and Phyllis McClure, "Title I of ESEA: Is It Helping Poor Children?" (Washington, D.C.: Washington Research Project, NAACP Legal Defense and Educational Fund, 1969); Superfine, "The Politics of Accountability: The Rise and Fall of Goals: 2000."

179 See, e.g., Center on Education Policy, "From the Capital to the Classroom: State and Federal Efforts to Implement the No Child Left Behind Act," (Washington, D.C.: Center on Education Policy, 2003); Lynn Olsen, ""Approved" Is a Relative Term for Ed. Department," *Education Week*, August 6, 2003. http://www.edweek.org (accessed January 9, 2006).

180 Center on Education Policy, "State High School Exit Exams: A Challenging Year," (Washington, D.C.: Center on Education Policy, 2006).

181 Center on Education Policy, "Standards Differ from the No Child Left Behind Act," (Washington, D.C.: Center on Education Policy, 2006).

182 Center on Education Policy, "State High School Exit Exams: A Challenging Year."

183 Steven W. Raudenbush, "Learning from Attempts to Improve Schooling: The Contribution of Methodological Diversity," *Educational Researcher* 34, no. 5 (2005): 25–31. This sentiment has been echoed by other prominent researchers, such as Maris Vinovskis, "Missed Opportunities: Why

the Federal Response to a Nation at Risk Was Inadequate," in *A Nation Reformed?* ed. David T. Gordon (Cambridge, MA: Harvard Education Press, 2003).

184 David Tyack and Larry Cuban, *Tinkering toward Utopia: A Century of Public School Reform* (Cambridge, MA: Harvard University Press, 1995).

Chapter Three

1 Americans with Disabilities Act of 1990, 42 U.S.C. § 12101 et seq. (1990); Civil Rights Act of 1964, 42 U.S.C. § 2000 et seq. (1964); Equal Educational Opportunities Act, 20 U.S.C. § 1701 et seq. (1976); Section 504 of the Rehabilitation Act, 29 U.S.C. § 794 et seq. (1973).

2 *Debra P. v. Turlington*, 644 F.2d 397 (5th Cir., 1981); *GI Forum v. Texas Education Agency*, 87 F. Supp. 2d 667 (W.D. Tex., 2000). In discussing and organizing the major areas in which high-stakes testing has occurred, this chapter draws from National Research Council, *High Stakes: Testing for Tracking, Promotion, and Graduation,* ed. Jay P. Heubert and Robert M. Hauser (Washington, D.C.: National Academy Press, 1999).

3 *Richmond v. Croson*, 488 U.S. 469 (1989); *Adarand Constructors, Inc. v. Pena*, 515 U.S. 200 (1995).

4 See, e.g., *Grutter v. Bollinger*, 539 U.S. 306 (2003).

5 *People Who Care v. Rockford Board of Education*, 851 F. Supp. 905 (N.D. Ill., 1994).

6 *Washington v. Davis*, 426 U.S. 229 (1976).

7 *Debra P. v. Turlington*, 644 F.2d 397 (5th Cir., 1981).

8 *People Who Care v. Rockford Board of Education*, 111 F.3d 528 (7th Cir., 1997).

9 U.S. Constitution, Amendment XIV.

10 Equal Educational Opportunities Act, 20 U.S.C. § 1701 et seq. (1976).

11 *Green v. County School Board*, 391 U.S. 430, 439 (1968).

12 In response to such an argument, the Supreme Court stated, "If the State perpetuates policies and practices traceable to its prior system that continue to have segregative effects . . . and such policies are without sound educational justification and can practically be eliminated, the State has not satisfied its burden of proving that it has dismantled its prior system." *United States v. Fordice*, 505 U.S. 717 (1992). See also *McNeal v. Tate County School District*, 508 F.2d 1017 (5th Cir., 1975); *Debra P. v. Turlington*, 644 F.2d 397 (5th Cir., 1981).

13 See, e.g., *McNeal v. Tate County School District*, 508 F.2d 1017 (5th Cir., 1975); *Georgia State Conference of Branches of NAACP v. Georgia*, 775 F.2d 1403 (11th Cir., 1985).

14 *Debra P. v. Turlington*, 644 F.2d 397 (5th Cir., 1981).

15 National Research Council, *High Stakes: Testing for Tracking, Promotion, and Graduation*. To be sure, there have been some recent cases in which

plaintiffs have continued to employ this kind of argument. See, e.g., *GI Forum v. Texas Education Agency*, 87 F. Supp. 2d 667 (W.D. Tex., 2000).

16 34 C.F.R. § 100.3(b)(2) (2000); 34 C.F.R. § 106.31 (2000); 34 C.F.R. § 104.4(b) (2000); 28 C.F.R. § 35.130(b)(3)(i) (2000).

17 *Watson v. Fort Worth Bank and Trust*, 487 U.S. 977 (1988).

18 In *Groves v. Alabama State Board of Education*, a district court described many of the different statistical tests that have been used for this purpose. See *Groves v. Alabama State Board of Education*, 776 F. Supp. 1518, 1526–28 (M.D. Ala., 1991).

19 Ibid.

20 *Larry P. v. Riles*, 793 F.2d 969 (9th Cir., 1984).

21 Ibid.

22 See *Wards Cove Packing Company v. Antonio*, 490 U.S. 642 (1989); *New York Urban League v. New York*, 71 F.3d 1031 (2d Cir., 1995).

23 *Larry P. v. Riles*, 793 F.2d 969 (9th Cir., 1984); *Georgia State Conference of Branches of NAACP v. Georgia*, 775 F.2d 1403 (11th Cir., 1985); *Sharif v. New York State Department of Education*, 709 F. Supp. 345 (S.D.N.Y., 1989).

24 *Larry P. v. Riles*, 793 F.2d 969, 983 (9th Cir., 1984).

25 Jennifer Mueller, "Facing the Unhappy Day: Three Aspects of the High-Stakes Testing Movement," *Kansas Journal of Law and Public Policy* 11, no. 2 (2001): 201–78.

26 *Groves v. Alabama State Board of Education*, 776 F. Supp. 1518 (M.D. Ala., 1991); *United States v. Fordice*, 505 U.S. 717 (1992). To be sure, the *AERA Standards* would include an examination of cut score placement and whether high-stakes decisions are predicated on the results of one particular test as part of a validity analysis. However, courts have sometimes carved out such examinations from their formal validity analyses in the process of determining whether a testing practice is educationally necessary.

27 *Larry P. v. Riles*, 793 F.2d 969, 980 (9th Cir., 1984).

28 Mueller, "Facing the Unhappy Day: Three Aspects of the High-Stakes Testing Movement."

29 Benjamin M. Superfine, "At the Intersection of Law and Psychometrics: Explaining the Validity Clause of No Child Left Behind," *Journal of Law and Education* 33 (2004): 475–513.

30 *Richardson v. Lamar County Board of Education*, 729 F. Supp. 809 (M.D. Alabama, 1989); *New York Urban League v. New York*, 71 F.3d 1031 (2d Cir., 1995).

31 Wards Cove Packing Company v. Antonio, 490 U.S. 642 (1989); Sharif v. New York State Department of Education, 709 F. Supp. 345 (S.D.N.Y., 1989).

32 National Research Council, *High Stakes: Testing for Tracking, Promotion, and Graduation.*

33 American Educational Research Association, American Psychological Association, and National Council on Measurement in Education, "Standards for Educational and Psychological Testing," (Washington, D.C.: American Educational Research Association, 1999).

34 In *Lau v. Nichols*, the Supreme Court specifically ruled that a district's policy of teaching LEP students only in English violated Title VI because students were deprived of their opportunities to graduate. *Lau v. Nichols*, 414 U.S. 563 (1974). In a later case, *Castaneda v. Pickard*, a federal appeals court relied on the Equal Educational Opportunities Act to specify steps that schools must take to help LEP students participate in a district's educational program. *Castaneda v. Pickard*, 648 F. 2d 989 (5th Cir., 1981). The court generally held that schools serving LEP students must adopt an educational program that is recognized as sound by experts in the field, implement that program effectively, and evaluate the effectiveness of the program on an ongoing basis. Several courts have subsequently followed the holding of *Castaneda*. See, e.g., *Idaho Migrant Council v. Board of Education*, 647 F.2d 69 (9th Cir., 1981); *Gomez v. Illinois Board of Education*, 811 F.2d 1030 (7th Cir., 1987); *Flores v. Arizona*, 48 F.Supp.2d 937 (D. Ariz., 1999).

35 American Educational Research Association, American Psychological Association, and National Council on Measurement in Education, "Standards for Educational and Psychological Testing."

36 34 C.F.R. § 104.35(b) (2005).

37 34 C.F.R. § 104.35(c) (2005).

38 *Alexander v. Sandoval*, 532 U.S. 275 (2001).

39 *Erik V. v. Causby*, 977 F.Supp. 384 (E.D.N.C., 1997); *Debra P. v. Turlington*, 644 F.2d 397 (5th Cir., 1981).

40 Decker F. Walker, "What Constitutes Curricular Validity in a High-School-Leaving Examination?" in *The Courts, Validity, and Minimum Competency Testing*, ed. George Mandaus (Boston, MA: Kluwer-Nijhoff Publishing, 1983).

41 See, e.g., William S. Koski, "Educational Opportunity and Accountability in an Era of Standards-Based School Reform," *Stanford Law and Policy Review* 12 (2001): 301–15; Rachel Moran, "Sorting and Reforming: High-Stakes Testing in the Public Schools," *Akron Law Review* 34 (2000): 107–35; Jennifer Mueller, "Facing the Unhappy Day: Three Aspects of the High-Stakes Testing Movement."

42 Fla.Stat. § 229 et seq. (1976).

43 Fla.Stat. § 232.246 (1978).

44 Walt Haney, "Validity and Competency Tests: The *Debra P.* Case, Conceptions of Validity, and Strategies for the Future," in *The Courts, Validity, and Minimum Competency Testing*, ed. George F. Madaus (Boston, MA: Kluwer Nijhoff Publishing, 1983). To be clear, the concept of

validity has shifted over time, and psychometricians still argue about how validity should be defined. Under one influential construction of validity, the concept is unified and consists of various aspects, including content validity. See Samuel Messick, "Validity," in *Educational Measurement*, ed. Robert L. Linn (New York, NY: American Council on Education, 1989).

45 Haney, "Validity and Competency Tests: The *Debra P.* Case, Conceptions of Validity, and Strategies for the Future."

46 *Debra P. v. Turlington*, 474 F.Supp. 244 (M.D. Fla., 1979).

47 Judge Carr particularly cited *Goss v. Lopez* for support that the plaintiffs possessed a property right in a diploma. *Goss v. Lopez*, 419 U.S. 565 (1975). Notably, Judge Carr also determined that all the plaintiffs had a liberty interest at stake as well because failure to receive a diploma would result in adverse stigma that would affect the economic and psychological development of the plaintiffs.

48 *Debra P. v. Turlington*, 474 F.Supp. 244, 265 (M.D. Fla., 1979).

49 *Debra P. v. Turlington*, 644 F.2d 397 (5th Cir., 1981).

50 Ibid., 404.

51 *Debra P. v. Turlington*, 654 F.2d 1079 (5th Cir., 1981).

52 *Debra P. v. Turlington*, 564 F.Supp. 177 (M.D. Fla., 1983).

53 It is important to note that Judge Carr also held a second trial on the issue of perpetuating the effects of past segregation. Although the discussion of the remand does not cover this second trial for sake of space, Judge Carr found that sufficient time had passed for all students to receive a sufficient education and that the graduation requirement accordingly would not continue to perpetuate the effects of past segregation.

54 *Debra P. v. Turlington*, 564 F.Supp. 177, 183 (M.D. Fla., 1983).

55 Ibid., 186.

56 *Debra P. v. Turlington*, 730 F.2d 1405 (5th Cir., 1984).

57 *GI Forum v. Texas Education Agency*, 87 F. Supp. 2d 667 (W.D. Tex., 2000).

58 Keith L. Cruse and Jon S. Twing, "The History of Statewide Achievement Testing in Texas," *Applied Measurement in Education* 13, no. 4 (2000): 327–31.

59 In 1998–1999, Texas also replaced the Essential Elements with the Texas Essential Knowledge and Skills, standards that are arguably more rigorous than the Essential Elements.

60 Walt Haney, "The Myth of the Texas Miracle in Education," *Education Policy Analysis Archives* 8, no. 41 (2000). http://epaa.asu.edu (accessed July 9, 2006).

61 Still, Judge Prado did note that such considerations cannot be used to "tie a court's hands" when a state uses its power to impermissibly disadvantage minority students. *GI Forum v. Texas Education Agency*, 87 F. Supp. 2d 667, 668 (W.D. Tex., 2000).

62 Plaintiffs' Response and Brief in Opposition to Defendants' Motion for Summary Judgment, Ibid.

63 Defendants' Motion for Summary Judgment and Brief in Support, Ibid.

64 Defendants' Motion for Summary Judgment and Brief in Support, Ibid. Plaintiffs' Response and Brief in Opposition to Defendants' Motion for Summary Judgment, Ibid.

65 Judge Prado particularly looked to the "Four-Fifths Rule" used by the Equal Employment Opportunity Commission in the context of employment discrimination. Under this test, a plaintiff can make a *prima facie* case of disparate impact if the passage rate for minorities is less than 80 percent of the passage rate for whites.

66 *GI Forum v. Texas Education Agency*, 87 F. Supp. 2d 667, 681 (W.D. Tex., 2000).

67 Susan E. Phillips, "*GI Forum v. Texas Education Agency*: Psychometric Evidence," *Applied Measurement in Education* 13, no. 4 (2000): 343–85.

68 Superfine, "At the Intersection of Law and Psychometrics: Explaining the Validity Clause of No Child Left Behind." By examining the potential effects of the TAAS on student motivation, Judge Prado implicitly examined the "consequential aspect" of validity to determine the justifiability of the administration of the TAAS. The extent to which a validity analysis should include an analysis of the consequences of testing practices has been hotly debated among psychometricians and is currently unresolved.

69 Phillips, "*GI Forum v. Texas Education Agency*: Psychometric Evidence."

70 See, e.g., William A. Mehrens, "Defending a State Graduation Test: *GI Forum v. Texas Education Agency*: Measurement Perspectives from an External Evaluator," *Applied Measurement in Education* 13, no. 4 (2000): 387–401; Phillips, "*GI Forum v. Texas Education Agency*: Psychometric Evidence."; Ann Smisko, Jon S. Twing, and Patricia Denny, "The Texas Model for Content and Curricular Validity," *Applied Measurement in Education* 13, no. 4 (2000): 333–42; Haney, "The Myth of the Texas Miracle in Education."

71 See, e.g., Audrey L. Amerin and David C. Berliner, "High-Stakes Testing, Uncertainty, and Student Learning," *Education Policy Analysis Archives* 10, no. 18 (2002). http://epaa.asu.edu (accessed July 9, 2006); Martin Carnoy and Susanna Loeb, "Does External Accountability Affect Student Outcomes? A Cross-State Analysis," *Educational Evaluation and Policy Analysis* 24, no. 4 (2002): 305–31; Laurence A. Toenjes and A. G. Dworkin, "Are Increasing Test Scores in Texas Really a Myth, or Is Haney's Myth a Myth?," *Education Policy Analysis Archives* 10, no. 17 (2002). http://epaa.asu.edu (accessed July 9, 2006).

72 Moran, "Sorting and Reforming: High-Stakes Testing in the Public Schools."

73 Ibid. For an example of recent high-stakes litigation where the plaintiffs met limited success, see *O'Connell v. Superior Court*, 47 Cal.Rptr.3d 147 (Cal.App. 1 Dist., 2006).

74 Moran, "Sorting and Reforming: High-Stakes Testing in the Public Schools."

75 Moran also highlighted the limited potential of high-stakes testing litigation to address the underlying causes of poor or inequitable performance. Ibid.

76 James Crawford, "A Diminished Vision of Civil Rights: No Child Left Behind and the Growing Divide in How Educational Equity Is Understood," *Education Week*, June 6, 2007. http://www/edweek.org (accessed January 9, 2006).

77 Testimony of Peter Zamora, Washington, D.C. Regional Councel, MALDEF, House Education and Labor Committee, Early Childhood, Elementary and Secondary Education Subcomittee, "Impact of NCLB on English Language Learners." March 23, 2007.

Chapter Four

1 Section 1983 actions are discussed in detail later in this chapter.

2 *Association of Community Organizations for Reform Now v. New York City Department of Education*, 269 F. Supp. 2d 338 (S.D.N.Y., 2003).

3 New York State Education Department, *Schools in New York*. http://usny.nysed.gov/citizens/nyschools.html (accessed July 10, 2007).

4 Complaint, *Association of Community Organizations for Reform Now v. New York City Department of Education*, 269 F. Supp. 2d 338 (S.D.N.Y., 2003).

5 Foundation for Education Reform and Accountability, "Survey of NYC Parents: Strong Support for Increased Parental Options as Klein Gets Ready to Overhaul School System," (Clifton Park, NY: Foundation for Education Reform and Accountability, 2002).

6 Joe Williams, "School Transfer Delays Slammed," *New York Daily News*, September 20, 2002. http://www.lexis.com (accessed July 9, 2006).

7 Complaint, *Association of Community Organizations for Reform Now v. New York City Department of Education*, 269 F. Supp. 2d 338 (S.D.N.Y., 2003).

8 Complaint, Ibid.

9 Complaint, Ibid.

10 Abby Goodnough, "Free Tutoring Fails to Draw Many Students," *New York Times*, September 4, 2002. http://www.lexis.com (accessed July 9, 2006).

11 Complaint, *Association of Community Organizations for Reform Now v. New York City Department of Education*, 269 F. Supp. 2d 338 (S.D.N.Y., 2003).

12 Complaint, Ibid.

13 For more information on whether a statute contains an implied cause of action, see *Cort v. Ash*, 422 U.S. 66 (1975).

14 *Gonzaga University v. Doe*, 536 U.S. 273 (2002).

15 42 U.S.C. § 1983 (2006).

16 Bradford C. Mank, "Suing under Section 1983: The Future after *Gonzaga University v. Doe*," *Houston Law Review* 39 (2003): 1417–82.

17 *Blessing v. Freestone*, 520 U.S. 329 (1997).

18 *Gonzaga University v. Doe*, 536 U.S. 273 (2002).

19 See, e.g., Marsha S. Berzon, "Rights and Remedies," *Louisiana Law Review* 64 (2004): 519–44; Melanie Natasha Henry, "No Child Left Behind? Educational Malpractice Litigation for the 21st Century," *California Law Review* 92 (2004): 1117–71.

20 *Association of Community Organizations for Reform Now v. New York City Department of Education*, 269 F. Supp. 2d 338 (S.D.N.Y., 2003).

21 *Fresh Start Academy v. Toledo Board of Education*, 363 F.Supp.2d 910 (N.D. Ohio, 2005); *Alliance for Children, Inc. v. City of Detroit Public Schools*, 475 F.Supp.2d 655 (E.D. Mich., 2007).

22 Transcript of Hearing before Pennsylvania Department of Education, *Reading School District v. Pennsylvania Department of Education*, 855 A.2d 166 (Pa. Commw. Ct., 2004) (*Reading I*).

23 Transcript of Hearing before Pennsylvania Department of Education, Ibid.

24 Transcript of Hearing before Pennsylvania Department of Education, Ibid.

25 *Reading School District v. Pennsylvania Department of Education*, No. 472 M.D. 2005 (Pa. Commw. Ct., 2004) (*Reading II*).

26 Pennsylvania Department of Education, "2007 Accommodations Guidelines," (Harrisburg, PA: Pennsylvania Department of Education, 2006).

27 *Reading School District v. Pennsylvania Department of Education*, 855 A.2d 166 (Pa. Commw. Ct., 2004) (*Reading I*). Many statisticians would consider the term "N number" to be redundant. To statisticians, "N" generally refers to a number. However, because the *Reading I* court uses the term "N number," I have used this term to avoid further confusion.

28 Transcript of Hearing before Pennsylvania Department of Education, Ibid.

29 Caroline M. Hoxby, "Inadequate Yearly Progress: Unlocking the Secrets of NCLB," *Education Next* 5, no. 3 (2005): 46–51; Robert L. Linn, Eva L. Baker, and Damian W. Betebenner, "Accountability Systems: Implications of Requirements of the No Child Left Behind Act of 2001," *Educational Researcher* 31, no. 6 (2002): 3–16,

30 Matthew Bender & Company, "Education Law," (New York, NY: Matthew Bender & Company, 2004), § 12.03.

31 *Sell v. Worker's Compensation Appeal Board*, 771 A.2d 1246, 1250–51 (Pa., 2001).

32 No Child Left Behind Act of 2001, 20 U.S.C. § 6317 (2002).

33 No Child Left Behind Act of 2001, 20 U.S.C. § 6316(c)(8)(B) (2002); 34 C.F.R. § 200.52(b) (2003).

34 *Reading School District v. Pennsylvania Department of Education*, 855 A.2d 166, 171 (Pa. Commw. Ct., 2004) (*Reading I*).

35 No Child Left Behind Act of 2001, 20 U.S.C. § 6311 (c)(3)(C)(ix)(III) (2002).

36 Transcript of Hearing before Pennsylvania Department of Education, *Reading School District v. Pennsylvania Department of Education*, 855 A.2d 166 (Pa. Commw. Ct., 2004) (*Reading I*).

37 *Reading School District v. Pennsylvania Department of Education*, 855 A.2d 166, 172 (Pa. Commw. Ct., 2004) (*Reading I*).

38 No Child Left Behind Act of 2001, 20 U.S.C. § 6311(b)(2)(C)(v)(2) (2002).

39 34 C.F.R. § 200.7 (2003).

40 *Reading School District v. Pennsylvania Department of Education*, No. 472 M.D. 2005 (Pa. Commw. Ct., 2005) (*Reading II*).

41 *Reading School District v. Pennsylvania Department of Education*, 2278 C.D. 2004 (Pa. Commw. Ct., 2005) (*Reading III*).

42 Ibid., 3. The court particularly asked whether PDE's limits on the grounds on which it would allow school districts to appeal AYP determinations violates the due process guarantees of the Fourteenth Amendment of the U.S. Constitution.

43 *Center for Law and Education v. United States Department of Education*, 209 F. Supp. 102 (D.D.C., 2002) (*CLE I*); *Center for Law and Education v. United States Department of Education*, 315 F. Supp. 2d 15 (D.D.C., 2004) (*CLE II*).

44 34 C.F.R. § 200.3(a)(2) (2004). For more information on the properties of criterion-referenced tests, norm-referenced tests, and augmented norm-referenced tests, see Sasha Zucker, "Using Augmented Norm-Referenced Assessments for NCLB Compliance" (San Antonio, TX: Harcourt Assessment, Inc., 2004).

45 34 C.F.R. § 200.2(b)(7) (2005).

46 *Center for Law and Education v. United States Department of Education*, 315 F. Supp. 2d 15, 21 (D.D.C., 2004) (*CLE II*).

47 Editorial Projects in Education, "Education Counts Research Center." http://www.edweek.org/rc (accessed September 8, 2007).

48 Negotiated Rulemaking Act, 5 U.S.C. § 561 et seq. (2004).

49 "Notice of Meetings to Conduct a Negotiated Rulemaking Process." *Federal Register* 67: 40 (28 February, 2002) pp. 9223–24.

50 Appendix to Plaintffs' Memorandum of Points and Authorities in Opposition to Defendants' Motion to Dismiss or for Summary Judgment or, in the Alternative, Plaintiffs Rule 56(F) Motion to Defer Ruling on Summary Judgment, *Center for Law and Education v. United States Department of Education*, 315 F. Supp. 2d 15 (D.D.C., 2004) (*CLE II*).

51 Ibid.

52 *Lujan v. Defenders of Wildlilfe*, 504 U.S. 555 (1992).

53 *Center for Law and Education v. United States Department of Education*, 315 F. Supp. 2d 15 (D.D.C., 2004) (*CLE II*).

54 *Board of Education of Ottawa Township High School District 140 v. U.S. Department of Education*, 2007 U.S. Dist. LEXIS 24057 (N.D. Ill., 2005).

55 *Reading School District v. Pennsylvania Department of Education*, 2278 C.D. 2004 (Pa. Commw. Ct., 2005) (*Reading III*).

56 *School District of Pontiac v. Spellings*, 2005 U.S. Dist. LEXIS 29253 (E.D. Mich., 2005); *State of Connecticut v. Spellings*, 453 F.Supp.2d 459 (E.D. Mich., 2006).

57 See, e.g., U.S. Congress. Senate Committee on Health Education Labor and Pensions, *Hearing Examining State and Community Perspectives on the Implementation of Title I of H.R. 1, to Close the Achievement Gap with Accountability, Flexibility, and Choice, So That No Child Is Left Behind* (September 10, 2002).

58 Bess Keller, "NEA Takes Stand against Bush Education Law," *Education Week*, July 7, 2003. http://www.edweek.org (accessed September 8, 2006).

59 National Education Association et al., "Joint Organizational Statement on 'No Child Left Behind' Act," (Washington, D.C.: National Education Association, 2004).

60 Center on Education Policy, "From the Capital to the Classroom: Year 2 of the No Child Left Behind Act," (Washington, D.C.: Center on Education Policy, 2004).

61 *School District of Pontiac v. Spellings*, 2005 U.S. Dist. LEXIS 29253 (E.D. Mich., 2005).

62 Complaint, Ibid.

63 No Child Left Behind Act of 2001, 20 U.S.C. § 7907(a) (2002).

64 *Pennhurst State School and Hospital v. Halderman*, 451 U.S. 1 (1981).

65 Complaint, *School District of Pontiac v. Spellings*, 2005 U.S. Dist. LEXIS 29253 (E.D. Mich., 2005).

66 Complaint, Ibid.

67 National Conference of State Legislatures, "Task Force on No Child Left Behind: Final Report," (Washington, D.C.: National Conference of State Legislatures, 2005).

68 Jennifer Imazeki and Andrew Reschovsky, "Does No Child Left Behind Place a Fiscal Burden on States? Evidence from Texas," (Madison, WI: La Follette School of Public Affairs, 2005).

69 *State of Connecticut v. Spellings*, 453 F.Supp.2d 459 (E.D. Mich., 2006).

70 Education Week, "Quality Counts at 10: A Decade of Standards-Based Education," (Washington, D.C.: Education Week, 2006).

71 Soncia Coleman, "Background on Connecticut's No Child Left Behind Act Law Suit," (Hartford: CT, Office of Legislative Research, Connecticut General Assembly, 2006).

72 *School District of Pontiac v. Spellings*, 2005 U.S. Dist. LEXIS 29253 (E.D. Mich., 2005).

73 Ibid., *4.

74 Ibid.

75 *Pontiac v. Spellings*, N. 05-2708 (6th Cir., Jan. 7, 2008).

76 Sam Dillon, "Court Revives Lawsuit against No Child Left Behind," *New York Times*, January 8, 2008. http://www.lexis.com (accessed January 9, 2008).

77 *State of Connecticut v. Spellings*, 453 F.Supp.2d 459, 487 (E.D. Mich., 2006).

78 In addition, Judge Kravitz concluded that, even if the court did have "subject matter" jurisdiction to hear the claim, he would deny jurisdiction because the claim would not be ripe – that is, the claim needed further factual development for the claim to be decided by a court unless undue hardship on one of the parties would be imposed.

79 *State of Connecticut v. Spellings*, 453 F.Supp.2d 459, 499 (E.D. Mich., 2006).

80 For a discussion about the methodologies used in cost studies and the validity of cost studies, see Chapter Five.

81 *Californians for Justice Education Fund v. California State Board of Education*, 2003 Cal. App. Unpub. LEXIS 11713 (Ct. App. Cal. 2003) (*CJE*).

82 *Kegerreis v. United States*, 2003 WL 22327188 (D. Kan., 2003).

83 Elizabeth DeBray-Pelot, "NCLB's Transfer Policy and Court-Ordered Desegregation: The Conflict between Two Federal Mandates in Richmond County, Georgia, and Pinellas County, Florida," *Educational Policy* 21, no. 5 (2007): 717–46.

84 *Alliance for Children, Inc. v. City of Detroit Public Schools*, 475 F.Supp.2d 655 (E.D. Mich., 2007). The supplemental services provider in *Alliance for Children* also sued Detroit Public Schools under (a) the Fourteenth Amendment for terminating its contract with the provider without cause and under (b) the First Amendment for retaliating against the provider by refusing to award another contract for speaking out against its treatment with regard to the previous contract. The court dismissed both of these claims. Because the relationship between these arguments

and the core elements of standards-based reform and accountability policies is so attenuated, this chapter does not address these arguments in any more detail.

85 Connecticut State Conference of NAACP Branches, "CT NAACP Urges State to Avoid Wasting Additional Funds Pursuing NCLB Suit," (Connecticut State Conference of NAACP Branches, 2006). The Lawyers' Committee for Civil Rights Under Law joined the NAACP in press release.

86 20 U.S.C. § 3401 et seq. (1979).

87 Notably, NCLB does include some sections addressing particular educational strategies. For example, NCLB provides grants to states under its Reading First program to help states implement reading programs that comport with specific criteria articulated in NCLB.

Chapter Five

1 Michael Griffith, "School Finance Litigation and Beyond," http://www.ecs.org/clearinghouse/60/26/6026.htm (accessed August 10, 2006).

2 William N. Evans, Sheila E. Murray, and Robert M. Schwab, "The Impact of Court-Mandated Finance Reform," in *Equity and Adequacy in Education Finance: Issues and Perspectives*, ed. Helen F. Ladd, et al. (Washington, D.C.: Brookings Institution Press, 1999); Bradley W. Joondeph, "The Good, the Bad and the Ugly: An Empirical Analysis of Litigation Prompted School Finance Reform," *Santa Clara Law Review* 35 (1995): 763–824.

3 Patricia F. First and Louis F. Miron, "The Social Construction of Adequacy," *Journal of Law and Education* 20 (1991); Joondeph, "The Good, the Bad and the Ugly: An Empirical Analysis of Litigation Prompted School Finance Reform."

4 Michael Heise, "Equal Educational Opportunity, Hollow Victories, and the Demise of School Finance Equity Theory: An Empirical Perspective and Alternative Explanations," *Georgia Law Review* 32: 543–631; Joondeph, "The Good, the Bad and the Ugly: An Empirical Analysis of Litigation Prompted School Finance Reform."

5 The Fourteenth Amendment of the U.S. Constitution states, "No state shall make or enforce any law which shall abridge the privileges or immunities of citizens of the Unites States; nor shall any state deprive any person of life, liberty, or property, without due process of law; nor deny to any person within its jurisdiction the equal protection of the laws." the equal protection of the laws." U.S. Constitution, Amendment XIV.

6 The "wave" metaphor has been commonly employed by scholars to describe the different types of school finance litigation. William Thro first popularized the metaphor. William Thro, "To Render Them

Safe: The Analysis of State Constitutional Provisions in School Finance Litigation," *Virginia Law Review* 75 (1989): 1639–79. The wave metaphor has been adopted by a host of others. For example, see Michael Heise, "State Constitutions, School Finance Litigation, and the 'Third Wave': From Equity to Adequacy," *Temple Law Review* 68 (1995): 1151–76; Levine Gail F. Levine, "Meeting the Third Wave: Legislative Approaches to Recent Judicial School Finance Rulings," *Harvard Journal on Legislation* 28 (1991): 507–542. Each of the three waves is discussed in chronological order in this chapter. Although William Koski has questioned the accuracy of the wave metaphor, I use the wave metaphor here because it is useful for structuring a brief overview of the major issues in almost 40 years of school finance reform litigation. William S. Koski, "Of Fuzzy Standards and Institutional Constraints: A Re-Examination of the Jurisprudential History of Educational Finance Reform Litigation," *Santa Clara Law Review* 43 (2003): 1185–1298.

7 *San Antonio Independent School District v. Rodriguez*, 411 U.S. 1 (1973). Applying a traditional equal protection analysis to Texas's school financing scheme, the Supreme Court found that, under the U.S. Constitution, education does not constitute a fundamental right and wealth does not constitute a suspect class. Thus, the Supreme Court applied the rational basis test instead of strict scrutiny and concluded that the U.S. Constitution does not constitute a viable basis for equalizing differences in education funding.

8 Robert F. Williams, "Equality Guarantees in State Constitutional Law," *Texas Law Review* 63 (1985): 1195–1223.

9 Peter Enrich, "Leaving Equality Behind: New Directions in School Finance Reform," *Vanderbilt Law Review* 48 (1995): 101–194. In contrast to state constitutions, the U.S. Constitution does not contain an education clause and includes no explicit mention of education anywhere in its text. As discussed in the footnotes of Chapter One, Mississippi's state constitution is the only one that arguably does not contain an education clause.

10 For an example of plaintiffs relying solely on an equal protection clause in the second wave, see *Serrano v. Priest*, 557 P.2d 929 (Cal. 1976). For an example of plaintiffs relying primarily on an education clause in the second wave, see *Robinson v. Cahill*, 351 A.2d 713 (N.J. 1975). For an example of plaintiffs relying on both types of clauses taken together, see *Washakie County School District Number One v. Herschler*, 606 P.2d 310 (1980).

11 In describing the problems facing school finance reform litigation in the second wave, this chapter draws heavily from Peter Enrich, "Leaving Equality Behind: New Directions in School Finance Reform."

12 See, e.g., *Danson v. Casey*, 299 A.2d 360 (Pa. 1979); *Abbott v. Burke*, 575 A.2d 359 (N.J. 1990).

13 See, e.g., *McDaniel v. Thomas*, 285 S.E.2d 156 (Ga. 1981).

14 See, e.g., *Olsen v. State*, 55 P.2d 139 (Or. 1976); *Levittown Union Free School District v. Nyquist*, 439 N.E.2d 359 (N.Y. 1982).

15 Richard F. Elmore and Milbrey McLaughlin, *Reform and Retrenchment: the Politics of California School Finance Reform* (Cambridge, MA: Ballinger, 1982); Government Accountability Office, "School Finance: State Efforts to Equalize Funding between Wealthy and Poor School Districts," (Washington, D.C.: Government Printing Office, 1998); Mark Jaffe and Kenneth Kersch, "Guaranteeing a State Right to a Quality Education: The Judicial-Political Dialogue in New Jersey," *Journal of Law and Education* 20 (1991): 271–300.

16 *Rose v. Council for Better Education*, 790 S.W.2d 186 (K.Y. 1989).

17 During the 1980s, Kentucky ranked 50th among the states in adult literacy and adults with high school diplomas, 49th in the rate of students continuing to college, and 48th in per pupil expenditures on public schools. Moreover, only 68 percent of ninth graders were graduating from high school in four years, and in the Appalachian counties, over 48 percent of the population was functionally illiterate. Molly Hunter, "All Eyes Forward: Public Engagement and Education Reform in Kentucky," *Journal of Law and Education* 28 (1999): 485–516.

18 The *Rose* court stated that an efficient system of education must have as its goal to provide each and every child with at least the seven following capacities: (i) sufficient oral and written communication skills to enable students to function in a complex and rapidly changing civilization; (ii) sufficient knowledge of economic, social, and political systems to enable the student to make informed choices; (iii) sufficient understanding of governmental processes to enable the student to understand the issues that affect his or her community, state, and nation; (iv) sufficient self-knowledge and knowledge of his or her mental and physical wellness; (v) sufficient grounding in the arts to enable each student to appreciate his or her cultural and historical heritage; (vi) sufficient training or preparation for advanced training in either academic or vocational fields so as to enable each child to choose and pursue life work intelligently; and (vii) sufficient levels of academic or vocational skills to enable public school students to compete favorably with their counterparts in surrounding states, in academics or in the job market. *Rose v. Council for Better Education*, 212.

19 Kentucky Education Reform Act, Ky. Rev. Ann. § 156.005 et seq. (1991).

20 C. Scott Trimble and Andrew C. Forsaith, "Achieving Equity and Excellence in Kentucky Education," *University of Michigan Journal of Law Reform* 28 (1995): 599–653. In the year after KERA's enactment, total education revenues in Kentucky increased by 38 percent, and the range of per pupil revenue among districts decreased by 45.9 percent.

21 Kentucky Education Reform Act, Ky. Rev. Ann. § 156.005 et seq. (1991).

22 Ibid., § 156.6453 (1991).

23 Ibid., § 156.6455 (1991).

24 Ibid.

25 *McDuffy v. Secretary of the Executive Office of Education*, 615 N.E.2d 516 (Mass. 1993).

26 National Access Network, "School Funding Decisions since 1989." (New York: NY: National Access Network, 2006).

27 In detailing the benefits of adequacy arguments over equity-based arguments, this section draws heavily from Enrich, "Leaving Equality Behind: New Directions in School Finance Reform."

28 *Dupree v. Alma School District Number 30*, 651 S.W.2d 90, 93 (Ark. 1983).

29 Since as early as *Rodriguez*, courts have indicated that, when they hear school finance reform suits, they deal in an area without clear standards and where courts have "traditionally deferred to legislatures." *San Antonio Independent School District v. Rodriguez*, 40. For example, overturning the judgment of a lower court specifically in an adequacy suit, the Rhode Island Supreme Court emphasized, "[T]he judgment fails to recognize the role of the Judiciary in our tripartite system of government. By retaining jurisdiction for purposes of enforcement, the Superior Court self-imposed a role in this state's education system far beyond the Judiciary's constitutional powers or institutional capacity. *City of Pawtucket v. Sudlun*, 662 A.2d 40, 55 (R.I. 1995).

30 *Baker v. Carr*, 369 U.S. 186 (1962). The six criteria for a non-justiciable political question are: (1) a textually demonstrable commitment of the issue to a coordinate political department; (2) a lack of judicially discoverable and manageable standards for resolving it; (3) the impossibility of deciding without an initial policy determination of a kind clearly for non-judicial discretion; (4) the impossibility of a court's undertaking independent resolution without expressing lack of the respect due coordinate branches of government; (5) an unusual need for unquestioning adherence to a political question already made; and (6) the potentiality of embarrassment from multifarious pronouncement by various departments on one question.

31 *Committee for Educational Rights v. Edgar*, 672 N.E.2d 1178, 1192 (1996).

32 For example, the New Hampshire Supreme Court also used the *Rose* capabilities to define an adequate education but deferred to the other branches of government to "promptly develop and adopt specific criteria implementing these guidelines." *Claremont School District v. Governor*, 703 A.2d 1353, 1360 (N.H. 1997). See also *Brigham v. State*, 692 A.2d 384 (Vt. 1997); *Columbia Falls Elementary School District No. 6 v. State*, 109 P.3d 304 (Mt. 2005).

33 *Claremont School District v. Governor*, 794 A.2d 744, 745–46 (N.H. 2002).

34 See *Abbott v. Burke*, 748 A.2d 82 (N.J., 2002).

35 Improving America's Schools Act, 20 U.S.C. § 6301 et seq. (1994). See Chapter Two for more detail on this law.

36 U.S. Department of Education, "High Standards for All Students: A Report from the National Assessment of Title I on Progress and Challenges since the 1994 Reauthorization," (Washington, D.C.: U.S. Government Printing Office, 2001).

37 *Leandro v. State*, 488 S.E.2d 249 (N.C., 1997).

38 Public School Forum of North Carolina, "Local School Finance Study," (Raleigh, NC: Public School Form of North Carolina, 1994).

39 North Carolina State Board of Education, "Report Card: The State of School Systems in North Carolina," (Raleigh, NC: North Carolina State Board of Education, 1994).

40 *Leandro v. State*, 1995 WL 17804112 (N. C. Super., 1995).

41 *Leandro v. State*, 468 S.E.2d 543 (N.C. Ct. App., 1996).

42 *Leandro v. State*, 488 S.E.2d 249 (N.C., 1997).

43 Ibid., 254.

44 Ibid., 259.

45 Ibid., 259–60.

46 Ibid. Still, it is important to note that the North Carolina Supreme Court expressly stated that the value of standardized tests is the subject of much debate and must not be treated as absolutely authoritative on the issue of adequacy. Ibid., 260.

47 *Hoke County Board of Education v. State*, 95 CVS 1158 (N.C. Super. Ct., Oct. 12, 2000) (*Hoke I*).

48 Ibid., 109.

49 Ibid.

50 Ibid., 11.

51 *Hoke County Board of Education v. State*, 95 CVS 1158 (N.C. Super. Ct., Oct. 26, 2000) (*Hoke II*). A more detailed discussion of the trend of courts hearing school finance cases to order preschool appears later in this chapter.

52 *Hoke County Board of Education v. State*, 95 CVS 1158 (N.C. Super. Ct., Mar. 26, 2001) (*Hoke III*).

53 *Hoke County Board of Education v. State*, 95 CVS 1158, 78 (N.C. Super. Ct., Oct. 12, 2000) (*Hoke I*).

54 Ibid., 89.

55 Ibid., 90.

56 *Hoke County Board of Education v. State*, 95 CVS 1158 (N.C. Super. Ct., Apr. 4, 2002) (*Hoke IV*). In the third opinion, Judge Manning actually ordered North Carolina and the plaintiffs to conduct self-examinations

of how funds were allocated and to produce a plan that focuses resources and funds towards meeting the needs of all children. However, in the wake of a strong, hostile political response, Judge Manning announced that this order was interlocutory, or a temporary order issued during litigation, and issued a slightly different order in the fourth opinion.

57 *Hoke County Board of Education v. State of North Carolina*, 599 S.E.2d 365 (N.C., 2004).

58 Tico A. Almeida, "Refocusing School Finance Litigation on At-Risk Children: *Leandro v. State of North Carolina*," *Yale Law and Policy Review* 22 (2004): 525–69.

59 *Campaign for Fiscal Equity, Inc. v. State of New York*, 655 N.E.2d 661 (N.Y., 1995).

60 The New York Court of Appeals had addressed equality arguments and found them unpersuasive in the previous case *Levittown Union Free School District v. Nyquist*, 439 N.E.2d 359 (N.Y., 1982). In this case, however, the Court of Appeals specifically hinted that adequacy-based arguments may prove more successful in a future lawsuit.

61 *Campaign for Fiscal Equity, Inc. v. State of New York*, 655 N.E.2d 661, 666 (N.Y., 1995).

62 Ibid., 667.

63 Campaign for Fiscal Equity, Inc., "The State of Learning in NY: The State of Learning in New York State Public Schools," (New York, NY: Campaign for Fiscal Equity, Inc., 2001).

64 *Campaign for Fiscal Equity, Inc. v. State of New York*, 719 N.Y.S.2d 475, 483 (Sup. Ct., 2001).

65 Ibid., 484.

66 Ibid., 550.

67 Ibid., 550–51.

68 *Campaign for Fiscal Equity, Inc. v. State of New York*, 744 N.Y.S.2d 130 (N.Y. App. Div., 2002).

69 Ibid., 134.

70 Ibid., 138.

71 Shaila K. Dewan, "Pataki Attacks June Ruling That 8th Grade Education Is Enough," *New York Times*, Sept. 13, 2002. http://www.lexis.com (accessed January 28, 2006).

72 *Campaign for Fiscal Equity, Inc. v. State of New York*, 744 N.Y.S.2d 130 (N.Y. App. Div., 2003).

73 *Campaign for Fiscal Equity, Inc. v. State of New York*, 801 N.E.2d 326 (N.Y., 2003).

74 Ibid., 345.

75 Ibid., 349.

76 Jay G. Chambers et al., "The New York Adequacy Study: Determining

the Cost of Providing All Children in New York an Adequate Education," (Washington, D.C.: American Institutes for Research Management Analysis and Planning, Inc., 2004).

77 Standard & Poor's School Evaluation Services, "Resource Adequacy Study for the New York State Commission on Education Reform," (New York: Standard & Poor's, 2004).

78 New York State Department of Education, "Estimating the Additional Cost of Providing an Adequate Education," (Albany, NY: New York State Department of Education, 2004).

79 John D. Feerick, E. Leo Milonas, and William C. Thompson, "Report and Recommendations of the Judicial Referees," (New York, NY: 2004).

80 *Campaign for Fiscal Equity Inc. v. State of New York*, Order No. 111070/93 (N.Y. Sup. Ct., Mar. 16, 2005).

81 *Campaign for Fiscal Equity, Inc. v. State*, 29 A.D.3d 175 (N.Y. App. Ct., 2006).

82 *Campaign for Fiscal Equity, Inc. v. State of New York*, 861 N.E.2d 50 (N.Y., 2006).

83 Eliot Spitzer, "A Contract for Excellence," (Albany, NY: 2007).

84 Ibid.

85 *DeRolph v. State*, 677 N.E.2d 733, 738 (Ohio, 1997) (*DeRolph I*).

86 Patricia F. First, "The Meaning of Educational Adequacy: The Confusion of *DeRolph*," *Journal of Law and Education* 32 (2003): 185–215.

87 In conducting the 1997 cost study for Ohio, Dr. Auglenblick screened out districts that fell in the top 5 percent and bottom 5 percent of property value per pupil and districts that fell in the top 5 percent and bottom 5 percent of median household incomes. Ibid.

88 *DeRolph v. State*, 728 N.E.2d 993, 1019 (Ohio 2000) (*DeRolph II*).

89 *DeRolph v. State*, 728 N.E.2d 993, 1019 (Ohio 2000) (*DeRolph II*).

90 Ibid., 1019–20.

91 First, "The Meaning of Educational Adequacy: The Confusion of *DeRolph*." This article contains a detailed description of the cost studies conducted during the *DeRolph* litigation, and this section relies heavily on the description of the cost studies in this article.

92 *DeRolph v. State*, 754 N.E.2d 1184, 1189 (Ohio, 2001) (*DeRolph III*). After *DeRolph II* was handed down, several legislators denounced the decision "Reaction Swift, Strong to State Court Decision," *Dayton Daily News*, May 12, 2000. http://www.lexis.com (accessed January 28, 2006). Justice Alice Resnick, the author of the majority opinion in *DeRolph II* received particularly negative press for her role in the case. Larry J. Obhof, "*DeRolph v. State* and Ohio's Long Road to an Adequate Education," *Brigham Young University Education and Law Journal* 2005, no. 1 (2005): 83–149.

93　*Derolph v. State*, 780 N.E.2d 529 (Ohio, 2004) (*DeRolph IV*).

94　*McDuffy v. Secretary of the Executive Office of Education*, 615 N.E.2d 516 (Mass., 1993).

95　Like Judge Manning, Judge Botsford examined several different types of output data in addition to student performance on state tests, such as dropout rates and SAT scores.

96　*Hancock v. Driscoll*, 2004 WL 877984, *118 (2004).

97　Ibid., *112.

98　In describing the cost study, Judge Botsford indicated four areas that "must be considered" for a determination of cost, such as preschool programs for children that would be unable to pay.

99　*Hancock v. Driscoll*, 822 N.E.2d 1134 (Mass., 2005).

100　Ibid., 1152.

101　Ibid., 1160.

102　Notably, Judge Greaney did not go so far as to support Judge Botsford's recommendation that Massachusetts implement whatever funding changes are necessary under the cost study to provide students with an adequate education. Judge Greaney instead indicated that, if more money is needed and is not forthcoming, there would be sufficient time to discuss the matter of appropriations in a nonadversarial way.

103　Ibid., 1170.

104　*Williams v. State of California*, No. 312236 (Ca. Sup. Ct., filed May 17, 2000).

105　While California uses the API to satisfy certain NCLB requirements, AYP under NCLB is calculated differently than the API.

106　See, e.g., W. N. Grubb, Laura Goe, and Luis A. Huerta, "The Unending Search for Equity: California Policy, The "Improved School Finance," And the *Williams* Case," *Teachers College Record* 106, no. 11 (2004): 2081–101; Thomas B. Timar, "School Governance and Oversight in California: Shaping the Landscape of Equity and Adequacy," *Teachers College Record* 106, no. 11 (2004): 2057–80.

107　Complaint, *Williams v. State of California*, No. 312236 (Ca. Sup. Ct., filed May 17, 2000).

108　Order, *Williams v. State of California*, No. 312236 (Ca. Sup. Ct., Nov. 14, 2000).

109　The experts' reports for *Williams v. State of California* are available at http://www.decentschools.org. accessed August 27, 2007.

110　The bills in California were: S.B. 550 (2004); A.B. 2727 (2004).

111　The bills in California were: A.B. 1550 (2004), A.B. 3002 (2004), S.B. 6 (2004).

112　William S. Koski and Hillary Anne Weis, "What Educational Resources Do Students Need to Meet California's Educational Content Standards? A Textual Analysis of California's Educational Content Standards and

Their Implications for Basic Educational Conditions and Resources," *Teachers College Record* 106, no. 10 (2004): 1907–35.

113 ACLU Foundation of Southern California and Public Advocates, Inc., "*Williams v. California*: The Statewide Impact of Two Years of Implementation," Los Angeles, CA: ACLU Foundation of Southern California, 2007.

114 *Columbia Falls Elementary School District Number 6 v. State of Montana*, 2004 WL 844055, *21 (Mont. Dist. 2004).

115 Ibid., *22–23. Dr. John Augenblick, the creator of a cost study heavily relied upon by the Ohio legislature to reform its school funding system, is a founder of Augenblick & Meyers.

116 Ibid., *21.

117 See, e.g., *Claremont School District v. Governor*, 794 A.2d 744 (N.H., 2002); *Lake View School District No. 20 v. Huckabee*, 91 S.E.3d 472 (Ark., 2002); *Neeley v. West Orange Cove Consolidated Independent School District*, 176 S.W.3d 746 (Tex., 2005).

118 James E. Ryan, "The Future of School Finance Litigation," *Texas Law Review* (in press). According to Professor Ryan, only the Kansas Supreme Court has expressly relied on standards to define adequacy. As discussed in this chapter, the North Carolina Supreme Court arguably relied on standards to define adequacy as well. The highest court in New York expressly refused to use standards to define adequacy (though, this court did rely heavily on tests scores linked to standards), the highest court in Massachusetts overturned Judge Botsford's opinion, and *Williams v. State of California* resulted in a settlement.

119 Campaign for Fiscal Equity, Inc., "Costing Out Chart," (New York, NY: Campaign for Fiscal Equity, Inc., 2006).

120 Although some approaches to conducting cost studies are discussed earlier in this chapter, this note includes descriptions of the four dominant approaches for easy reference. The most common approach uses the "professional judgment" method, which relies on experts, such as teachers, to determine the resources necessary to produce a specified level of achievement. See American Institutes for Research and Management and Planning, Inc., "New York Adequacy Study: Providing All Children with Full Opportunity to Meet the Regents Learning Standards," (New York, NY: American Institutes for Research, 2004). A second method looks to the literature of "effective schools" to determine the resources needed to produce specified educational outcomes. See Lawrence O. Picus and Associates, "A State-of-the-Art Approach to School Finance Adequacy in Kentucky," (Lawrence O. Picus and Associates, 2003). A third method looks at the resources deployed in school districts that are deemed successful via various performance measures. See John Augenblick, John Meyers, and Justin

Silverstein, "Alternative Approaches for Determining a Base Figure and Pupil-weighted Adjustments for Use in a School Finance System in New Hampshire," (Augenblick & Meyers, Inc., 1998). A fourth method, employing a "cost function" analysis, determines, through various cost indices and performance measures, how much a district would have to spend, relative to an average district, to obtain set performance goals. See Andrew Rechovsky and Jennifer Imazeki, "Achieving Adequacy through School Finance Reform," (Philadelphia, PA: Center for Policy Research in Education, 2000). A more comprehensive summary of different types of cost studies can be found in Campaign for Fiscal Equity, Inc., "A Costing Out Primer," (New York, NY: Campaign for Fiscal Equity, Inc., 2005).

121 See, e.g., *Hancock v. Driscoll*, 2004 WL 877984 (Mass. Super., 2004).

122 Eric A. Hanushek, "Pseudo-Science and a Sound Basic Education," *Education Next* 4 (2005): 67–73; Michael A. Rebell, "Professional Rigor, Public Engagement and Judicial Review: A Proposal for Enhancing the Validity of Education Adequacy Studies," *Teachers College Record* 109, no. 6 (2007): 1303–73.

123 Hanushek, "Pseudo-Science and a Sound Basic Education."

124 *Alabama Coalition for Equity, Inc. v. Hunt*, No. CV-90- 883-R (appendix of Opinion of the Justices, 624 So.2d at 128) (citing Alabama Education Improvement Act of 1991, 1991 Ala. Acts 602).
      The discussion of input standards in Alabama is, in part, drawn from William S. Koski, "Educational Opportunity and Accountability in an Era of Standards-Based School Reform," *Stanford Law and Policy Review* 12 (2001): 301–15. In this article, Koski looked to legislative texts in places such as Alabama as a potential basis for litigation, particularly with regard to students' opportunities to learn.

125 1993 Mich. Pub. Acts 335, § 380.1282(2) (codified at Mich. Stat. Ann. § 15.41282(2) (Callaghan 1996). Koski also discussed these legislative standards in Ibid.

126 Courts have ordered the implementation of class size reduction programs in at least New Jersey and Wyoming. See *Abbott v. Burke*, 710 A.2d 450 (N.J., 1998); *Campbell County School District v. State of Wyoming*, 907 P.2d 1238 (Wyo., 1998). Courts have ordered the implementation of whole school reform programs in at least New Jersey. See *Abbott v. Burke*, 710 A.2d 450 (N.J., 1998). Courts have ordered the implementation of preschool programs in at least Arkansas (discussing the unpublished opinion of the trial court), Massachusetts, New Jersey, North Carolina, and South Carolina. See *Hoke County Board of Education v. State*, 95 CVS 1158 (N.C. Super. Ct., Oct. 26, 2000) (*Hoke II*); *Abbott v. Burke*, 710 A.2d 450 (N.J., 1998); *Lake View School District No. 20 v. Huckabee*, 91 S.E.3d 472 (Ark., 2002); *Hancock v. Driscoll*, 2004 WL

877984 (Mass. Super., 2004); *Abbeville County School District v. State*, No. 31-0169 (S.C. Ct. Comm. Pl., 2005).

127 Benjamin M. Superfine and Roger Goddard, "The Expanding Role of the Courts in Education Policy: The Preschool Remedy and an Adequate Education," *Teachers College Record* (in press).

128 Kelly Thompson Cochran, "Beyond School Financing: Defining the Constitutional Right to an Adequate Education," *North Carolina Law Review* 78 (2000); James S. Liebman and Charles F. Sabel, "Changing Schools: A Public Laboratory Dewey Barely Imagined: The Emerging Model of School Governance and Legal Reform," *New York University School of Law Review of Law and Social Change* 28 (2003): 183–304.

129 James S. Liebman, "Implementing Brown in the Nineties: Political Reconstruction, Liberal Recollection, and Litigatively Enforced Legislative Reform," *Virginia Law Review* 76 (1990): 349–345.

130 Aaron J. Saiger, "Legislating Accountability: Standards, Sanctions, and School District Reform," *William and Mary Law Review* 46 (2005): 1655–1732.

131 Michael Heise, "The Courts, Education Policy, and Unintended Consequences," *Cornell Journal of Law and Public Policy* 11 (2002): 636–663.

132 James E. Ryan, "The Future of School Finance Litigation."

Chapter Six

1 See, e.g., Robert F. Nagel, "Separation of Powers and the Scope of Federal Equitable Remedies," *Stanford Law Review* 661 (1978): 661–724.

2 Charles F. Sabel and William H. Simon, "Destabilization Rights: How Public Law Litigation Succeeds," *Harvard Law Review* 117 (2004): 1015–101.

3 Malcom M. Feeley and Edward L. Rubin, *Judicial Policy Making and the Modern State: How the Courts Reformed America's Prisons* (Cambridge: Cambridge University Press, 1998).

4 Sabel and Simon, "Destabilization Rights: How Public Law Litigation Succeeds," 1020.

5 Helen Hershkoff, "Positive Rights and State Constitutions: The Limits of Federal Rationality Review," *Harvard Law Review* 112 (1999): 1131–96.

6 Edward L. Rubin and Malcom M. Feeley, "Judicial Policy Making and Litigation against the Government," *University of Pennsylvania Journal of Constitutional Law* 5 (2003): 617–64, Feeley and Rubin, *Judicial Policy Making and the Modern State: How the Courts Reformed America's Prisons*.

7 *Holt v. Sarver*, 300 F. Supp. 825, 828 (E.D. Ark., 1969).

8 Rubin and Feeley, "Judicial Policy Making and Litigation against the Government," 656.

9 Ibid.

10 *Sheppard v. Phoenix*, 210 F. Supp. 2d 450 (S.D.N.Y., 2002); Sabel and Simon, "Destabilization Rights: How Public Law Litigation Succeeds."

11 In their work, Feeley and Rubin devoted significant attention to the argument that the new mode of "judicial policymaking" in public law litigation is theoretically justifiable. Feeley and Rubin, *Judicial Policy Making and the Modern State: How the Courts Reformed America's Prisons*.

12 Michael C. Dorf and Charles F. Sabel, "A Constitution of Democratic Experimentalism," *Columbia Law Review* 98 (1998): 267–361.

13 Sabel and Simon, "Destabilization Rights: How Public Law Litigation Succeeds."

14 Rubin and Feeley, "Judicial Policy Making and Litigation against the Government."

15 James S. Liebman and Charles F. Sabel, "Changing Schools: A Public Laboratory Dewey Barely Imagined: The Emerging Model of School Governance and Legal Reform," *New York University School of Law Review of Law and Social Change* 28 (2003): 183–304; Sabel and Simon, "Destabilization Rights: How Public Law Litigation Succeeds."

16 Gary Orfield, *The Reconstruction of Southern Education: The Schools and the 1964 Civil Rights Act* (New York, NY: John Wiley and Sons, 1969); Michael A. Rebell, "Poverty, 'Meaningful' Educational Opportunity, and the Necessary Role of the Courts," *North Carolina Law Review* 85 (2007): 1467–543, Liebman and Sabel, "Changing Schools: A Public Laboratory Dewey Barely Imagined: The Emerging Model of School Governance and Legal Reform."

17 Molly Hunter, "All Eyes Forward: Public Engagement and Education reform in Kentucky," *Journal of Law and Education* 28 (1999): 485–516.

18 Liebman and Sabel, "Changing Schools: A Public Laboratory Dewey Barely Imagined: The Emerging Model of School Governance and Legal Reform."

19 Rebell, "Poverty, "Meaningful" Educational Opportunity, and the Necessary Role of the Courts."

20 Michael Lipsky, *Street-Level Bureaucracy: Dilemmas of the Individual in Public Services* (New York, NY: Russell Sage Foundation, 1980); David Tyack and Larry Cuban, *Tinkering toward Utopia: A Century of Public School Reform* (Cambridge, MA: Harvard University Press, 1995).

21 Mark A Smylie and Robert L. Crowson, "Working within the Scripts: Building Institutional Infrastructure for Children's Service Coordination in Schools," *Educational Policy* 10, no. 1 (1996): 3–21.

22 Kristen Tosh Cowan and Leigh M. Manasevit, *The New Title I: Balancing Accountability with Flexibility* (Washington, D.C.: Thompson Publishing Group, 2002).

23 National Reading Panel, *Teaching Children to Read: An Evidence-Based Assessment of the Scientific Research Literature on Reading and Its Implications for Reading Instruction* (Washington, D.C.: National Institute of Child Health and Human Development, 2000); No Child Left Behind Act of 2001, 20 U.S.C. § 6301 et seq. (2002).

24 Education Sciences Reform Act of 2002, 20 U.S.C. § 9501 et seq. 2002.

25 U.S. Department of Education, Institute of Education Sciences, "What Works Clearinghouse," (Institute of Education Sciences, 2007). http://www.whatworks.ed.gov (accessed July 27, 2007).

26 Kathleen Kennedy Manzo, "Senate Report Details "Reading First" Conflicts of Interest," *Education Week*, May 9, 2007. http://www.edweek.org (accessed January 28, 2006).

27 Margaret Eisenhart and Lisa Towne, "Contestation and Change in National Policy On 'Scientifically Based' Education Research," *Educational Researcher* 32, no. 7 (2003): 32–38.

INDEX

Rosenberg, Gerald, 12
Rubin, Edward, 182, 183, 184,
  186, 246*n11*
Ryan, James, 161, 243*n118*